Programming the IBM PC
User Interface

Also by Henry Simpson

Design of User-Friendly Programs for Small Computers

Programming the IBM PC User Interface

Henry Simpson

McGraw-Hill Book Company

New York   St. Louis   San Francisco   Auckland   Bogotá
Hamburg   Johannesburg   London   Madrid
Mexico   Montreal   New Delhi   Panama
Paris   São Paulo   Singapore
Sydney   Tokyo   Toronto

Library of Congress Cataloging in Publication Data

Simpson, Henry.
 Programming the IBM PC user interface.

 Includes index.
 1. IBM Personal Computer—Programming. 2. IBM PC*jr*
(Computer)—Programming. 3. Microcomputers—Programming.
I. Title.
QA76.8.I2594S575 1985   001.64'2   85-7924
ISBN 0-07-057297-6

1234567890 DOC/DOC 898765

ISBN 0-07-057297-6

*The editors for this book were Stephen G. Guty and Susan Killikelly,
the designer was Naomi Auerbach, and the production supervisor
was Sara L. Fliess. It was set in Century Schoolbook by Achorn Graphic Services, Inc.*

Printed and bound by R. R. Donnelley & Sons Company.

Contents

Preface   vii

1. Design Principles 1

Define the Users   1
Minimize the Operator's Work   2
Keep the Program Simple   3
Be Consistent   4
Give Adequate Feedback   4
Give the Operator Control   4
Do Not Overstress Short-Term Memory   5
Minimize Dependence on Recall Memory   6
Help the Operator Remain Oriented   6
Follow Prevailing Design Conventions   8
Manage Errors   8
Build a Turnkey System   9

2. Outside-In Design 10

Outside-In Versus Inside-Out Design   10
Applying the Outside-In Design Method   10

3. Display Screen Formatting 21

Alternative Screen-Generation Methods   21
Layout Shortcuts   22
Moving among Screens   24
Screen-Printing Mechanics   31
Screen Layout   48
Using Color   66

4. Information Presentation 74

Use of Language   74
Presenting Numeric Information   78
Display Conventions   88
Special Video Modes   92

5. User Input 98

> BASIC Data-Input Statements   98
> The Input-Validation Sequence   114
> Handling Syntax-Dependent Entries—Dates, Times, Phone Numbers   137

6. Data-Input Screens 144

> Data-Input Screens, Data-Input Forms, and Database-Review Screens   144
> Scrolling Prompt Screen   145
> Single-Row Input   146
> Full-Screen Input   153

7. Error Management 166

> Preventing Programming Errors   166
> Preventing Operator Errors   167
> Error Handling   170

8. Program Control with Menus 186

> Overview of Program Control   186
> Designing a Menu   188
> Creating Menus with BASIC   192
> Menu-Control Networks   210

Index   225

Preface

This book is directed at programmers who develop software for the various models of the IBM Personal Computer (PC), and compatibles. The book illustrates techniques for effective user-interface design. Its main objective is to help programmers design programs that are easy for operators to learn and use, and are minimally subject to operator errors. In other words, this is a book on how to design "user-friendly" programs.

The book illustrates these techniques with the BASIC language. Although BASIC has many limitations in terms of speed, portability, and readability, it is the most widely used PC language and the language of choice for most PC programmers—it is the common language of the PC community. If you are a BASIC programmer, then you can use the techniques in this book directly in your programs. If your language of choice is *not* BASIC—if you use assembler, Pascal, C, FORTH, or another language—this book still contains much that will be useful to you, for this is not so much a book about BASIC programming. as about user-interface design. The techniques illustrated apply to all PCs and to all small computers, although their implementation will vary with the language used.

The book assumes that you have a system with at least one disk drive, a minimum of 128 kilobytes of random-access memory, a monochrome or color monitor that enables 80-column display, and an 80-column printer. Some of the code examples require DOS 2.1 and advanced BASIC (or PC*jr* cartridge BASIC), but most examples do not. The use of color on video displays is covered in Chapter 4, but most of the code assumes a monochrome display.

The book consists of eight chapters that cover a wide range of topics. Chapter 1 presents twelve design principles whose observance makes for friendly programs. Chapter 2 describes "outside-in" design, and presents a procedure for developing user-friendly programs. Chapter 3 shows how to format displays. Chapter 4 shows how to present information in a clear and understandable way. Chapter 5 discusses user input. Chapter 6 shows how to create data-input screens, with the emphasis on full-screen input. Chapter 7 describes the errors that dog programs and presents a strategy for preventing them and handling them when they occur. Chapter 8 shows how to design effective menu-driven programs.

The best strategy for reading is to start at the beginning and read straight through to the end. You do not need a computer for the first two chapters, but you definitely do from Chapter 3 on. Try things out on your computer; that is the best way to make them come to life.

Thanks to IBM Corporation, Microsoft Corporation, Alison Software Corporation, and Fogle Computing Corporation for supplying technical information and providing illustrations used in this book.

Programming the IBM PC
User Interface

1

Design Principles

This chapter presents twelve principles that support the design of user-friendly programs. These are rules of thumb to follow in designing a program. Most of them are based on human factors, and others on that rare thing called common sense. Each principle is defined and then illustrated with one or more concrete examples.

Define the Users

The first step in program design is to identify the audience—*who* will use the program. Different audiences have different needs and expectations. If you ignore them, you will disappoint their expectations or, worse, fail to meet their needs.

Form as real a picture of users as possible. One way to start is with operator stereotypes. Four common operator stereotypes are (1) computer professionals, (2) professionals without computer experience, (3) naive users, and (4) skilled clerks (Figure 1-1). These types are points on a continuum, not narrow categories, but they are useful classifications for thinking about your program's audience. Computer professionals are the most demanding in terms of program flexibility, the least patient, and the least in need of prompting and other operator help. The requirements of skilled clerks are similar. Naive users are at the other extreme, often in need of constant hand-holding and likely to make every blunder in the book as well as many no one put in the book. Somewhere in between are professionals without computer experience, whose needs vary depending on where they fall in the continuum.

Define the audience, and design accordingly. Often you must write for more than one audience—typically, for some combination of professionals without computer experience and naive users. If so, anticipate the needs of both audiences. There are two basic approaches to designing such programs: (1) write for the lowest common denominator and (2) provide different features for different audiences. The first approach is the simplest but is unsatisfactory for sophisticated users. The second approach is more difficult for the programmer but preferable for program users; it requires the program to provide for operator

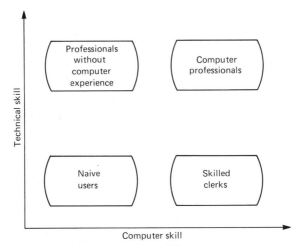

Figure 1-1   One way to categorize operators is in terms of their relative technical and computer skills. The four extremes are marked by the operator types shown in this graph.

growth. A program may do this in many ways; for example, by providing an operator-selectable prompting level.

Minimize the Operator's Work

In designing a program, you will find that there are many points at which your choices make things easier either for yourself or for the program user (Figure 1-2). Make the choice in favor of the user. Minimize both mental and physical work. *Mental* work is that involved in recalling things, performing mental calculations, making decisions, and the like. *Physical* work is that involved in pressing keys, inserting and removing floppy disks, and the like.

Design objectives can usually be met in many different ways. Often you may meet the letter of a design specification by providing a program feature, but that feature may be so cumbersome to exercise that operators will avoid it. Consider, for example, the various ways to provide access for editing a database. At the worst, raw, unformatted information is thrown up on the screen, without title or

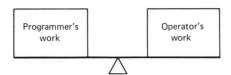

Figure 1-2   A program should be designed to minimize the amount of physical and mental work the operator must perform. This usually means more work for the programmer, who must provide additional features to reduce the operator's work.

headings, and operators must first decipher it. At the other extreme is a database access program that presents the data in the format in which it was first entered—replicating original data-input forms. By designing the program the second way, you make things easier for the operator.

Keep the Program Simple

Simplicity may be the oldest universal principle. It has found its way into the aesthetic of many different domains, including the arts, sciences, and engineering. When is something simple enough? There is no easy (or simple) answer. As you design, stop every so often and ask yourself such questions as these:

- Is there an easier way to do this?
- Are there any ways in which this might confuse the operator?
- Is this really necessary?
- How could I simplify this for the operator?

Look for ways to unclutter displays, reduce the number and complexity of keyboard entries, and get rid of the unnecessary or superfluous. Since this is akin to editing, it is important to get help from others—both designers and program users. After you design a program, let others try it out and see if they can find any ways to simplify it further (Figure 1-3). In short, plan for simplicity, design for simplicity, and test for simplicity.

Simplicity does not mean simplistic. It is more like economy of means. It

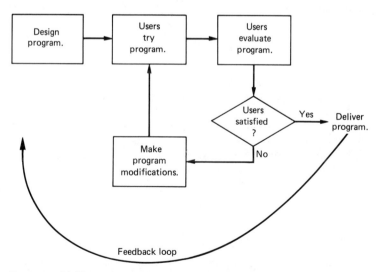

Figure 1-3 Making a program simple requires that you make a conscious effort during the planning and design stages. Further, the program should be tested by operators to evaluate whether it is simple enough.

emerges from careful planning, relentless pruning, and systematic testing and revision.

Be Consistent

Consistency, like simplicity, is a universal principle. Consistency makes a program easier to learn and results in fewer operator errors, mainly because it reduces the amount of information the operator must learn. For example, suppose that you are designing a program with several different data-input routines. If all routines work the same way, then the operator only has to learn how to make data entries *one* time, in *one* part of the program. The skill developed from the first data-input routine then transfers to other routines. On the other hand, if every data-input routine is slightly different from every other one, then the learning task is magnified. The operator must learn each routine separately. The ability to generalize from a single learning experience is what psychologists call "transfer of training." Inconsistency reduces transfer and may even result in "negative transfer," e.g., the operator attempts to apply a technique learned one place in another, and it does not work.

The consistency principle applies to most aspects of user-interface design. It is especially important, for example, in the display of information, and dictates that the format and information content of displays be consistent.

Give Adequate Feedback

Feedback is information received by the operator from the computer, indicating that a previous operator action has had an effect. In the absence of such feedback, the operator may be unsure. For example, the operator may know that he or she intended to press a particular key; however, if there is no overt sign (or *echo*) from the computer, there is no way for the operator to be sure what happened. As a consequence, the action may be repeated, perhaps producing some unintended result.

When you design a program, keep in mind that any action the operator takes should produce some explicit response from the computer to show that it has received the instruction and acted. For example, in a data-input program, typed-in data should be displayed on the screen opposite the prompt. When editing, the operator should be able to back up the cursor, remove what was entered earlier, type in the correction, and have it displayed on the screen. Though such simple requirements should be obvious, in many programs what is typed in at the keyboard never appears on the screen and must be maintained in the operator's short-term memory.

Give the Operator Control

There is a limit to the rate at which the operator can process information. This rate is dictated mainly by human short-term memory. The operator can use your program successfully only if you do not exceed his or her processing limit. Individual operators vary in the rate at which they can process information. Also, the rate changes with learning and experience. In short, your program needs to be flexible to deal with the differing preferences and skills of different operators. One size does not, as they sometimes say, fit all.

It is equally important not to give operators the idea that the computer is controlling what they do. Many inexperienced computer operators already feel threatened by computers. If the computer seems to be making unreasonable demands on them, they have a very strong negative reaction—their latent fears are simply being reinforced. More-experienced operators are not threatened, but they get angry when they feel that the computer—which they regard as simply a tool—seems to be bossing them around. In commonsense terms, this principle reduces to a number of different admonitions, such as the following:

- *Do not present information too quickly.* Let operators control the rate at which they receive information by letting them start and stop the information as necessary.

- *Do not present too much information at once.* Present what is needed for accomplishing the task at hand, and let operators access other information as they need it.

- *Filter information.* Select the relevant information, and display only that; do not dump your database on users unless they request it.

- *Do not allow your program to seem to express human emotions.* Keep error messages and the like brief and factual, and word them so that they do not sound scolding or humorous.

Do Not Overstress Short-Term Memory

Human short-term memory is like a computer's processing buffer. Both have limited capacity and only hold the information being processed momentarily. Human short-term memory has a capacity of about seven items (Miller's magic number, 7 ± 2) and holds onto information for about 15 seconds. These limitations are important to keep in mind as you design. Human operators may be able to work with up to nine things in memory at one time, but this is stretching their capacity to the limit. In designing something, you would be smarter to play it safe and work with the lower end of this range—with a capacity of, say, five items. As you design, take into account the operator's task and do not require the operator to process more than five items at one time. In addition, do not expect retention of anything you present on the screen for more than about 15 seconds.

Let us consider a specific example of how these limitations might be applied in designing a hypothetical real estate–investment program. To use this program, a real estate salesperson must enter data concerning purchase price, loans, interest rates, appreciation rates, commissions, length of time the investment is held, and so forth to calculate the rate of return on the investment. A display screen then appears showing the results of the analysis. After reviewing the results, the salesperson will usually want to modify some of the initial entries in order to fine-tune the results to achieve the rate of return requested by the customer. The problem with this design is that data entries are made on a screen that is separate from displayed results. Thus, program users must retain one screen in their heads while viewing the other. Most users cannot really do this; what they do remember from one screen will be lost shortly after they move to the next. A better design would permit program users to view all information—inputs and results—simultaneously (as you can with a spreadsheet program).

Minimize Dependence on Recall Memory

People find it easier to *recognize* familiar information than to *recall* it from memory. In designing a program, you will be called upon to make decisions that determine whether operators will be required to recognize or to recall information. For example, suppose that you are designing a part of a program that requires operators to specify which of a series of data files should be loaded. Such routines are usually designed in one of two ways:

1. A prompt requests the name or number of the file (Figure 1-4a). The operator then types this in from memory. If the user cannot recall the name of the file exactly, the file cannot be loaded, and there will be a delay until he or she figures out a way to examine the file directory as a memory jog.
2. A directory is presented on the screen that lists the files from which a selection may be made (Figure 1-4b). The operator then selects the one wanted by typing in its name or number. This makes use of recognition memory and does not require the operator to recall the file name exactly.

The second method is usually preferable for the program user.

The same principle applies to the selection of a program control method. Two of the most common control methods are as follows:

1. The program user specifies the desired program by typing in its name, number, or a code recalled from memory.
2. A list of program options (i.e., a menu) is displayed and the user selects the one desired. This technique makes use of recognition memory.

The argument made earlier suggests that menu selection (method 2) would be best. In many designs, particularly with complex programs used by sophisticated operators, menus are not the best control method because they sacrifice program flexibility and speed. However, menus do make sense for many microcomputer programs that are used by less-sophisticated operators—and for certain programs used infrequently by sophisticated operators.

Help the Operator Remain Oriented

In using a computer program, the operator attempts to build a sort of mental map or model of the program's organization. While we would be misguided to think too literally about little maps inside of people's heads, the mental map is a useful and relevant metaphor. The control structure of many menu-driven programs can also be thought of as a road with one branch point (i.e., menu) at the top that has several more branches further along the road, and so on. (See Figure 8-2 for an

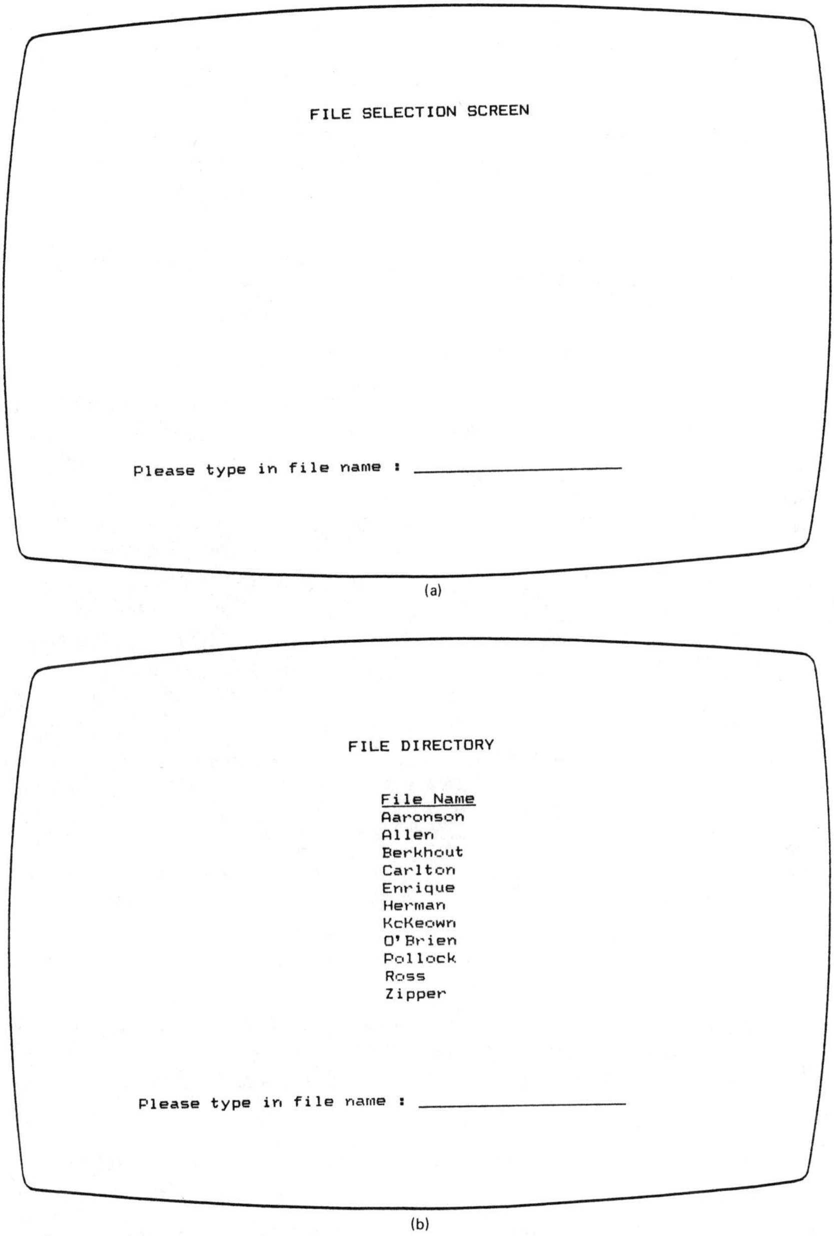

```
                    FILE SELECTION SCREEN









        Please type in file name :  _____
```

(a)

```
                       FILE DIRECTORY

                         File Name
                         Aaronson
                         Allen
                         Berkhout
                         Carlton
                         Enrique
                         Herman
                         KcKeown
                         O'Brien
                         Pollock
                         Ross
                         Zipper




        Please type in file name :  _____
```

(b)

Figure 1-4 Two screens requesting file name. (a) Screen requires the operator to type the name in from memory; (b) screen displays a directory to help the operator identify the file.

illustration.) Menu networks can, of course, be designed in many other ways, but the point is that the network looks a lot like a map and that operators must learn the map well enough to find their way around the program.

Programs using other types of control techniques—for example, command languages—also require operators to build mental maps. Learning is aided by (1) organizing the control structure logically, (2) explaining this structure in user documentation, and (3) providing "street signs" (i.e., screen labels) within the program to tell operators where they are. These three things aid operator orientation. The object, of course, is to make it easy for the operator to learn the program's organization and to keep from getting lost while using it.

Follow Prevailing Design Conventions

To a certain extent, we are all prisoners of the worlds we have grown up in. Through experience, we learn to expect certain things and take them for granted. This is true in most realms of human experience, including the use of computer programs. There are many conventions concerning the way operators are supposed to interact with computers. Conventions have become conventions through their wide acceptance. Usually, though not always, such acceptance reflects the fact that the convention has passed the test of working successfully in the real world. One such convention is that of displaying columns of numbers aligned on the decimal point. It would probably take very little to convince you that this makes the information easier to read.

Colors also tend to be used in conventional ways. For example, green usually means to go, or represents a safe condition; yellow stands for caution; red means to stop, or represents a hazardous condition. On visual displays, information is usually presented from left to right and from top to bottom. Similarly, movement in a clockwise direction usually stands for an increase and counterclockwise movement for a decrease. Not all conventions are good. Bad conventions—such as the use of abbreviations instead of complete words on display screens—should be abandoned. But make your program conform to the sensible conventions.

Manage Errors

Books have been written about errors, academic careers have been built on the subject, ships have gone down because of them, and some folks wax positively eloquent on the subject. The poor programmer must deal with them constantly. Consider:

- The programmer's PC sometimes makes errors via a bug in BASIC or DOS. Thankfully, such errors occur rarely.

- The programmer makes errors in coding the program. Programmer errors are not as rare as PC errors, and they depend upon programmer skill and the amount and effectiveness of program testing.

- Operators make errors in using the program. They do such things as attempt to write data to a program disk, and destroy the only copy of their database. These errors are fairly common, even for skilled operators.

But what to do about errors? To start with, you need an appropriate error-management philosophy. The recommended one in this book is fairly simple. First, assume that Murphy's Law holds and that everything will go wrong. Second, attempt to prevent errors by anticipating them, protecting against them (with error-trapping routines, key-deactivation routines, and data-input error tests), educating operators, and thoroughly testing the program before releasing it to operators (who will, no doubt, prove that errors still exist, despite everything you did).

Error management is one of the key factors in designing a user-friendly program and is one of the first things to look for in evaluating someone else's program. Bear in mind that any program that contains errors which compromise its effectiveness cannot be considered friendly in even the narrowest sense. It automatically fails the test the moment it crashes, allows the user to destroy a data base, or permits other mischief to occur.

Build a Turnkey System

A *turnkey* system is one that requires the very minimum of operator intervention—either physical or mental—to work properly. This does not mean that it does everything for the operator, but it does do everything that it feasibly can. A turnkey system is intended to (1) reduce the operator's work, (2) be easier to learn, and (3) reduce errors. It reduces work by letting the computer perform certain functions that the operator might otherwise do. For example, it will automatically activate BASIC and begin to execute a program when the computer is turned on.

The less that the operator must do to use the program correctly, the easier it is to learn that program. This is fairly obvious, and reduces to the rather simple idea that it is easier to learn less of something than more. Turnkey systems also reduce errors. It stands to reason that the less the operator must do, the less the likelihood that something incorrect will be done. This is sometimes referred to as the "exposure factor" and is the reason that you can reduce the cost of your automobile insurance by driving fewer miles each year.

Turnkey systems are not strictly for novices. No one likes to exert unnecessary effort, and this includes experts. Saving the expert's time and energy is just as important as saving the novice's.

Chapter

2

Outside-In Design

"Outside-in" design is a systematic approach to program design. The "outside" in the name stands for the program's displays. "Inside" stands for the inner workings of the program—what drives those displays. Outside-in design works in the order indicated—outside first, inside second. Since the method starts with what the user will see, it is a user-oriented approach to design and an effective way to design user-friendly programs. This chapter describes the outside-in design method and presents a step-by-step procedure for applying it in design problems.

Outside-In Versus Inside-Out Design

The computer operator often thinks of a program as consisting of a series of screens. One screen is used to indicate the beginning of the program, a sort of home base; another is used to enter data; others display computed results; and so on. Clearly, the content of individual screens and the way the screens are organized will have a significant impact on how effectively the operator can use the program. During program design, screens are one of the first—if not *the* first—things to consider.

When you begin design with a program's displays, you are performing a type of design referred to as "outside-in" design (Figure 2-1). This type of design focuses first on the design of screens (and printed reports) and later on the design of the parts of the program required to produce those displays. Opposed to this approach is the more traditional one of inside-out design, which involves designing a program's innards first and later designing the screens (Figure 2-2). Outside-in design generally produces better programs for the simple reason that operator needs drive the design.

Applying the Outside-In Design Method

To apply outside-in design to a real-world problem, it must first be translated into a procedure. The sequence of steps in such a procedure is shown in Figure 2-3. This procedure shows the general sequence of activities in outside-in design and

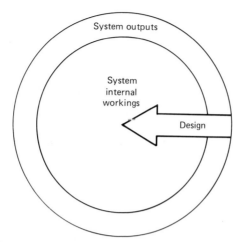

Figure 2-1 Outside-in design starts with system outputs—screens and printed reports—and later focuses on the system internal workings required to generate those outputs.

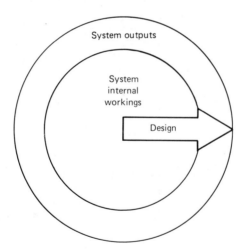

Figure 2-2 Inside-out design starts with the internal workings of the system and later focuses on the system outputs—screens and printed reports—which can be generated.

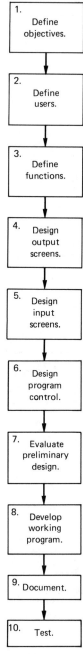

Figure 2-3 Sequence of steps in outside-in design of a computer program.

is not meant to be followed in rigid, cookbook fashion. Start with this procedure, and adapt it to your working style and the design problem you are attempting to solve. Each step of the procedure is described below and illustrated with the design of a simple checkbook balancing and reconciliation program called Checkbook.

Step 1. Define the Program's Objectives

Program objectives are high-level statements concerning the goals of the program. They are stated before you worry about the more technical aspects of design such as equipment configuration, programming language used, file sizes, or any other design constraints. The objectives may be modified or changed later based on these factors but should not be constrained by them at the beginning.

For example, the objectives of Checkbook are as follows:

- Permit users to maintain a computerized record of their checkbook.
- Help users reconcile their checkbook and manage their money.

Step 2. Define the Program's Users

Consider all possible users and their characteristics. Consider the probable characteristics of each type of user in terms of such factors as the following:

- Frequency of use of program
- Computer sophistication
- Education, intelligence, and subject-matter expertise
- Motivation
- Patience
- Computerphobia

Checkbook is targeted at an individual for personal use and perhaps at some small-business owners. The typical user of this program would lack computer sophistication and would enter all data and review all displays personally.

Step 3. Define the Program's Functions

A *function* is a class of things that a program must do. Here are the functions that Checkbook must perform:

1. Maintain records of up to 200 checks and 50 deposits per month for 12 months.
2. Provide screen and hard-copy checkbook reconciliation displays.
3. Provide a running balance of the account by date and income/expense item.
4. Permit users to locate checks by number, payee, or expense category and to locate income items by payor or income category.

Functions are derived from the program's objectives (see step 1). Functions are specific and have direct design implications. For example, the first function implies the existence of files for maintaining records of checks and deposits; this means that data must be entered and that at least one data-input screen is required. The second and third functions have implications for screen and hardcopy displays. The fourth function implies the existence of database searching routines to be used with output screens.

Step 4. Design Output Screens

Program functions must be systematically translated into the output screens used in the program. Each function must be analyzed to determine what types of data to present and how these data should be organized into one or more output screens.

Consider the functions given above. The first function relates to database content and file size and does not affect the content of any output screen. However, since up to 200 checks and 50 deposits can be stored in the database for a single month, it is clear that not all data can be displayed at once; paging, scrolling, or another access technique must be used to locate the desired information.

Functions 3 and 4 relate to the content of displays. Let us consider these two functions and make up a list of *data elements* to be included in the displays. A data element is an item of information to be presented on the display. The element may derive directly from the database or be computed from some combination of data and operator entries. Function 3 calls for one or more displays to "provide a running balance of the account by date and income/expense item." Function 4 requires that checks be accessible by number, payee, or expense category; and income items by payor or income category. Thus, to accomplish Functions 3 and 4, these displays must contain the following information:

- Expenses—from database
    Check number
    Check date
    Check payee
    Check amount
    Expense category
    Payor (optional)
    Tax deductibility (optional)

- Income—from database
    Deposit payor (i.e., paycheck, gift, etc.)
    Deposit date
    Deposit amount
    Deposit category

- Account balance—computed from above
    Account balance (by date)
    Cumulative expenses (optional)
    Cumulative income (optional)

Function 3 requires a display to maintain a running balance of the account, and function 4 requires a display for account reconciliation. It is possible that one display could serve both purposes. It is probable that the user will want to generate a hard copy of the displays as a permanent record. Thus, at least two displays—screen and hard copy—are required. In addition, it is probable that the user will find it useful to be able to generate displays listing only income or expense items and to break these down further by category. Thus, based on the list of data elements given above, one could foresee at least five types of displays:

1. Checkbook Summary/Reconciliation display

2. Overall Income Summary display

3. Overall Expense Summary display

4. Categorical Income display

5. Categorical Expense display

Since one of the major goals of the program is to help users manage their money, these displays would be linked to one another in levels as shown in Figure 2-4. The main display would be the Checkbook Summary/Reconciliation display,

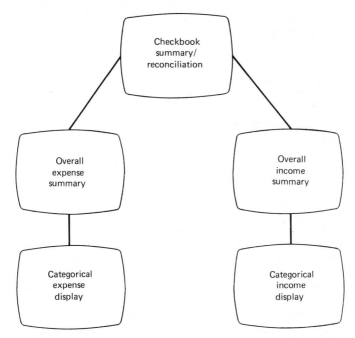

Figure 2-4 Relationships among CHECKS' output displays. The Checkbook Summary/Reconciliation display presents expense and income data in cumulative, summary form. To investigate expense or income data, the user accesses either the Overall Expense Summary or Overall Income Summary display. Particular expense or income items are explored with categorical displays.

which would present both income and expense data in cumulative, summary form. To investigate expenses alone, the user would call the Overall Expense Summary display. To investigate particular categories of expenses, the user would access the Categorical Expense display. Income data would be investigated analogously. Each of these displays would have a corresponding hardcopy display, which could be specified from the particular screen.

Each of the five displays would contain various combinations of the data elements listed above. The designer would be required to decide which of these or other displays to use based on the users' and the program's objectives. In addition to the displays mentioned, it is likely that the program would include one or more database-review and -editing screens and data-input screens, as well as menu screens. Data-input screens and control screens are covered in the next two steps.

Step 5. Design Input Screens

At least one data-input screen will be required for any program that employs a database. The input screen will be used to enter the data comprising the program's database.

The data that must be entered are derived from the list of data elements (see above). If the program simply stores a database and then displays portions of that database back to the user, then input data elements are the same as output data elements. If the database is transformed before being displayed, then the input data elements differ from output data elements. Checks is a simple database program that displays back the information entered—except for the data element *running balance,* which is computed—and so input data elements and output data elements are the same. Checks employs at least two classes of inputs: (1) expenses and (2) income. These two classes imply two data-input screens or a single screen with two data-input areas or input modes. It would be desirable to use a single screen, if possible, to simplify movement between screens during the data-input process.

In addition to the screen(s) for entering data, the program must permit the user to define the income and expense categories and the projected monthly amounts for the program to use. For example, the user will need to define expense categories of particular amounts for rent, electricity, food, and the like, and analogous categories and amounts for income. Since there are two classes of inputs, two category definition screens are implied: (1) expenses and (2) income. In this case, it is probably wise to use two separate screens, rather than one, to enable the user to keep the two classes of inputs separate. These two screens permit the user to define the budget. Since the budget must be balanced—projected expenses and income must be combined to arrive at a bottom line total—a third screen might be used. A logical way to organize these screens is in the form of a tree (Figure 2-5), which enables the user to start with the Balance screen, review the bottom line, and then access the Expense or Income definition screens to adjust categories and amounts to balance the budget.

Most programs employ at least one "setup" screen in which the user enters information concerning the particular equipment configuration—number of disk drives, printer column width, and so forth. This screen is seldom used, and so can

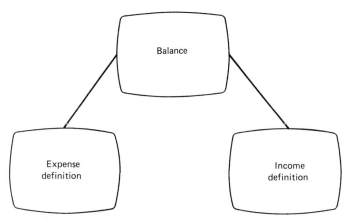

Figure 2-5 Relationships among displays for defining and balancing the budget in CHECKS program. The Balance screen combines projected expenses and income to arrive at a bottom line total. Expense or income items are then adjusted by accessing the Expense or Income Definition screens.

and should be kept out of the main path of the program. Checks would require one such screen.

Finally, it is common for a database program to include a database-review and -editing routine that permits the user to get at data that have been entered, review them, and make changes if desired. Normally, such a routine will also permit the user to print out part or all of the database on a printer.

The foregoing analysis leads to the conclusion that Checks requires at least six input screens:

1. Income/Expense Input
2. Expense Definition
3. Income Definition
4. Balance
5. Database Edit
6. Setup

The most frequently used of these screens is Income/Expense Input. Expense and Income Definition and Balance screens will be used less often. The Database Edit will also be used infrequently. The Setup screen will be used least of all. Probable frequency of use should be taken into account in designing the program's control, as described below.

Step 6. Design Program Control

For purposes of this discussion, *program control* is the manner in which the various screens are linked together, and the control method (such as menu or command language) used to move among screens.

Assume that the program will be menu-driven. The program will start with a Main Menu, which will provide access to the program's various subprograms. In general, menus should list programs in the order of their probable frequency of use. For example, the various programs in Checks are listed in order of their probable frequency of use, from highest to lowest, below.

Income/Expense Input

Checkbook Summary/Reconciliation

Expense Definition, Income Definition, and Balance

Database Edit and Printout

Setup

These programs, with one addition, Exit program, could be used as the options on Checks' Main Menu. The resulting menu and Checks' overall control structure are shown in Figure 2-6.

Step 7. Evaluate Preliminary Design

The program's user interface may be thought of as its various screens and the user inputs required to get to and to use those screens. Steps 4, 5, and 6 lead to the definition of this interface. In general, the screens should be laid out on paper first before they are coded. They should then be presented to typical users for critique before they are translated into a working program. Following critique, the program design should be modified, as necessary, to answer user criticisms. This critique enables user input into the design process and ensures that the design will gain user acceptance. Recognize that although the steps in outside-in design are analytical, they require the designer to make many subjective decisions. The only way to ensure that the designer has not made any wrong turns or blunders is to test the design with users.

Step 8. Develop a Working Program

After the user interface has been designed, the program's internal workings are designed and developed so as to support that interface. In general, it is a good idea to develop a design specification for use by programmers during program development. The specification is a compilation of all the design information that has been generated up to this step in the design process, as well as information that can be logically derived therefrom. It should contain information concerning program objectives, users, hardware requirements, input screens, output screens, and program control, as well as derivative information concerning data structures and files, program modularization, and other design factors.

You should focus early on the program's data structures and files. These can be readily derived from the data elements defined during steps 4 through 6. Program modules and submodules must be defined. Often these reflect the program's control organization, as determined during step 6. The program is then developed, usually on a modular basis. As each module is developed, it is tested, debugged, refined, and then linked to existing modules.

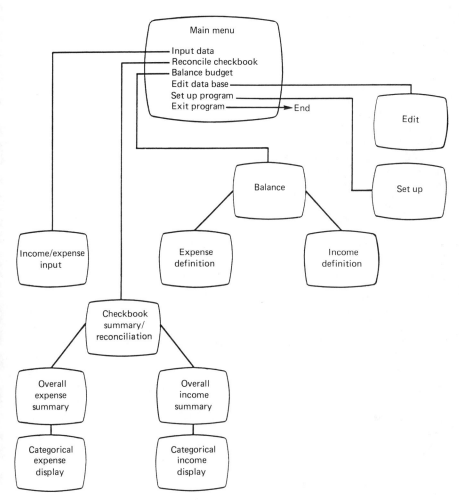

Figure 2-6 Main Menu and relationships among various subprograms in CHECKS.

Step 9. Document the Program

There are two general types of program documentation. The first is *systems* documentation. This is technical documentation aimed at the programmer who must maintain the program. Systems documentation should be developed concurrently with the program. The second type of documentation is *user* documentation. User documentation tells program users what they need to know to make the program work properly. The program user's guide is the most familiar example of this type of documentation. In addition, user documentation may be contained within the program in the form of help screens, directions, detailed prompts, and other user-aiding features. User documentation should be developed as soon after the program is completed as possible. It is desirable to develop user documentation concurrently with the program.

Step 10. Test the Program

The program must be thoroughly tested before its release for general use. Testing occurs at different stages. The programmer will test the routines used in each program module, then test the module, and eventually test several modules together. Such testing is often done informally and may leave many errors undetected. Beyond such testing, the individual modules and completed program should be subjected to more formal testing by other programmers, who will uncover errors that the original programmer overlooked.

Next, the program should be subjected to rigorous and controlled testing by the type of operators who will be expected to use it when it is delivered. Those users should be provided with user documentation and be required to perform the tasks the program was designed to accomplish.

3

Display Screen Formatting

This chapter provides an introduction to display screen formatting. Topics covered are alternative screen-generation methods, layout shortcuts, moving among screens, screen printing mechanics, screen layout, and using color. In this chapter, as later in the book, the term "display" refers to hardware (video display or printer) and "screen" refers to the information presented on the display.

Alternative Screen-Generation Methods

This book shows how to generate screens using BASIC. BASIC methods are illustrated for cursor positioning, the printing of titles and headings, the drawing of lines, and so forth, to generate screens on the video display. BASIC is easy to use, and programs can be developed quickly in it. Execution speed of BASIC programs is slower than that of programs written in assembly language. BASIC also takes more memory within the program and more storage on disk than assembly language.

If you are a skilled assembly-language programmer, then you may prefer to develop all or part of your programs in it. If you are a BASIC programmer, you can access assembly-language routines within a BASIC program to perform certain functions, and this often makes a good deal of sense. For example, BASIC sorts are notoriously slow, and no sane programmer would use them to sort more than a dozen or so items; it would make much more sense to use an assembly-language routine. Screen generation is another case in point, although the use of assembly language here is more problematical than in sorting. Assembly-language techniques can be used to generate screens very quickly and to store them in high memory where they can be recalled instantaneously for display. This technique is beyond the scope of the present text, but readers interested in it should consult the *IBM Technical Reference** manual and books on assembly-

---

*IBM Corporation, 1983.

language programming. Any program that requires quick access to many screens is a logical candidate for assembly-language screen generation.

Another tool to simplify programming is the screen-generation program. There are a number of these on the market, differing somewhat in capabilities, although in general they allow you to compose a screen through the keyboard, save the screen, and then recall it for display later. In other words, you do not have to write the code to generate the screen—merely compose the screen and save it. The mechanics of how such programs work vary. For example, the Screen Design Facility (SDF) published by Fogle Computing Corporation permits the screen to be typed in through the keyboard. SDF then generates the BASIC code required to display the screen. The resulting code is merged with a program to produce the desired screens. SDF's screens are quite sophisticated. Standard, high intensity, and reverse video can be used. Data-input screens created with SDF have protected input fields, permit tabbing between fields, and allow insertion, deletion, and other common control and editing functions.

Other programs may use a similar screen-creation technique—typed in through the keyboard—but store the screens in binary files. The screens can then be produced within the program by reading the binary files and displaying their contents. In general, recalling and displaying a screen in this manner is somewhat slower than direct generation with BASIC, although it is more economical in terms of program memory and disk storage.

In other words, regard the BASIC programming techniques shown in this and subsequent chapters as a starting point. Tools such as screen-generation programs can make programming easier, and the intelligent use of assembly-language routines can increase the speed of your BASIC program.

Layout Shortcuts

It is wise to plan each screen carefully before attempting to write the code to generate it. The more vague the screen's design, the more time you will waste attempting to compose it at your PC. Two alternative layout shortcuts are to use (1) a matrix or (2) a word processor or text editor.

A common way to lay out a screen is with paper and pencil, using a matrix such as that shown in Figure 3-1. Once the screen has been designed, the code to generate it can be written very quickly—and *mechanically*. By using a matrix, you separate the act of design from that of coding. This is good; coding should be a mechanical act that involves converting information from one domain (written, on paper) to another (BASIC code).

Another approach to screen layout is to use a word-processing program or text editor to compose the screen on your video display and then to translate the content and information coordinates of the screen into BASIC code. To make this easier, it is best first to build a box representing the screen (similar to a screen design matrix), with row and column numbers marked for reference (Figure 3-2). Then simply type in the new screen within the boundaries of the box. After completing the screen, print a hard copy of it and use that as the basis for writing the screen-generation code. This approach is more flexible than using paper and pencil and allows you to modify the screen with the same ease as using your word processor.

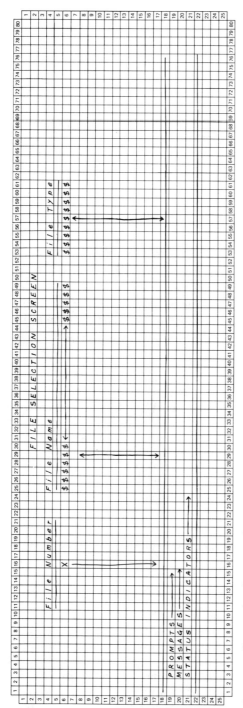

Figure 3-1 Screen plan drawn on planning matrix.

```
          10        20        30        40        50        60        70
----------|---------|---------|---------|---------|---------|---------|---------
|                                                                             |
|                          FILE SELECTION SCREEN                              |
|                                                                             |
|        File Number    File Name                    File Type                |
-         -----------    ---------------             ---------                -
|              X         $$$$$$$$$$$$$$$$$$$$$$$$     $$$$$$$$$$$$$$            |
|              X         $$$$$$$$$$$$$$$$$$$$$$$$     $$$$$$$$$$$$$$            |
|              X         $$$$$$$$$$$$$$$$$$$$$$$$     $$$$$$$$$$$$$$            |
|              X         $$$$$$$$$$$$$$$$$$$$$$$$     $$$$$$$$$$$$$$            |
-              X         $$$$$$$$$$$$$$$$$$$$$$$$     $$$$$$$$$$$$$$            -
|              X         $$$$$$$$$$$$$$$$$$$$$$$$     $$$$$$$$$$$$$$            |
|              X         $$$$$$$$$$$$$$$$$$$$$$$$     $$$$$$$$$$$$$$            |
|              X         $$$$$$$$$$$$$$$$$$$$$$$$     $$$$$$$$$$$$$$            |
|              X         $$$$$$$$$$$$$$$$$$$$$$$$     $$$$$$$$$$$$$$            |
-              X         $$$$$$$$$$$$$$$$$$$$$$$$     $$$$$$$$$$$$$$            -
|              X         $$$$$$$$$$$$$$$$$$$$$$$$     $$$$$$$$$$$$$$            |
|              X         $$$$$$$$$$$$$$$$$$$$$$$$     $$$$$$$$$$$$$$            |
|  -------------------------------------------------------------------------  |
|  PROMPTS..............................                                       |
-  MESSAGES.........................................................          -
|  STATUS INDICATORS...............................................           |
|  -------------------------------------------------------------------------  |
|                                                                             |
|                                                                             |
|                                                                             |
----------|---------|---------|---------|---------|---------|---------|---------
```

Figure 3-2 Screen plan produced with word processing program.

In composing screens, keep in mind that row 25 of the screen on IBM PCs is reserved for the display of function key definitions. When this row is active, no information can be printed on row 25. Row 25 can be turned off by using the KEY OFF statement, thereby permitting display in this area. It can be reactivated by using the KEY ON statement. Therefore, if you intend to use function keys in a program and display their definitions, do not attempt to display information in row 25. In fact, in general it is good practice to avoid both rows 24 and 25 of the display, regardless of the situation. When the function key definitions are displayed, attempting to print something at row 24 produces an extra line feed, causing the display to scroll; this also happens when the definitions are not displayed and you attempt to print something in row 25. For the same reason, it is best not to print anything in the rightmost column being displayed (40 or 80) and to limit the display area to 39 or 79 columns.

Moving among Screens

Three common ways to move from screen to screen are scrolling, paging, and windowing.

Scrolling

In scrolling (Figure 3-3), the new screen is printed row by row, usually starting at the bottom of the display, and rolls up to replace the existing screen. As scrolling occurs, the screen moves up the display, and for the brief period of its motion, neither the old screen nor its replacement is readable. It is quite easy to use the scrolling technique with BASIC code, and this is perhaps why its use is so widespread, particularly among inexperienced programmers.

A scrolling screen is produced when you begin printing a replacement screen

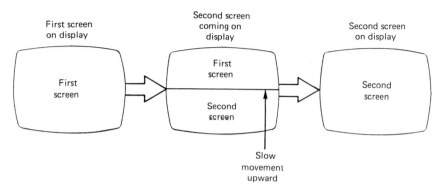

Figure 3-3 Stages in scrolling: Process starts with first screen on display. Second screen scrolls up from bottom, displacing and eventually replacing first screen. During transition, movement makes both screens unreadable.

at the bottom of an existing screen. This causes the existing screen to scroll up as the replacement screen takes its place. To produce a scrolling screen, code is required to generate the first and second screen (Figure 3-4). When this code is executed, it begins generating the new screen on the video display at the current location of the cursor, which is typically at the bottom of the display.

Scrolling is widely used on timesharing systems, where the operator carries on an interactive dialog with the computer that consists of a sequence of request, response, question, and the like. Many people who come from a timesharing background see nothing wrong with scrolling screens and may in fact think that they are the norm. In general, however, scrolling is not the best way to introduce a screen (see below).

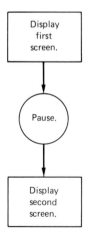

Figure 3-4 Code blocks required to scroll: First screen is displayed and, after a pause, second screen is displayed.

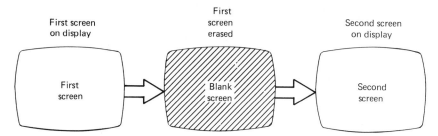

Figure 3-5 Stages in paging: First screen is displayed and then erased before presenting second screen.

Paging

Paging is aptly named and is like flipping through the pages of a book. The key requirement is to clear the first screen before presenting the second (Figure 3-5). Since the first screen is erased, the second is generated starting at the top of a blank display onto a "clean slate," and the displayed information shows no apparent movement.

The code required to page is nearly as simple as that to scroll. The only additional requirement is to clear the first screen (with a CLS statement) before generating the second (Figure 3-6).

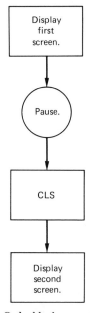

Figure 3-6 Code blocks required to page: First screen is displayed and, after a pause, it is erased and second screen is displayed.

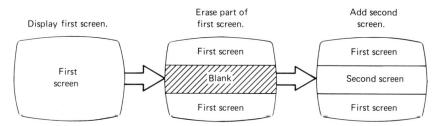

Display first screen.   Erase part of first screen.   Add second screen.

Figure 3-7 Stages in partial paging: First screen is displayed. Part of first screen is erased, and second screen added in its place.

Paging does not require that the entire display be cleared. In fact, it often involves retaining part of the first screen while the second appears. For example, the first screen might contain a directory of names and telephone numbers. If the directory is too long, then additional information can be paged onto the display while retaining the first screen's title, headings, and other pertinent information (Figure 3-7). (Partial scrolling is likewise possible.) Partial paging requires selective screen-clearing and screen-generation code (Figure 3-8).

Since part or all of the screen is cleared during paging, there is a brief period of time during which the display goes completely blank and is unreadable. The length of this period depends on how long it takes to generate the new screen. With complex screens, it may last several seconds. The blank screen phenome-

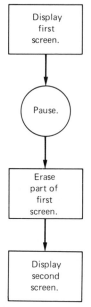

Figure 3-8 Code blocks required for partial paging. First screen is displayed and, after a pause, part of it is erased. Second screen is then displayed.

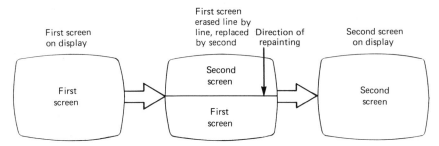

Figure 3-9 Stages in row-by-row clearing of screen. First screen is displayed. It is then erased, one row at a time, and replaced by second screen.

non can be eliminated by clearing the old screen and replacing it with the new one one row at a time, rather than clearing the entire old screen at the start (Figure 3-9). The code for doing such clearing requires you to erase each row of the old screen as you generate the new screen. This can be accomplished by positioning the cursor with the LOCATE statement, clearing the row by printing a row of blank spaces, repositioning the cursor with a second LOCATE statement, and then printing a row of information on the display. This process is repeated for each row of the screen, until the entire screen has been painted on the display (Figure 3-10).

Windowing

Windowing (Figure 3-11) is the most sophisticated screen access technique; it amounts to being able to move the screen window across an information landscape. In its most sophisticated form, it permits the user to combine selected portions of different information landscapes together.

To permit windowing, the program must contain a display-management module that presents the information in the way that the operator specifies (Figure 3-12). This module controls what information is presented and how it is presented.

Is it possible to say which of these three screen access techniques—scrolling, paging, windowing—is best? To a certain degree, yes.

To start with, scrolling is not usually good. Research studies have shown that operators prefer paging to scrolling and perform better when using screens that page. Paging eliminates the apparent movement of information up the screen and helps reduce eyestrain. It also provides a better separation between the first two screens; if one screen scrolls into another, then the implication is that the two are part of the same thing, which may or may not be true.

Of course, if the two screens actually *are* related, then it is a different matter. In the example given earlier, of an interactive dialogue between operator and computer, the conversation consists of a sequence of statements—first the operator, then the computer, then the operator, and so forth. In this case, scrolling provides the operator with a visual history of the recent conversation and may be quite helpful. Such dialogs do not ordinarily occur between people and PCs, however, and so the utility of scrolling is more limited.

Windowing has undeniable advantages, particularly in programs that integrate different software functions into the same package. At the same time, it is costly

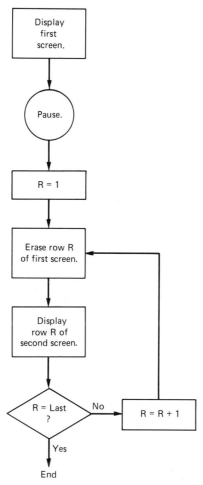

Figure 3-10 One way to illustrate code blocks required to clear a screen row by row. First screen is displayed. After a pause, its top row is erased and replaced by the top row of the second screen. The row is then incremented by one and the process repeated. Replacement continues until the last row of the first screen has been replaced by the last row of the second.

to write programs that have these capabilities, and they are not really necessary in most programs. Windowing becomes increasingly important as the information load on the operator increases, and it obviously increases when the operator attempts to keep on top of a spreadsheet, word processor, and database all at the same time. In a simpler program, the information load is smaller, and windowing is unnecessary.

For most programs, paging or scrolling will work just fine. And, in general, you

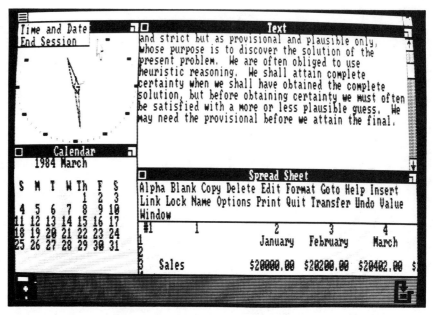

Figure 3-11 With a "windowed" display, the boundaries between separate screens are eliminated, as in this example, which contains separate windows for clock, calendar, word-processer, and spreadsheet. (*Photo courtesy of Microsoft Corporation.*)

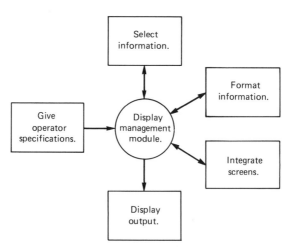

Figure 3-12 Windowing requires a display management module, which carries out an operator display specification by selecting and formatting information to display, integrating screens, and displaying the output.

should page rather than scroll. The code required to page complete screens and partial screens will be illustrated later in this chapter. But first we must cover the mechanics of screen printing and build some tools to work with.

Screen-Printing Mechanics

Before building actual screens, let us cover a few of the mechanics of screen generation. This subject has little to do with user-friendliness, but a great deal to do with how easily and effectively you can translate a screen design into BASIC code.

The simplest way to generate a screen with BASIC is to print it one row at a time, from top to bottom. The cursor is not positioned systematically but moves down one row as each row is printed. Such screen-generation code is extremely limited and only good for generating very simple screens. Usually it is more effective—and better practice—to position the cursor before printing each element of the screen. This requires cursor-positioning code. Thus, the first topic covered in this section is cursor positioning and screen generation.

It is often useful to clear part of a screen. The CLS statement lets you clear an entire screen but nothing less. Yet partial clearing of a screen—part of a single row, or a range of rows—is necessary in many different situations. Thus, we must devise some ways to do this and put them in our bag of tricks. The second topic in this section is clearing part of the screen.

In many situations, you need to introduce a temporary pause into a program, a sort of *Waiting for Godot* routine that will hold things still until the user decides to continue. The pause is the third topic in this section.

After covering these topics, we will have the tools necessary to illustrate paging and partial paging—the final topic in this section.

Cursor Positioning and Screen Generation

Top-bottom–left-right screen generation. The most common way to generate a screen is from top to bottom and from left to right (Figure 3-13). The display is first cleared, and then each row of the screen is generated using PRINT statements. If some of the information is printed to the right of column 1, then the

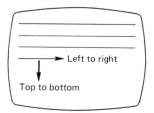

Figure 3-13 Top-bottom–left-right screen generation. The most common way to generate a screen is one row at a time, from top to bottom, with each row being printed from left to right.

```
5 KEY OFF
10 CLS
20 PRINT
30 PRINT TAB(30)"FILE SELECTION SCREEN"
40 PRINT
50 PRINT TAB(11)"File Number   File Name                     File Type"
60 PRINT TAB(11)"-----------   ------------------------      ---------"
70 FOR ROW=6 TO 17
80 PRINT TAB(16)"X        $$$$$$$$$$$$$$$$$$$$$$$$$$$    $$$$$$$$$"
90 NEXT
100 PRINT"-----------------------------------------------------------------
-----"
110 PRINT"  PROMPTS"
120 PRINT "  MESSAGES"
130 PRINT"  STATUS INDICATORS"
140 PRINT"-----------------------------------------------------------------
-----"
```

Figure 3-14   Program to generate screen shown in Figure 3-1 in the top-bottom–left-right manner.

cursor is moved there before printing with a TAB or LOCATE statement. To illustrate, Figure 3-14 shows some simple BASIC code for generating the screen shown in Figure 3-1 using the *top-bottom–left-right* method. This code has the obvious advantage that it is very simple. However, it has some serious drawbacks. For example:

- The code makes only one "pass" through the screen. Everything that is to be printed on row 1, 2, etc. must be printed during that single pass. There is no going back to add additional information or change anything.

- If you want to replace part of the screen and rewrite it with something new, you must rewrite the entire display.

Exercising cursor control during screen generation.   It is often desirable to generate the elements of a screen in some order other than top-bottom–left-right. For example, suppose that you want to create a screen consisting of a series of headings and data fields such as that shown in Figure 3-15. The headings are to remain on the display, but the data fields will change. In this case, it makes more sense to generate the headings first, and then go back and fill in the data fields, printing everything in the order shown in Figure 3-16.

Obviously, in order for the display to be printed in this order, the screen-generation code must consist of two separate parts: (1) screen-template generator and (2) data-field generator. The code is shown in Figure 3-17. This code is still quite simple. The screen template is created with a series of PRINT statements. The data fields are then filled in by first positioning the cursor with LOCATE statements and then printing in the new fields.

Such code can become considerably more involved, however. For example, if you want to clear part of the display and print an entirely new block there, then you must perform a screen-clearing operation first (Figure 3-18).

The foregoing illustrates some typical display situations, and all of them underline the importance of being able to generate the screen in the order that *you* want and find convenient, rather than the usual top-bottom–left-right manner. (The final example also illustrated the importance of being able to perform selective clearing of the display, about which more will be said later in this section.)

The key to being able to create screens this way is to maintain control of the

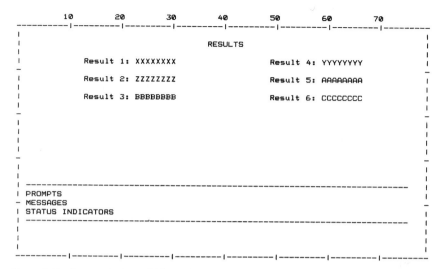

Figure 3-15 Screen design which requires cursor positioning for efficient generation.

cursor, rather than letting the cursor's position be decided by the providence of BASIC. Fortunately, it is easy to exercise this control through BASIC's TAB and LOCATE statements. Let us briefly consider the properties of these two statements and their use for cursor positioning.

Using TAB. Let us first consider TAB. To begin with, TAB positions the cursor in only one dimension, the horizontal. TAB is always used with a PRINT statement, and their combined syntax is as follows:

```
PRINT TAB (n) output
```

n is the cursor position, which may range from 1 to 255, but which will normally be in the range 1 to 80, since values above 80 wrap to the next row. *Output* is the information to be printed. Use of this statement is extremely simple, and most programmers master it in their first few hours of programming. To print something at, say, column 24, you use an expression of this form:

```
PRINT TAB (24) output
```

When this statement is executed, BASIC will obediently print *output* starting at column 24. (Incidentally, PC BASIC is nice in that the TAB argument n corresponds to the *column* rather than *column-1* as in some other BASICs.)

TAB has some drawbacks, however.

First, unlike the LOCATE statement, it does not permit you to position the cursor in the vertical dimension. Hence, in the vertical dimension at least, you are still at BASIC's mercy.

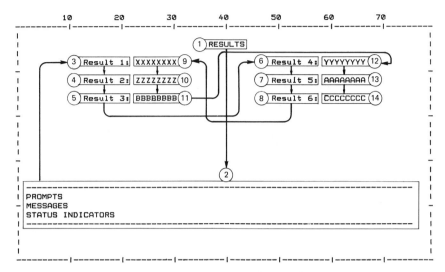

Figure 3-16 Desired order in which to generate different elements of screen shown in Figure 3-15. The screen template is generated first, and then the field contents are filled in.

```
5 KEY OFF
10 CLS
20 REM--Print Screen Template--
30 REM-Print Heading-
40 LOCATE 2,37
50 PRINT"RESULTS"
60 REM-Print Prompt & Message Area-
70 LOCATE 18,2
80 PRINT"----------------------------------------------------------------
----"
90 PRINT" PROMPTS"
100 PRINT" MESSAGES"
110 PRINT" STATUS INDICATORS"
120 PRINT"----------------------------------------------------------------
-----"
130 REM-Print Result Headings-
140 LOCATE 4,13:PRINT"Result 1:"
150 LOCATE 6,13:PRINT"Result 2:"
160 LOCATE 8,13:PRINT"Result 3:"
170 LOCATE 4,49:PRINT"Result 4:"
180 LOCATE 6,49:PRINT"Result 5:"
190 LOCATE 8,49:PRINT"Result 6:"
200 REM--Print Data Fields--
210 LOCATE 4,23:PRINT"XXXXXXXX"
220 LOCATE 6,23:PRINT"ZZZZZZZZ"
230 LOCATE 8,23:PRINT"BBBBBBBB"
240 LOCATE 4,59:PRINT"YYYYYYYY"
250 LOCATE 6,59:PRINT"AAAAAAAA"
260 LOCATE 8,59:PRINT"CCCCCCCC"
```

Figure 3-17 Program which uses cursor positioning to generate screen in the order shown in Figure 3-16.

```
5 KEY OFF
10 CLS
20 REM--Print Screen Template--
30 REM-Print Heading-
40 LOCATE 2,37
50 PRINT"RESULTS"
60 REM-Print Prompt & Message Area-
70 LOCATE 18,2
80 PRINT"-------------------------------------------------------------------------
----"
90 PRINT" PROMPTS"
100 PRINT" MESSAGES"
110 PRINT" STATUS INDICATORS"
120 PRINT"-------------------------------------------------------------------------
-----"
130 REM-Print Result Headings-
140 LOCATE 4,13:PRINT"Result 1:"
150 LOCATE 6,13:PRINT"Result 2:"
160 LOCATE 8,13:PRINT"Result 3:"
170 LOCATE 4,49:PRINT"Result 4:"
180 LOCATE 6,49:PRINT"Result 5:"
190 LOCATE 8,49:PRINT"Result 6:"
200 REM--Print Data Fields--
210 LOCATE 4,23:PRINT"XXXXXXXX"
220 LOCATE 6,23:PRINT"ZZZZZZZZ"
230 LOCATE 8,23:PRINT"BBBBBBBB"
240 LOCATE 4,59:PRINT"YYYYYYYY"
250 LOCATE 6,59:PRINT"AAAAAAAA"
260 LOCATE 8,59:PRINT"CCCCCCCC"
270 REM--Temporary Pause--
280 COLOR 31,0:REM high-intensity blinking
290 LOCATE 23,1
300 PRINT"Press any key to continue"
310 COLOR 7,0
320 A$=INKEY$:IF A$="" GOTO 310
330 LOCATE 23,1:PRINT SPACE$(25):REM erase prompt
340 REM--Erase and Reprint Data Fields--
350 REM-Erase-
360 LOCATE 4,23:PRINT"         "
370 LOCATE 6,23:PRINT"         "
380 LOCATE 8,23:PRINT"         "
390 LOCATE 4,59:PRINT"         "
400 LOCATE 6,59:PRINT"         "
410 LOCATE 8,59:PRINT"         "
420 REM-Reprint-
430 LOCATE 4,23:PRINT"New 1"
440 LOCATE 6,23:PRINT"New 2"
450 LOCATE 8,23:PRINT"New 3"
460 LOCATE 4,59:PRINT"New 4"
470 LOCATE 6,59:PRINT"New 5"
480 LOCATE 8,59:PRINT"New 6"
```

Figure 3-18   Modified version of program shown in Figure 3-17. This version fills in the data fields and then introduces a pause. When the user terminates the pause, the data fields are erased and rewritten with new data.

Second, it does not allow you to overprint two adjacent statements. To illustrate, type in and run the following lines.

```
10 PRINT TAB (20) "THIS IS THE FIRST STATEMENT";
20 PRINT TAB (28) "this is the second statement"
```

Note the semicolon at the end of line 10, which is intended to suppress the carriage return and line feed; one might expect the second statement to overprint the first, like this:

```
THIS IS this is the second statement
```

But that is not what happens. Instead, you get this:

```
THIS IS THE FIRST STATEMENT
this is the second statement
```

Since the two statements would overlap if printed as TAB directed, BASIC generates a line feed and carriage return and prints the second statement on the next row. Assuming that the programmer intended for the two rows to be overprinted, then luck fails, since BASIC does not allow it.

Third, TAB does not permit you to print from right to left when printing a given row. For example, type in and try these lines:

```
10 PRINT TAB (20) "JONES";
20 PRINT TAB (16) "TOM"
```

If you expect to get TOM JONES, you are soon disappointed; what you get is

```
     JONES
TOM
```

Using LOCATE.   The LOCATE statement has none of the drawbacks just demonstrated. That is, it (1) positions the cursor in both the vertical and horizontal coordinates, (2) permits overprinting, and (3) allows printing from right to left. Moreover, unlike TAB, LOCATE is not linked inextricably with the PRINT statement. You can use it to move the cursor anywhere you like without printing anything; this comes in handy for doing such things as positioning the blinking cursor.

The syntax of the LOCATE statement is as follows:

```
LOCATE row, column, cursor, start, stop
```

The first two arguments position the cursor to the row and column specified by the arguments *row* and *column*. The *row* argument may take on values in the range 1 to 25 and the *column* argument from 1 to 80 or 1 to 40, depending upon display width. The last three arguments set the visibility and size of the cursor (more on this later). In positioning the cursor, only the first two arguments are needed. For example, to position the cursor to row 7 and column 21, this statement would be used:

```
LOCATE 7,21
```

Once both arguments have been defined, subsequent LOCATE statements need only specify one argument. For example, to move the cursor from the position set above to row 8 of the same column, this statement would be used:

```
LOCATE 8
```

Similarly, the cursor could be moved to column 39 of a particular row with this statement:

```
LOCATE ,39
```

After this sequence of LOCATE statements has been executed,

```
LOCATE 10,20
LOCATE 15
LOCATE ,24
```

the cursor will be located at row 15, column 24. All of which gives you great flexibility and ease in cursor positioning.

Unlike TAB, LOCATE allows you to overprint. To illustrate, type in and run the following lines, which are based on those used earlier to attempt overprinting, except that now we are using the LOCATE statement instead of TAB:

```
10 LOCATE 10,20:PRINT "THIS IS THE FIRST STATEMENT";
20 LOCATE 10,28:PRINT "this is the second statement"
```

What you should get is this:

```
THIS IS this is the second statement
```

This time overprinting occurred.

Now let us print something from right to left on a given row. Type in and run these lines:

```
10 LOCATE 10,20:PRINT "JONES";
20 LOCATE ,16:PRINT "TOM"
```

What you should get is this:

```
TOM JONES
```

This time the printing occurred from right to left.

As you can see, LOCATE is more powerful than TAB for positioning the cursor. But how useful are these features? Positioning the cursor in both vertical and horizontal dimensions is very useful, especially when you are composing displays in the manner described earlier. It is less important to be able to overprint or to print from right to left, although these features do come in handy. At any rate, it is nice to know that you can do these things if you want to. LOCATE has two main shortcomings: (1) it cannot be used in printing reports and (2) it is a little more trouble to use. This means that you must print out hard-copy reports in the traditional manner—left-right–top-bottom—and that you may want to re-serve LOCATE's use for when it is really necessary. It is often simpler to generate certain types of displays with PRINT and PRINT TAB (n) statements than to use LOCATE every time you need to position the cursor.

Using LOCATE to control cursor size.   LOCATE has a second use that is often overlooked, namely, to control the size and visibility of the cursor. In this statement,

```
LOCATE row, column, cursor, start, stop
```

cursor turns the cursor on or off, and *start* and *stop* set the start and stop scan line.

The cursor is turned on with a *cursor* value of 1 and off with a *cursor* value of 0. (A word of friendly advice: do not turn it off.)

You can increase or decrease the size of the cursor by redefining *start* and *stop*. The cursor consists of scan lines, and the number of scan lines differs depending upon whether your display is generated with the Color/Graphics adapter or the Monochrome/Printer adapter (if you have a PC*jr*, your display behaves like one generated by the Color/Graphics adapter). The Color/Graphics adapter generates eight scan lines (0 to 7) per row and the Monochrome/Printer adapter generates 14 (0 to 13), as shown in Figure 3-19.

You control the size of the cursor by setting *start* to the location of the top line and *stop* to the location of the bottom line. For example, if you have the Monochrome/Printer adapter and want the cursor to be as large as possible, you would set the top scan line to 0 and the bottom line to 13, like this:

```
LOCATE ,,,0,13
```

Monochrome/Printer adapter   Color/Graphics adapter

```
 0 ————————        0 ————————
 1 ————————
 2 ————————        1 ————————
 3 ————————
 4 ————————        2 ————————
 5 ————————
 6 ————————        3 ————————
 7 ————————        4 ————————
 8 ————————
 9 ————————        5 ————————
10 ————————
11 ————————        6 ————————
12 ————————
13 ————————        7 ————————
```

Figure 3-19 The cursor is composed of scan lines. The Monochrome/Printer adapter generates fourteen scan lines, numbered 0 to 13 (left). The Color/Graphics adapter generates eight scan lines, numbered 0 to 7 (right).

With the Color/Graphics adapter, the same effect can be achieved with this statement:

```
LOCATE ,,,0,7
```

With either adapter, you can set the cursor to a single line at the top of the character position with this statement:

```
LOCATE ,,,0,0
```

You can "split" the cursor in two by setting *stop* to a greater value than *start*. To illustrate, try this:

```
LOCATE ,,,5,2
```

Are these tricks useful for anything?

Actually, yes. Most PC users never complain about the "normal" single-line cursor which blinks unobtrusively away, but the fact is that it is small and fairly difficult to find, unless you know where to look. For this reason, it is recommended that you increase its size to make life easier for the operator—and yourself as well. It is suggested that you set its size to extend from the top to the bottom of the character position, excluding superscripts and subscripts. If you have a Monochrome/Printer adapter, this translates to scan lines 5 to 13; with the Color/Graphics adapter it translates to scan lines 0 to 6. In other words, early in your program, execute one of the following LOCATE statements:

```
LOCATE ,,,5,13 (Monochrome/Printer adapter)
```

or

```
LOCATE ,,,0,6 (Color/Graphics adapter or PCjr)
```

Doing this will make the cursor much more visible and help the operator find it.

In addition, it is sometimes useful to change the cursor's shape within the program depending upon which mode the program is in or which function is being performed. As you have probably noticed, the size of the cursor increases when you press the Ins key in order to enter insert mode. The size change is a simple way to show that the mode has changed, and that keyboard entries will have a different effect than they did before. If your program will make use of such mode changes, altering the cursor's appearance is a sure way to make the operator aware of the new condition.

You can make the cursor take on a variety of appearances (Figure 3-20). If you do decide to change the way it looks, do not get carried away. Use a maximum of 3 to 5 *distinctly different* cursor shapes, and use fewer than this if possible. As you increase the number of cursors used, you make it more difficult for the operator to decode and make sense of them.

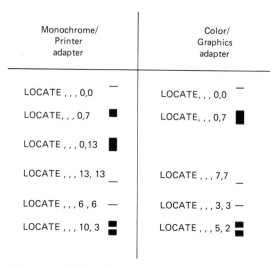

Figure 3-20   Effect of various LOCATE statements upon the appearance of the cursor.

Clearing Part of the Screen

Screens should not be thought of as static things whose information, once presented, must remain forever in place. Though many screens may, indeed, remain the same, once they are written, it is very often useful to replace various screen elements with new ones.

For example, you might want to retain a display template on the screen while erasing and rewriting the data fields corresponding to different file records (Figure 3-21).

In another situation, you might want to present portions of a directory on the screen, allowing the operator to page through the directory at will. The content of this directory should be capable of being changed without the entire screen being rewritten. In this case you would want to retain headings and other identification information on the screen while displaying different portions of the directory as the operator pages through it (Figure 3-22).

In these and many other situations, you need to be able to clear selected portions of the screen. In the first case, it is necessary to clear each data field, and in the second it is necessary to clear portions of particular rows. Since these functions must be performed frequently, it is useful to have a simple, foolproof method to do the job—preferably in the form of a subroutine. What follows are descriptions of three such subroutines. In each case, the cursor is first positioned to a particular *row* and *column,* and then the subroutine performs the clearing operation. The three subroutines are, respectively, (1) clear part of a row, (2) clear to the end of a row, and (3) clear a range of rows (Figure 3-23a, b, c). In all subroutines, the starting row and column are defined by the arguments ROW and COL. (Incidentally, you can save a few bytes of memory by using the integer form of these variables—ROW% and COL%—but the author is using the real

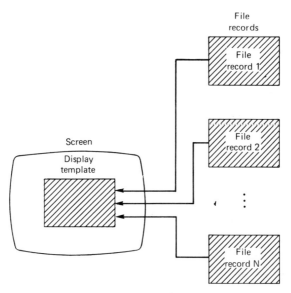

Figure 3-21 This screen consists of a display template and a central display area to present information. The central area is cleared, and then a file record is presented.

form to aid the clarity of the discussion. The same holds true for several other variables discussed in this and later chapters.)

Clearing part of one row.   Figure 3-24 contains the listing of a subroutine for clearing part of one row. After the clearing operation, the cursor is repositioned to the beginning of the field. Arguments of the subroutine are ROW, COL, and LENGTH, where LENGTH is the length of the field to be cleared.

To use this subroutine, the arguments are set and then the subroutine is called. For example, to clear a field of length 10 that is positioned at row 10 and column 20, code such as this would be used:

```
10 ROW = 10
20 COL = 20
30 LENGTH = 10
40 GOSUB 1000
```

This subroutine is useful for erasing a portion of a row before rewriting it. It might be used to clear a data field, as described earlier. For example, Figure 3-25 shows how you can display a heading and then erase and replace what follows that heading very easily.

In this listing, lines 20 to 40 set the arguments and line 50 calls the subroutine to clear the heading row. Line 60 prints the heading. Lines 70 to 110 then print the data field, which consists of all the characters with ASCII values 65 to 90 (the capital letters). Note that line 70 resets the COL argument to 31, which is one space to the right of the colon in the heading. Thus, the data field is cleared by the subroutine call at line 90 each time a character is printed.

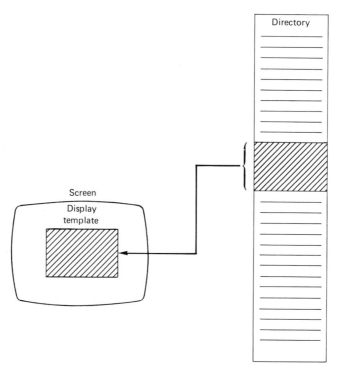

Figure 3-22 This screen consists of a display template and a central display area to present information. The central area is cleared before showing different segments of a long directory.

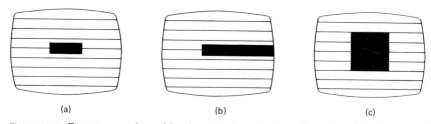

(a)   (b)   (c)

Figure 3-23 Functions performed by three display clearing subroutines: (*a*) clear part of one row, (*b*) clear to end of row, and (*c*) clear a range of rows and columns.

```
1000 REM--Clear Part of One Row--
1010 LOCATE ROW,COL:REM position cursor
1020 PRINT SPACE$(LENGTH):REM clear part of row
1030 LOCATE ROW,COL:REM reposition cursor
1040 RETURN
```

Figure 3-24 Subroutine to clear part of one row.

```
5 KEY OFF
10 CLS
20 ROW=10
30 COL=20
40 LENGTH=10
50 GOSUB 1000
60 PRINT"Character: "
70 COL=31
80 FOR ASCII=65 TO 90
90 GOSUB 1000
100 PRINT CHR$(ASCII)
110 NEXT
120 END
1000 REM--Clear Part of One Row--
1010 LOCATE ROW,COL:REM position cursor
1020 PRINT SPACE$(LENGTH):REM clear part of row
1030 LOCATE ROW,COL:REM reposition cursor
1040 RETURN
```

Figure 3-25 This program will print the heading "Character:", and then print the capital letters A through Z opposite.

A more interesting application of the subroutine is in data entry. Here it can be used (among other things) to erase an invalid entry and clear the row before printing an error message. Figure 3-26 is the listing of a simple data-input program to collect any number between 1 and 10 but to exclude numbers outside this range. In this listing, lines 10 to 30 set the arguments, with LENGTH being set to 32 (the length of the error message). Line 40 calls the row-clearing subroutine. Line 50 contains an INPUT statement which prints the prompt "Number" and then assigns the typed-in value to the variable N. Line 60 conducts a simple range test: The acceptable range is 1 to 10, and if the number passes the test, a GOTO sends control to line 110. If the test is failed, then lines 70 to 110 are executed. Line 70 calls the row-clearing subroutine, line 80 prints an error message, and line 90 uses a FOR-NEXT loop to introduce a time delay during which the message remains on the screen. After the delay, control drops to line 100, whose GOTO sends it back to line 40, starting the process over again. When this program is run, the user is prompted to enter a number. If an acceptable number is typed in, the program ends. If an unacceptable number is typed in, then the

```
5 KEY OFF
6 CLS
10 ROW=20
20 COL=1
30 LENGTH=32
40 GOSUB 1000
50 INPUT"Type in number (1-10): ";N
60 IF N)=1 AND N<=10 GOTO 110 ELSE 70:REM range test
70 GOSUB 1000
80 PRINT"Number must be between 1 and 10!":REM error message
90 FOR TIME=1 TO 6000:NEXT:REM time delay loop
100 GOTO 40
110 PRINT "Number=";N
120 END
1000 REM--Clear Part of One Row--
1010 LOCATE ROW,COL:REM position cursor
1020 PRINT SPACE$(LENGTH):REM clear part of row
1030 LOCATE ROW,COL:REM reposition cursor
1040 RETURN
```

Figure 3-26 This program uses the subroutine (lines 1000 to 1040) to erase the prompt and temporarily print an error message in its place if an out-of-range value is entered in response to the prompt.

```
1060 REM--Clear to End of Row--
1070 LOCATE ROW,COL:REM position cursor
1080 PRINT SPACE$(COLUMNS+1-COL):REM clear to end of row
1090 LOCATE ROW,COL:REM reposition cursor
1100 RETURN
```

Figure 3-27 Subroutine to clear to the end of a row.

error message is briefly displayed, and the user is required to make a new entry. (Incidentally, while Figure 3-26 illustrates the use of the row-clearing subroutine, it is not a good model of how to construct data-input programs. For better ones, refer to Chapters 5 and 6.)

Clearing to the end of a row. The second clearing subroutine (Figure 3-27) allows you to clear to the end of a row. Subroutine arguments are ROW, COL, and COLUMNS. The first two arguments are identical to those of the row-clearing subroutine (Figure 3-24). COLUMNS is the number of columns of the display (80 or 40). This subroutine allows you to erase everything to the right of the cursor in a given row. This might be used for applications similar to those of Figure 3-24—but when nothing is being printed to the right of the field being cleared.

This subroutine is similar to the earlier one except for line 1080:

```
1080 PRINT SPACE$(COLUMNS+1-COL)
```

This line calculates the number of spaces from COL to the right edge of the display, and then prints enough spaces to erase the row from COL to the edge. For example, if COL is 20, and COLUMNS is 80, then $80 + 1 - 20 = 61$ spaces are printed, starting at column 20 and ending at column 80. Since no LENGTH argument is required, this subroutine is somewhat simpler to use than that in Figure 3-24.

Clearing a range of rows. The third clearing subroutine (Figure 3-28) allows you to clear a range of rows. Subroutine arguments are ROW1 (starting row), ROW2 (ending row), COL, and WIDE (number of columns to clear).

This subroutine can be used to clear as many columns of as many rows as you want to specify; essentially, it erases a rectangle within the arguments specified, as shown in Figure 3-29.

As will be shown later in this chapter, this subroutine lets you do partial paging by moving different display blocks onto the screen against a display template that remains in place (more on this later).

Let us illustrate the subroutine's use by clearing columns 10 to 20 in rows 14 to

```
1110 REM--Clear Range of Rows--
1120 FOR ROW=ROW1 TO ROW2
1130 LOCATE ROW,COL:REM position cursor
1140 PRINT SPACE$(WIDE):REM clear part of row
1150 NEXT
1160 RETURN
```

Figure 3-28 Subroutine to clear a range of rows.

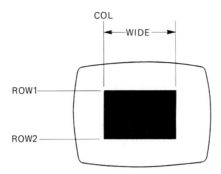

Figure 3-29 Arguments used by subroutine
shown in Figure 5-33.

20. To do this, the subroutine's arguments would be set and the subroutine called
like this:

```
10 COL = 10
20 WIDE = 10
30 ROW1 = 14
40 ROW2 = 20
50 GOSUB 1110
```

Figure 3-30 contains the listing of a little program that fills the screen with Xs and
then allows you to set the arguments to clear selected portions of the screen. Type
this in and try it out to get a feeling for the operation of the subroutine.

The three subroutines just described are very simple but, as you will see, they
can come in handy in many situations. The subsection that follows illustrates
their use to do partial paging.

The Pause

At various points during many programs you may want to halt the program until
the user gives an order to continue. Examples of such situations are while

```
5 KEY OFF
10 CLS
20 REM--Fill Screen with X's--
30 FOR ROW=1 TO 18
40 PRINT STRING$(79,"X"):REM use 39 for 40-column display
50 NEXT
60 REM--Collect Clearing Parameters--
70 LOCATE 20,1
80 INPUT"Type in COL: ";COL
90 INPUT"Type in ROW1, ROW2: ";ROW1,ROW2
100 INPUT"Type in WIDE: ";WIDE
110 GOSUB 1110
120 END
1110 REM--Clear Range of Rows--
1120 FOR ROW=ROW1 TO ROW2
1130 LOCATE ROW,COL:REM position cursor
1140 PRINT SPACE$(WIDE):REM clear part of row
1150 NEXT
1160 RETURN
```

Figure 3-30 Program to demonstrate use of subroutine shown in
Figure 3-28.

viewing a page of directions, before printing out a report, and after directing the user to insert a particular disk into a given disk drive. In each of these situations, the user must be given a chance to digest the information on the screen and perhaps act before the program proceeds.

Temporary pauses are very easy to insert into a program. The simplest way is with the INPUT statement, like this:

```
1000 INPUT "Press Enter key to continue ";A$
```

When the program comes to this line, it will print the prompt, followed by a blinking cursor, and then wait patiently until the Enter key is pressed, at which point the program will continue. While this will work, it will respond only to the Enter key and suffers from certain shortcomings that are inherent in using the INPUT statement (see Chapter 5 for the gory details); its use is not recommended.

It is much better to use the INKEY$ statement, and develop a routine such as this one:

```
1000 PRINT "Press any key to continue"
1010 A$=INKEY$:IF A$="" GOTO 1010
```

Here, the INKEY$ loop in line 1010 will respond to any of the standard keys that are pressed and allow the program to continue. The Enter key does *not* have to be pressed following the key.

You can, of course, also make the INKEY$ loop more selective. Suppose, for example, that you want the program to halt until the space bar is pressed. By changing line 1010 to read like this, the program will continue following a space bar press:

```
1010 A$=INKEY$:IF A$<>" " GOTO 1010
```

Likewise, by putting other characters or ASCII values after the <> sign, you can make the pause terminate after various other key presses. For example,

```
1010 A$=INKEY$:IF A$<>"A" GOTO 1010:REM "A" key
1010 A$=INKEY$:IF A$<>CHR$(13) GOTO 1010:REM Enter key
1010 A$=INKEY$:IF A$<>CHR$(27) GOTO 1010:REM ESC key
```

And so on.

Though these little pauses can be constructed in many different ways, two very useful pauses are those that respond to (1) any key and (2) space bar press. If you make the required key press more stringent than this, you sort of defeat the purpose of the pause which is, simply, to hold things up until the operator is ready to continue. When ready, it should not be necessary to search for some specific key to press, but should be as easy as, say, pressing any key or—what is nearly as simple—pressing the space bar.

Moreover, since it may be assumed that the operator will usually be observing the upper part of the display prior to giving the go-ahead signal, it makes sense to

```
1200 REM--Temporary Pause--
1210 LOCATE 23,28:REM (use LOCATE 23,8 for 40-column display)
1220 COLOR 31,0:REM high intensity blinking
1230 PRINT"Press Any Key to Continue"
1240 A$=INKEY$:IF A$="" GOTO 1240
1250 LOCATE 23,28
1260 PRINT SPACE$(25):REM erase prompt
1270 COLOR 7,0:REM normal video
1280 RETURN
```

Figure 3-31 Subroutine to introduce a temporary pause and print the blinking message "Press any key to continue" until any key is pressed.

display the go-ahead prompt at the bottom of the screen. If the function key definitions are displayed on row 25, then one of the lines above it may be used for the prompt. If function key definitions are not displayed, then row 25 may be used.

Figure 3-31 contains the listing of a simple subroutine to introduce a temporary pause into the program, until *any* key is pressed. When the subroutine is called, it prints the blinking message "Press any key to continue" on row 23 of the display. The subroutine, as written, is for a PC with 80-column display; the remark on line 1210 tells how to modify it for 40-column display.

Partial Paging

Now that the mechanics of screen generation and the elements of screen design have been covered, let us combine some of the pieces and look at the code required to do partial paging. Partial paging requires that you first print a screen *template* (the permanent part of the screen) on the video display. The remaining part of the screen is then printed, erased, and then rewritten with new information, and so on. The basic idea is illustrated in Figure 3-32*a, b, c*. The template is laid on the screen (Figure 3-32*a*), data set 1 is written to the display (Figure 3-32*b*), and then data set 1 is erased and data set 2 written to the screen (Figure 3-32*c*).

Partial paging can become considerably more imaginative than this. For example, part of the display template may be erased and rewritten, as well as the information on the display.

To illustrate the method more concretely, let us dive right in and solve a specific problem, namely, how to create the code used to generate the screens illustrated in Figure 3-32*a, b, c*. Figure 3-33 is a listing of the required code. In this listing, the following functions are performed:

Write template

Write data set 1

Pause

Erase data set 1

Write data set 2

You can extend the method just illustrated to more complex display problems—those requiring different parts of the template or information content of the screen to be erased and rewritten.

Screen Layout

There are four general rules for laying out screens:

1. Title and label them.
2. Center and balance the information.
3. Be consistent in the way you present information.
4. Separate the different types of information.

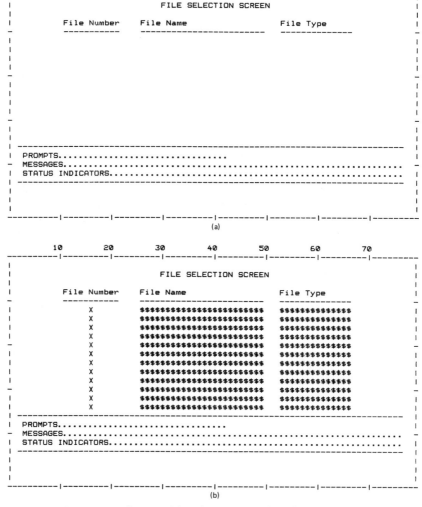

Figure 3-32 Appearance of screen (*a*) with screen template alone, (*b*) after data set 1 has been printed, and (*c*) after data set 1 has been erased and data set 2 has been printed.

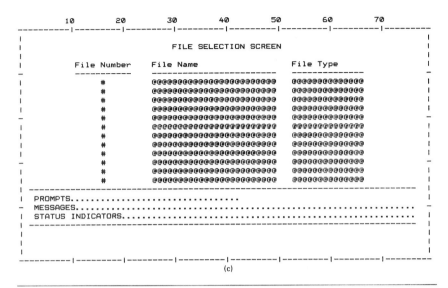

```
         10       20       30       40       50       60       70
---------I---------I---------I---------I---------I---------I---------I---------
I                          FILE SELECTION SCREEN                              I
I                                                                             I
I        File Number    File Name                    File Type               I
-        -----------    ---------------------------  --------------          -
I             #         @@@@@@@@@@@@@@@@@@@@@@@@@@@@  @@@@@@@@@@@@@@           I
I             #         @@@@@@@@@@@@@@@@@@@@@@@@@@@@  @@@@@@@@@@@@@@           I
I             #         @@@@@@@@@@@@@@@@@@@@@@@@@@@@  @@@@@@@@@@@@@@           I
I             #         @@@@@@@@@@@@@@@@@@@@@@@@@@@@  @@@@@@@@@@@@@@           I
-             #         @@@@@@@@@@@@@@@@@@@@@@@@@@@@  @@@@@@@@@@@@@@           -
I             #         @@@@@@@@@@@@@@@@@@@@@@@@@@@@  @@@@@@@@@@@@@@           I
I             #         @@@@@@@@@@@@@@@@@@@@@@@@@@@@  @@@@@@@@@@@@@@           I
I             #         @@@@@@@@@@@@@@@@@@@@@@@@@@@@  @@@@@@@@@@@@@@           I
I             #         @@@@@@@@@@@@@@@@@@@@@@@@@@@@  @@@@@@@@@@@@@@           I
-             #         @@@@@@@@@@@@@@@@@@@@@@@@@@@@  @@@@@@@@@@@@@@           -
I             #         @@@@@@@@@@@@@@@@@@@@@@@@@@@@  @@@@@@@@@@@@@@           I
I             #         @@@@@@@@@@@@@@@@@@@@@@@@@@@@  @@@@@@@@@@@@@@           I
I    -----------------------------------------------------------------       I
I  PROMPTS............................                                        I
-  MESSAGES........................................................          -
I  STATUS INDICATORS.............................................            I
I    -----------------------------------------------------------------       I
I                                                                             I
I                                                                             I
I                                                                             I
---------I---------I---------I---------I---------I---------I---------I---------
                                  (c)
```

Figure 3-32   (continued)

Titling and Labeling

Title each screen so that operators know what it is. Without a title, the screen has no name, and operators must make up one of their own. It is better if you do this for them. In addition, you cannot really talk about or deal with something that does not have a name, as you will find out when documentation is being prepared. For example, it is awkward to talk about the "screen that appears when you page from the screen selected with the third option of the main menu." Much better to talk about the "file definition" screen, or the like. It is suggested that you present this title in capital letters, centered at the top of the screen. Centering is traditional for titles, and it makes as much sense on screens as everywhere else. The use of capital letters is also traditional, although there may be occasions when you want to use upper- and lowercase, reverse video, underlining, or various combinations of these. (Chapter 4 gives guidelines for using the special video modes.)

Centering a title.   To center a title on the display, count the number of characters it contains, subtract this from the number of columns being displayed (80 or 40), divide by 2, add 1, round to the nearest whole number, and print the title at the column number computed. (Incidentally, the 1 is added so that the character string will be printed one column to the right of one-half the difference between the display width and the length of the title; if 1 is not added, the title will be printed too far to the left.)

For example, suppose that you want to center and print the title "DISPLAY TITLE" on an 80-column display. This title contains thirteen characters. Hence, the column number is computed as follows:

$$COL = (80 - 13)/2 + 1 = 34.5 \cong 35$$

```
5 KEY OFF
10 REM--Write Screen Template--
20 CLS
30 LOCATE 2,30
40 PRINT"FILE SELECTION SCREEN"
50 LOCATE 4,11
60 PRINT        "File Number    File Name              File Type"
70 PRINT TAB(11)"----------     ----------------------   ----------"
80 LOCATE 18,2
90 PRINT STRING$(76,"-")
100 PRINT"   PROMPTS"
110 PRINT "   MESSAGES"
120 PRINT"   STATUS INDICATORS"
130 PRINT STRING$(76,"-")
140 REM--Write Data Set 1--
150 FOR ROW=6 TO 17
160 LOCATE ROW,16
170 PRINT"X        $$$$$$$$$$$$$$$$$$$$$$$$$$$$   $$$$$$$$$"
180 NEXT
190 REM--Pause--
200 GOSUB 1200
210 REM--Erase Data Set 1--
220 ROW1=6
230 ROW2=17
240 COL=16
250 WIDE=50
260 GOSUB 1110
270 REM--Write Data Set 2--
280 FOR ROW=6 TO 17
290 LOCATE ROW,16
300 PRINT"#        @@@@@@@@@@@@@@@@@@@@@@@@@@@@   @@@@@@@@@"
310 NEXT
320 END
1110 REM--Clear Range of Rows--
1120 FOR ROW=ROW1 TO ROW2
1130 LOCATE ROW,COL:REM position cursor
1140 PRINT SPACE$(WIDE):REM clear part of row
1150 NEXT
1160 RETURN
1200 REM--Temporary Pause--
1210 LOCATE 23,28:REM (use LOCATE 23,8 for 40-column display)
1220 COLOR 31,0:REM high intensity blinking
1230 PRINT"Press Any Key to Continue"
1240 A$=INKEY$:IF A$="" GOTO 1240
1250 LOCATE 23,28
1260 PRINT SPACE$(25):REM erase prompt
1270 COLOR 7,0:REM normal video
1280 RETURN
```

Figure 3-33   Program required to generate sequence of screens shown in Figure 5-32a, b, and c.

And you would print the title with a statement such as

```
PRINT TAB(35) "DISPLAY TITLE"
```

or

```
LOCATE 1,35 : PRINT "DISPLAY TITLE"
```

You can make programming a little simpler by having a subroutine perform the above procedure for you. Figure 3-34 contains the listing of a subroutine that will calculate the column number and print the title on a video display. The argument of the subroutine is TITLE$. The subroutine then calculates the column number, assigns it to the variable COL, and prints the title on the display.

```
1300 REM--Center & Print Title (video display)--
1310 COL=(81-LEN(TITLE$))/2:REM (use 41 for 40-column display)
1320 LOCATE ,COL
1330 PRINT TITLE$
1340 RETURN
```

Figure 3-34 Subroutine to center and print a title on a video display.

Centering and printing a title is a simple matter of defining the title and making a subroutine call, like this:

```
10 TITLE$ = "DISPLAY TITLE"
20 GOSUB 1300
```

Creating a title page. The subroutine shown in Figure 3-34 does not position the cursor to a particular row. Hence, you can use it to center any character string at any row of the screen. This makes it handy for centering character strings in other applications. For example, suppose that you want to create a program title page containing the following program name, publisher, author's name, and copyright information:

```
PSYCHOLOGICAL PROFILE ANALYSIS PROGRAM
Softpsych Software, Inc.
Author: Morton Bayfig, Ph.D
Copyright 1985 by Softpsych Software, Inc.
```

Creating the title page is quite simple. Clear the screen with a CLS statement, locate the cursor at the starting row, and then assign the arguments and make the calls to the Center & Print subroutine. The code required is shown in Figure 3-35. The resulting screen will appear as shown in Figure 3-36.

The centering subroutine can be easily modified to center and print a title on a hardcopy display. Figure 3-37 shows a version of the subroutine with the required modifications. The LOCATE statement—which is nonfunctional with a printer—has been deleted and the print head is positioned with PRINT TAB (n).

```
5 KEY OFF
10 CLS
20 LOCATE 10
30 TITLE$="PSYCHOLOGICAL PROFILE ANALYSIS PROGRAM"
40 GOSUB 1300
50 TITLE$="Softpsych Software, Inc."
60 GOSUB 1300
70 TITLE$="Morton Bayfig, Ph.D"
80 GOSUB 1300
90 TITLE$="Copyright 1985 by Softpsych Software, Inc."
100 GOSUB 1300
110 END
1300 REM--Center & Print Title (video display)--
1310 COL=(81-LEN(TITLE$))/2:REM (use 41 for 40-column display)
1320 LOCATE ,COL
1330 PRINT TITLE$
1340 RETURN
```

Figure 3-35 Code required to generate a title page with centered titles.

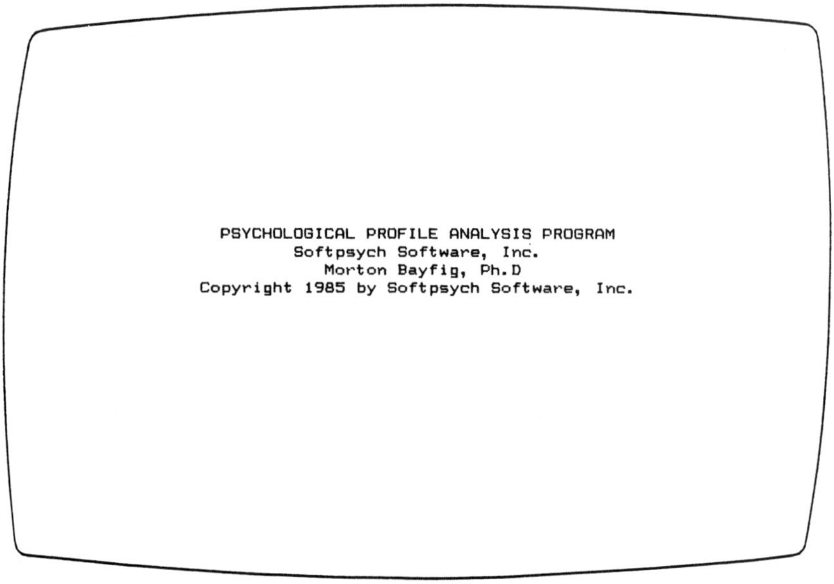

```
        PSYCHOLOGICAL PROFILE ANALYSIS PROGRAM
             Softpsych Software, Inc.
               Morton Bayfig, Ph.D
        Copyright 1985 by Softpsych Software, Inc.
```

Figure 3-36   Appearance of screen produced by code shown in Figure 3-35.

Right justification.   On occasion you may want to right-justify what you display—align everything you print on a common right margin—like this:

```
PSYCHOLOGICAL PROFILE ANALYSIS PROGRAM
            Softpsych Software, Inc.
         Author: Morton Bayfig, Ph.D
Copyright 1985 by Softpsych Software, Inc.
```

It is *not* good practice to do extensive right-justification since it makes text more difficult to read. However, on title pages and on certain other screens, you can make the screen more appealing with selective use of right-justification. To right-justify the text at a particular column, count the number of characters in the string, subtract this from the column number you want to justify to, and print the title at the column number computed. For example, to right-justify the character string "RIGHT STRING" to column 79, compute COL as follows:

```
COL = (79 - LEN ( "RIGHT STRING" ) ) = 67
```

Then print the string at the calculated column. It is quite easy to write a little subroutine that will right-justify the string to whatever column you want (Figure

```
1350 REM--Center & Print Title (printer)--
1360 COL=(81-LEN(TITLE$))/2
1370 LPRINT TAB(COL) TITLE$
1380 RETURN
```

Figure 3-37   Subroutine to center and print
a title with an 80-column printer.

```
1390 REM--Right Justify & Print Title--
1400 LOCATE ,(COL-LEN(TITLE$))
1410 PRINT TITLE$
1420 RETURN
```

Figure 3-38 Subroutine to right-justify a title.

3-38). The arguments of this subroutine are COL (column to right-justify to) and TITLE$, and these arguments are set and the subroutine called in the usual manner. The code required to generate the hypothetical title page described above is shown in Figure 3-39.

(Incidentally, you can often improve the appearance of a title page by using bars, lines, boxes, or color—see the discussion of "Separation of Information," which follows.)

Within-screen labels. The preceding discussion touched on two different types of screen titling or labeling: (1) screen title and (2) program title page. Each program should have a title page that tells what it is, and each screen needs its own title. In addition to these two types of titles, some screens require within-screen labels to identify the content of their different areas (Figure 3-40). While there are no strict rules about what to label, it is important to make sure that everything which is not self-evident *is* labeled—even if what it is seems totally obvious to you. Do not be concerned about labeling too much; it is far better to err in this direction than to leave doubt about what a particular area of the screen contains. Do not make operators decipher a screen. Using your program should not be a test of their intelligence or ingenuity. Make it easy for them.

In sum, keep in mind that there are three levels at which your program requires titles or labels: (1) program, (2) screen, and (3) within screen (Figure 3-41).

Centering and Balancing

Center information (Figure 3-42). Think of the screen as the page of a book. The information on a printed page does not start at the left edge of the paper. Rather, left and right margins are set, and then the information is centered. Figures and tables are centered as well. For partial pages, information is centered vertically. These conventions are followed because they make a page easier to interpret

```
5 KEY OFF
10 CLS
20 COL=60
30 LOCATE 10
40 TITLE$="PSYCHOLOGICAL PROFILE ANALYSIS PROGRAM"
50 GOSUB 1390
60 TITLE$="Softpsych Software, Inc."
70 GOSUB 1390
80 TITLE$="Morton Bayfig, Ph.D"
90 GOSUB 1390
100 TITLE$="Copyright 1985 by Softpsych Software, Inc."
110 GOSUB 1390
120 END
1390 REM--Right Justify & Print Title--
1400 LOCATE ,(COL-LEN(TITLE$))
1410 PRINT TITLE$
1420 RETURN
```

Figure 3-39 Code required to generate a right-justified title page.

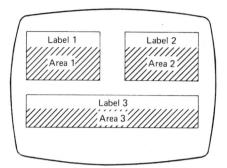

Figure 3-40 Use within-screen labels to identify different areas of the screen.

and more symmetric and pleasing to the eye. They are also the conventions that
every one of us has learned and gotten used to. It is natural for operators to expect
text conventions to be followed within computer programs. Yet, it is very common
to encounter a computer program whose screens are off-center—usually with
everything left-justified, since such screens can be created almost without thinking. For example, how many menus, blocks of numeric information, and text

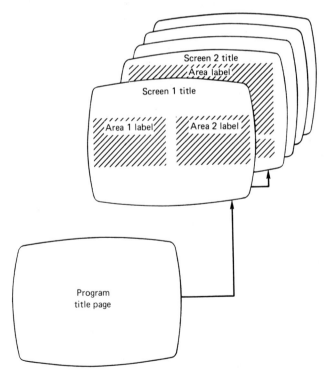

Figure 3-41 A screen requires three types of titles or labels: program title page, screen title, and within-screen labels.

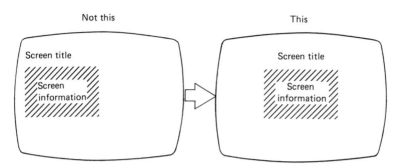

Figure 3-42   Center information on the screen.

examples have you seen that looked like the "Not this" versions shown in Figures 3-43*a, b,* and *c,* respectively? The centered versions of these screens have a much more attractive and professional appearance.

Admittedly, it is extra work to center everything, which is one of the reasons that a screen layout matrix (Figure 2-5) is important. If you left-justify everything, you can more or less forget about positioning things on the screen and simply let the information fall where it happens to fall. To center the information, you must estimate the size of the block and then allocate space to the left and right, and top and bottom, so that you can position the headings, numbers, words, and so forth appropriately (Figure 3-44). In general, the left and right margins should be the same, as should the top and bottom margins.

And if you must position more than one block, then you must make several estimates, including the size of each block and the distances between blocks. As before, keep the left and right margins the same, and top and bottom margins the same. Allow a minimum of two spaces between blocks, and more if there is room—preferably, there should be as much space between blocks as at the margins of the display (Figure 3-45). While there are no rigid rules about how to compose the screen, you must (1) allow adequate space between blocks and (2) give the screen an overall "balanced" appearance. Composing the screen requires that you exercise your aesthetic judgment to a certain extent; if you do not trust yours, get a friend to help you (a good idea in any case).

Consistency

Screens often contain different types of information, such as a title, directions, prompt line, error-message line, operating mode indicator, and so forth. A given *type* or class of information—a prompt line, for example—may appear on several different screens. Determine what types of information you will present, and then present this information consistently from screen to screen. Assign an *area* to each type of information. To the extent possible, keep each type of information in the same location, regardless of screen (Figure 3-46).

Note that the requirement for consistency may sometimes conflict with other design requirements. For example, it might conflict with the above recommendation to create "balanced" screens. In a particular type of program, you may present more information on some screens than on others. Creating a balanced

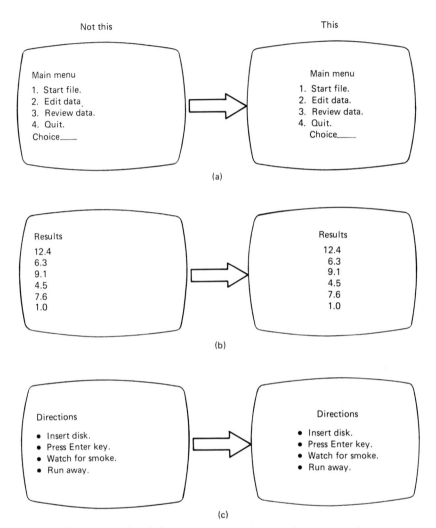

Figure 3-43 Three examples of alternative ways to present information on the screen (i.e., left-justified versus centered): (*a*) menu, (*b*) numeric information, and (*c*) text. The preferred screens are those with information centered.

screen might require you to change the margins and location of certain information items from screen to screen. But consistency requires that you present the same type of information in the same location from screen to screen. When such conflicts arise, design the screen for consistency. Balancing the screen is desirable, but it is primarily an aesthetic factor. Consistency will affect performance and is the more important factor of the two.

By being consistent, you make it easier for the operator to learn your rules for displaying information. If you follow these rules for all screens, then operators can learn them quickly. If you change the rules from screen to screen, then they

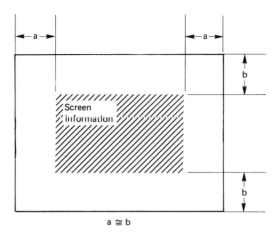

Figure 3-44 Attempt to keep upper and lower margins equal, and left and right margins equal. Ideally, all margins should be the same.

have more to learn and you make it more difficult for them. In addition, if you are not consistent, operators may mistake information appearing on a particular part of the screen for something that it is not. For example, if on one screen you present error messages on the second row, and on another screen you put the operating mode indicator there, operators may confuse one for the other.

Consistency is obviously an ideal and can rarely be accomplished fully. By necessity, some parts of the screen must be used for many different things. For example, the bottom rows of a screen are often used for prompts, error messages, and status indicators. Using an area for more than one thing does not pose a serious problem—the problem arises when you do something one way in one place and differently elsewhere. Then the rule apparently changes and may confuse operators.

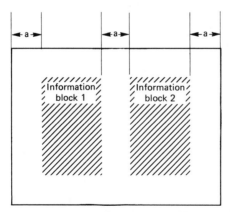

Figure 3-45 Space the information blocks to allow approximately the same amount of room between blocks as at the margins.

Edit Mode

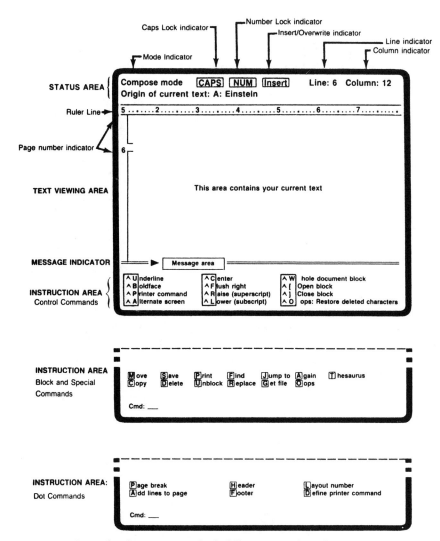

Figure 3-46 Example of a screen in which different areas have been assigned different functions. Also note the use of reverse video to highlight the status of the Caps Lock, Num Lock, and Ins keys. (*Courtesy of Alison Software.*)

Separation of Information

Format the screen so that the different blocks and types of information it contains are clearly separated from one another. If one thing runs into another, the implication is that both are parts of the same thing. When you follow the rule of consistency (noted above) the operator is helped in sorting things out, but you should go a step further by separating the screen areas *graphically*. That is, divide the screen up into different blocks, and separate the blocks by rows or columns of blank spaces, lines, or by color-coding the blocks themselves (Figure 3-47a, b, c). A combination of these techniques—though not usually required—makes the division between blocks even more obvious. The simplest way to separate blocks

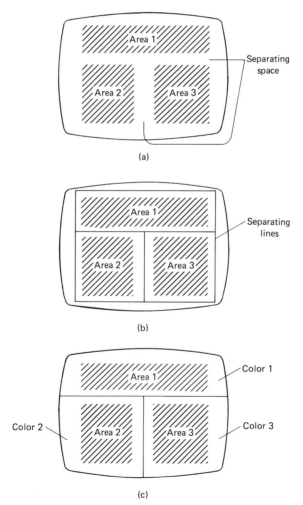

Figure 3-47 Separation of the information areas of the screen by (a) blank spaces, (b) lines, and (c) color.

is by leaving blank space between them (Figure 3-47a). It is more effective, and only slightly more difficult, to draw lines between blocks (Figure 3-47b). The use of color is the most effective way to separate screen areas (Figure 3-47c), but it requires a color display and great care to find acceptable color combinations. In general, leave blank space *and* use lines or color to separate the blocks. In the following discussion, we will first consider the use of lines and then the use of color for separating different areas of a screen.

Separation with lines and bars.   In text mode, simple BASIC statements enable you to draw horizontal and vertical lines quite easily. (To make the following discussion a little simpler, horizontal lines are referred to as "lines" and vertical lines as "bars.")

There are several ways to generate lines. The brute force method is to print a row of characters, like this:

```
PRINT "------------------"
```

This method is fine in short programs but costly in terms of memory, since each line takes up program memory. A more efficient technique is to define a particular character string and then to print that string when needed, like this:

```
10 Z$ = "------------------"
.
13450 PRINT Z$
.
26510 PRINT Z$
etc.
```

This method is less costly in terms of program memory since the string is defined once and then used repeatedly. String definition can be simplified through the use of the STRING$ statement. STRING$ enables you to define a string of up to 255 ASCII characters in a simple statement. The syntax of this statement is as follows:

```
Z$ = STRING$( n, char)
```

or

```
Z$ = STRING$ = ( n, char$)
```

The first argument, *n*, is the number of characters in the string. The second argument may be either (1) the ASCII code of a character or (2) a string. (ASCII codes of characters which can be displayed on the IBM PC or PC*jr* are given in

Appendix G of their BASIC manuals.*) Hence, to define Z$ as 20 dashes (ASCII code = 95), either of these expressions may be used:

```
Z$ = STRING$(20,95)
```

or

```
Z$ - 3TRING$(20,"-")
```

The STRING$ statement obviously makes it much easier to define a particular character string than by typing out the entire string on the right side of the equals sign. It also makes it easier to define strings consisting of characters which are not readily printable through the keyboard (see Appendix G, as noted). For example, to create a string of smiling faces, you define the line as follows:

```
FACES$ = STRING$(20,1)
```

Similarly, this statement will create a string consisting of 20 Greek omega signs:

```
OMEGA$ = STRING$(20,234)
```

While you may have little use for strings such as these, in constructing lines, bars, or boxes you will probably want to use the graphic characters whose ASCII codes range between 176 and 223. These characters cannot be printed directly through the keyboard, and a string of them can be defined only with the CHR$ or STRING$ statements.

Now, to print a line on a particular part of the display, you must do three things: (1) define the string, (2) position the cursor, and (3) print the line. You can do the positioning and printing directly in program code, like this:

```
100 Z$ = STRING$(20,219):REM create string of blanks
110 LOCATE 5,20:REM position cursor
120 PRINT Z$:REM print line
```

If you do very much of this—and you should if you are separating your displays properly—it comes in handy to have a subroutine that will perform these functions for you. Figure 3-48 is the listing of a simple line-printing subroutine. Arguments are ROW, COL, LENGTH, and CHAR (or CHAR$). ROW and COL are the row and column, respectively, at which the string begins to print; LENGTH is the string length; and CHAR is the ASCII code of the character the string is to consist of. CHAR$ can be used in place of CHAR by calling the subroutine at line 1450 instead of line 1440, which defines CHAR$ based on CHAR. Once CHAR$ has been defined, subsequent calls to this subroutine

---

*BASIC by Microsoft Corporation, IBM Corporation, 1982, and BASIC (PCjr) by Microsoft Corporation, IBM Corporation, 1984.

```
1430 REM--Print Line--
1440 CHAR$=CHR$(CHAR)
1450 LOCATE ROW,COL
1460 PRINT STRING$(LENGTH,CHAR$)
1470 RETURN
```

Figure 3-48   Subroutine to print a horizontal line.

require only the remaining arguments—ROW, COL, LENGTH—unless it is necessary to change the character composition of the string.

To illustrate the use of the subroutine, suppose that you want to draw the three lines, consisting of ASCII character 219, shown in Figure 3-49, starting at the coordinates indicated. Figure 3-50 contains the code required to generate these lines. Note that the use of this subroutine considerably simplifies the process of line generation.

Generating a bar (vertical line) requires a different approach, since, unfortunately, BASIC has nothing like the handy STRING$ function for placing vertical lines on the display. The easiest way to print a bar is to define a one-character string, and then to use a FOR-NEXT loop to print this character at a particular column while increasing the row by one each time the character is printed. The general idea is illustrated by this code:

```
10 CHAR$ = CHR$(219)
20 FOR ROW = 1 TO 10
30 LOCATE ROW,10
40 PRINT CHAR$
50 NEXT
```

This will print a vertical bar, 10 rows high, starting at row 1, column 10, and extending down to row 10. This procedure, like that for drawing a line, can be simplified by using a subroutine such as that shown in Figure 3-51. Arguments of this subroutine are ROW, COL, HIGH, and CHAR (or CHAR$). ROW and COL are the starting row and column, respectively; HIGH is the number of rows the bar should cover, and CHAR is the ASCII code of the character to use in the bar. As with the line-drawing subroutine, CHAR$ can be used instead of CHAR by accessing the subroutine at a different line number, and, once CHAR$ has been defined, it can be ignored in subsequent subroutine calls.

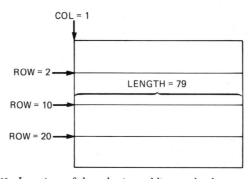

Figure 3-49   Locations of three horizontal lines to be drawn on display.

```
5 KEY OFF
10 CLS
20 CHAR=219
30 ROW=2
40 COL=1
50 LENGTH=79
60 GOSUB 1430:REM draw top line
70 ROW=10
80 GOSUB 1430:REM draw middle line
90 ROW=20
100 GOSUB 1430:REM draw bottom line
110 END
1430 REM--Print Line--
1440 CHAR$=CHR$(CHAR)
1450 LOCATE ROW,COL
1460 PRINT STRING$(LENGTH,CHAR$)
1470 RETURN
```

Figure 3-50 Code required to draw lines shown in Figure 3-49.

To illustrate the use of this subroutine, suppose that you want to draw the two bars consisting of ASCII character 219, as shown in Figure 3-52. The code required to draw these bars is shown in Figure 3-53. The use of this subroutine is similar to that of the subroutine for drawing horizontal lines—simply set the arguments, make the subroutine call, and the line or bar is drawn on the screen.

Blocking out the screen. Now that these two subroutines are available, it is very easy to block out the screen in any way that you want. Simply sketch the dividing lines and bars on a screen layout matrix, and then write the code to generate the dividing lines necessary. By combining the code used for drawing

```
1480 REM--Print Bar--
1490 CHAR$=CHR$(CHAR)
1500 LOCATE ROW,COL
1510 FOR R=ROW TO ROW+HIGH
1520 LOCATE R,COL
1530 PRINT CHAR$
1540 NEXT
1550 RETURN
```

Figure 3-51 Subroutine to draw a vertical bar.

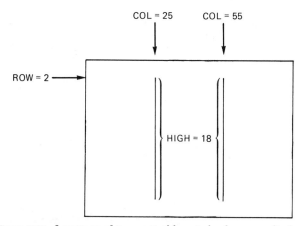

Figure 3-52 Locations of two vertical bars to be drawn on display.

```
5 KEY OFF
10 CLS
20 CHAR=219
200 ROW=2
210 COL=25
220 HIGH=18
230 GOSUB 1480:REM draw first bar
240 COL=55
250 GOSUB 1480:REM draw second bar
260 END
1480 REM--Print Bar--
1490 CHAR$=CHR$(CHAR)
1500 LOCATE ROW,COL
1510 FOR R=ROW TO ROW+HIGH
1520 LOCATE R,COL
1530 PRINT CHAR$
1540 NEXT
1550 RETURN
```

Figure 3-53 Code required to draw bars shown in Figure 3-52.

Figures 3-50 and 3-53, we can produce a screen that is divided into six parts, as shown in Figure 3-54. Further variations on this theme are left to the reader.

Separation with color. The use of color to separate the screen into different areas is an option available to those with color displays, although using color is, indeed, much trickier than using spaces, lines, bars, or boxes. Here are some guidelines for using color to separate the screen areas:

- Pick background colors that do not conflict with one another and cause interference at their borders (e.g., avoid combinations such as red and blue).

- Pick background colors that have similar brightness levels—avoid a screen with zebralike contrasts.

- Select and stick with a positive or negative image on all screen blocks—avoid light on dark in one area and dark on light in another.

- If some users of your program will have monochrome displays, assure that the borders between screen areas will be apparent to them—either via contrasting backgrounds or by using spaces and lines between areas in addition to color.

Color is discussed in detail in the final section of this chapter; if you intend to use color, review that section before proceeding.

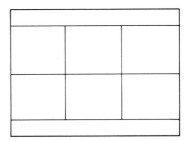

Figure 3-54 Appearance of screen when codes shown in Figures 3-50 and 3-53 are combined.

```
1560 REM--Draw Box--
1570 GOSUB 1430:REM draw top side
1580 GOSUB 1480:REM draw left edge
1590 ROW=ROW+HIGH
1600 GOSUB 1430:REM draw bottom side
1610 ROW=ROW-HIGH
1620 COL=COL+LENGTH
1630 GOSUB 1480:REM draw right edge
1640 RETURN
```

Figure 3-55 Subroutine to draw a box (requires solid characters).

Boxing.   Dividing up most screens will require you to draw one or more boxes. You can construct these from lines and bars, but it is often handy to have a subroutine to draw the box directly for you. Such a subroutine (Figure 3-55) can be readily constructed from the pieces described above. Arguments of the subroutine are ROW, COL, LENGTH, HIGH, and CHAR (or CHAR$), all of which have previously been defined. When these arguments are supplied, they will draw a box with the dimensions shown in Figure 3-56. Since this subroutine is simple, and constructed of pieces already described, we leave it to you to figure out.

Character selection.   One tricky part of using these and similar techniques is to select good characters for drawing your lines, bars, and boxes. As you will discover if you delve into this matter, the author has ducked the issue so far by using a very simple character—CHR$(219), a blank—that fills in the entire character matrix and is thereby symmetrical, and that works for both lines and bars. Many characters are available, and not all work well. Most characters do *not* fill the entire character matrix, and therefore will produce either broken lines or bars. Complicating the matter is that characters look different on 80- and 40-column displays—they are narrower on the former than on the latter—and thus the lines and bars are of different widths on one display than the other. The only solution to this dilemma is to decide what type of display will be used—80- or 40-column— and then to select characters that will produce lines and bars that look right.

To illustrate the character selection problem, let us modify the box-drawing subroutine shown in Figure 3-55 so that it will draw a nice box consisting of narrow lines instead of thick ones. Constructing such a box requires the use of six

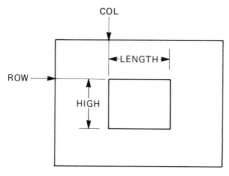

Figure 3-56 Arguments of box-drawing subroutine shown in Figure 3-55.

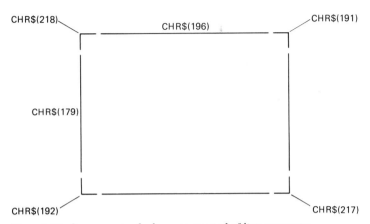

Figure 3-57   Components of a box constructed of line segments.

different characters—a separate character for each corner, a horizontal line, and a vertical line (Figure 3-57). The corner characters, respectively, are:

CHR$(218)   Upper left
CHR$(191)   Upper right
CHR$(192)   Lower left
CHR$(217)   Lower right

The horizontal line is CHR$(196) and the vertical line is CHR$(179).

Figure 3-58 shows the code required to generate the box. The subroutine consists of lines 1700 to 1970. (This subroutine calls the line- and bar-drawing subroutines, and they must also be present.) Arguments of the subroutine are V (starting row), H (starting column), HIGH (height), and LENGTH (width of box). These arguments are set, and then the subroutine is called in the usual manner.

The remarks within the code show what the subroutine actually does. Lines 1700 to 1780 print the four corners of the box. Then lines 1790 to 1840 print the top edge, lines 1850 to 1870 print the bottom edge, lines 1880 to 1930 print the left side, and lines 1940 to 1960 print the right side.

Using Color

The Mechanics of Setting Color

Character, background, and border colors.   To present information on any display, at least two colors must be used. These two colors must differ, or there is no contrast, and the information is illegible. The IBM machines—PC with Color/

```
5 KEY OFF
10 CLS
20 V=4
30 H=4
40 LENGTH=72
50 HIGH=16
60 GOSUB 1700:REM call box-drawing subroutine
70 END
1430 REM--Print Line--
1440 CHAR$=CHR$(CHAR)
1450 LOCATE ROW,COL
1460 PRINT STRING$(LENGTH,CHAR$);
1470 RETURN
1480 REM--Print Bar--
1490 CHAR$=CHR$(CHAR)
1500 LOCATE ROW,COL
1510 FOR R=ROW TO ROW+HIGH
1520 LOCATE R,COL
1530 PRINT CHAR$;
1540 NEXT
1550 RETURN
1700 REM--Draw Line Box--
1710 LOCATE V,H
1720 PRINT CHR$(218):REM top left corner
1730 LOCATE V+HIGH,H
1740 PRINT CHR$(192):REM bottom left corner
1750 LOCATE V,H+LENGTH
1760 PRINT CHR$(191):REM top right corner
1770 LOCATE V+HIGH,H+LENGTH
1780 PRINT CHR$(217):REM bottom right corner
1790 REM top edge
1800 ROW=V
1810 COL=H+1
1820 LENGTH=LENGTH-1
1830 CHAR= 196
1840 GOSUB 1430
1850 REM bottom edge
1860 ROW=V+HIGH
1870 GOSUB 1430
1880 REM left side
1890 ROW=V+1
1900 COL=H
1910 HIGH=HIGH-2
1920 CHAR=179
1930 GOSUB 1480
1940 REM right sic
1950 COL=H+LENGTH +
1960 GOSUB 1480
1970 RETURN
```

Figure 3-58 Subroutine to draw a box consisting of line segments.

Graphics adapter or PC*jr* with standard video output—permit you to set three display color parameters:

- *Character* color—referred to by IBM (for unknown reasons) as the "foreground" color.

- *Background* color—the color of the field comprising the display grid.

- *Border* color—the color at the edges of the display, on which no information is displayed.

These color areas are shown in Figure 3-59.

These three colors are set with the following BASIC statement:

```
COLOR character, background, border
```

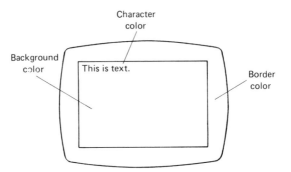

Figure 3-59 The IBM PC with Color/Graphics adapter, or the PC*jr*, has three separate color settings: character (or "foreground"), background, and border.

The *character, background,* and *border* colors are selected from those listed in Table 3-1. For example, to set characters to high-intensity white, background to magenta, and border to black, this statement would be used:

```
COLOR 15,5,0
```

Colors 8 through 15 are sometimes described as "light" versions of colors 0 through 7. This is true in most cases—colors 4 and 12 are, respectively, red and light red—but less true in the cases of cyan, magenta, and brown. The dark versions of these three colors are quite different from their light versions.

Note that the COLOR statement will affect the display differently, depending upon the type of interface and monitor being used. If the Color/Graphics adapter is in use and a color monitor is connected, then the COLOR statement will affect the color of the display as described. If a monochrome monitor is connected, then the various color values will translate into shades of gray. If the Monochrome/Printer adapter and the IBM monochrome monitor are connected, the COLOR statement will not affect display color, but will affect the display in terms of brightness, normal/reverse video, and blinking, as described later in

TABLE 3-1   IBM PC and PC*jr* Display Colors

Color (dark)		Color (light)	
0	Black	8	Gray
1	Blue	9	Blue (light)
2	Green	10	Green (light)
3	Cyan	11	Cyan (light)
4	Red	12	Red (light)
5	Magenta	13	Magenta (light)
6	Brown	14	Yellow
7	White	15	White (high-intensity)

Chapter 4. In addition, color output will be affected by the specific monitor in use and the settings of its hue and color intensity controls.

This discussion assumes that the Color/Graphics adapter (or PC*jr*) and a color monitor are in use. Given this, the color options available are further affected by the SCREEN statement currently active. The maximum number of colors is available in SCREEN 0 (text mode for both PC and PC*jr*), and fewer colors are available with other SCREEN settings (corresponding to graphics modes); since text mode offers the greatest flexibility, let us focus on it. Colors available in this mode are the following:

Character color: 0 to 15

Background color: 0 to 7

Border color: 0 to 15

Note that, while any color can be used for character or border, only the "darker" colors (0 to 7) can be used for the background. Thus, in selecting contrasting character and background colors, you are limited mainly to lighter colors against darker backgrounds. And, while it is possible to set the border to any color (0 to 15), there is no point—other than aesthetic—in setting the border to a different color than the background.

Color Selection

The most difficult part of using color is to select appropriate color combinations. One's aesthetic sense is not a good guide, since the colors interact in complex ways. A suggested approach is to decide first whether to use a positive or negative image, then decide on the desired image contrast, and leave color selection to last. Guidelines for making these decisions follow.

Positive versus negative images.   Decide whether to present a *positive* or *negative* image. A positive image consists of dark characters against a light background, and a negative image consists of light characters against a dark background. Deciding which to use is an issue riddled with tradition, personal preferences, and, to be sure, the uncertain application of logic and research findings. Computer video displays have traditionally presented negative images—most commonly, white characters against a black background. More recently, positive images have become more common, as with Apple Computer's Lisa and Macintosh computer systems. In addition, many people in the industry—system designers, programmers, operators, and others—have preferences for one type of image.

Some research studies have shown that operators suffer less visual fatigue when using positive images. Positive images are generally best if the program is used in normal ambient lighting because the eye makes fewer readjustments between the screen background and ambient illumination. Alternatively, if the program is used in a dark room, a negative image is better. It is usually difficult to predict exactly where your program will be used, although most programs are used in environments with *some* ambient lighting; this suggests that standard practice should be to use positive images. Moreover, the trend toward positive images appears to be increasing.

Image contrast. Image contrast is the brightness difference between the character color and background. The greater this difference, the higher the contrast. In general, medium-contrast images are preferable to either high-contrast or low-contrast images, both of which tend to cause eyestrain. Avoid selecting character and background colors that have extreme or small brightness differences, and select those with moderate differences. "Moderate" is not a precise term and is best illustrated by example.

Suppose that you want to present an image using *only* the colors black, gray, or white. Table 3-1 shows that you have these four shades of gray to work with:

   0   Black
   7   White
   8   Gray
  15   White (high-intensity)

Background colors are limited to 0 or 7, but any of the four colors can be used for presenting characters. (Note that color 7 is brighter than color 8, despite numbering.) The color combinations, and their relative contrast are summarized in Table 3-2. The contrasts produced by these six color combinations are approximated by Figure 3-60.

Contrast judgments are subjective and will vary with the monitor and its control settings. You can verify these judgments, or modify them to match your own, by typing in the short program whose listing is shown in Figure 3-61. This program will prompt you to type in the BACKGROUND and CHARACTER color, and it will then set the colors and fill your display with characters to show how the resultant screen appears.

The highest-contrast display is produced with background and character colors of 0 (black) and 15 (high-intensity white), respectively; this is not a good combination. The lowest-contrast display is produced with background and character colors of 0 (black) and 8 (gray), respectively; this is also a bad combination. Both of these combinations produce negative images. The background/character color combinations 0/7 and 8/15 both produce medium-contrast negative images, varying only in relative brightness, and both are superior to the first two combinations. The remaining two color combinations—7/0 and 7/8—both produce

TABLE 3-2   Image Contrast for Various Shades of Gray (IBM PC/PC*jr*)

Character color	Background	Contrast	Image
7	0	Medium	Negative
8	0	Low	Negative
15	0	High	Negative
0	7	Medium	Positive
8	7	Medium	Positive
15	7	Medium	Negative

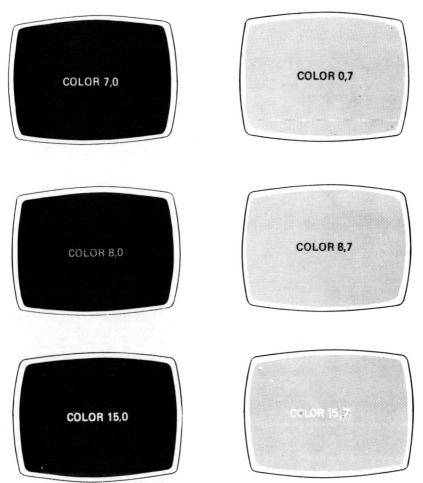

Figure 3-60   A crude illustration of the range of contrasts available with color monitor, using only the background colors 0 (black) or 7 (white), with character colors of 0 (black), 7 (white), 8 (gray), and 15 (high-intensity white).

medium-contrast positive images, varying only slightly in appearance. Both produce acceptable images.

Character colors.   Now let us consider character colors other than shades of gray. As these are discussed, it is suggested that you use the program shown in Figure 3-61 to create screens containing the various combinations and make your own judgments. Start with a background color of black (color 0). If you test the various character colors 1 to 7 and 9 to 14 against this background you will note that all produce readable displays, although character colors 1 (blue), 4 (red), and 5 (magenta) have little contrast against the background. The lighter versions of these colors (9, 12, 13) are an improvement but are still not very good. The best

```
5 KEY OFF
10 SCREEN 0,1
20 WIDTH 40
30 INPUT "Background: ";BACK
40 INPUT "Characters: ";CHAR
50 COLOR CHAR,BACK,BACK
60 CLS
70 FOR X=1 TO 20
80 PRINT"ABCDEFGHIJKLMNOPQRSTUVWXYZ01234567890";
90 NEXT
100 PRINT
110 PRINT
120 GOTO 30
```

Figure 3-61   This program, for PC with Color/Graphics adapter, or PC*jr*, permits you to set *background* and *character* color and observe the effect on your display.

character colors, for most purposes, are light green (10) and light yellow (14). This result is no surprise. The human eye is less sensitive to the reds and blues, which makes them poor choices for character colors. The eye is more sensitive to white, yellow, and green, which makes them better choices. (Most monochrome monitors use one of these as a phosphor color.)

Now consider a background color of white (color 7). If you test character colors 1 to 7 and 9 to 14 against this background, you will find that colors 1 to 5 produce readable displays, but that the remaining colors have too little contrast. The colors red, blue, and cyan are better now than they were with a dark background because they are dark enough to produce a good contrast. The best color against a background of white is black (color 0).

Selecting a character color is more difficult when the background color can be something other than a shade of gray. Any color 0 through 7 can be used as a background color. Leaving out the first and last of these colors (which were demonstrated earlier), six remain:

1 Blue
2 Green
3 Cyan
4 Red
5 Magenta
6 Brown

Any of these is acceptable as a background color, including the three colors earlier identified as poor choices for character colors, red, blue, and magenta. There are no simple rules for combining these colors, although certain color combinations should be avoided at all costs since the colors interfere at their boundaries. Undesirable combinations are the following:

Red + green

Red + yellow

Blue + green

Blue + red

Blue + yellow

```
5 KEY OFF
10 SCREEN 0,1
20 WIDTH 40
30 KEY OFF
40 FOR BACKGROUND=0 TO 7
50 COLOR 15,BACKGROUND,BACKGROUND
60 CLS
70 LOCATE 1,12
80 PRINT "BACKGROUND COLOR=";BACKGROUND
90 PRINT
100 FOR CHARACTER=0 TO 15
110 COLOR CHARACTER
120 PRINT CHARACTER;": ABCDEFGHIJKLMNOPQRSTUVWXYZ"
130 NEXT
140 COLOR 7,0
150 LOCATE 23,1
160 INPUT"PRESS RETURN KEY TO CONTINUE";A$
170 NEXT
180 KEY ON
190 COLOR 7,0,0
200 CLS
210 END
```

Figure 3-62 This program, for PC with Color/Graphics adapter, or PC*jr*, permits you to generate screens showing all possible background-character color combinations.

Making the selection is not a scientific activity. In the end, you must create display screens that present the candidate colors, and evaluate the alternatives subjectively. You can get a pretty good sense of what will work and what will not by using the program shown in Figure 3-61. Figure 3-62 contains the listing of a program that will enable you to compare various color combinations; this program sets the background to a particular color and then prints one row each of the fifteen possible character colors.

One final point: If in doubt, be conservative in your use of color.

Information
Presentation

The previous chapter discussed screen formatting. The present chapter covers screen content. Topics covered are: use of language, presentation of numeric information, display conventions, and use of special video modes.

Use of Language

Some Don'ts

Computer programs have not been distinguished by their effective use of language. The following is a brief catalog of common but undesirable practices, along with suggested alternatives:

- *Printing everything in capital letters.* Solution: Use uppercase and lowercase. It is easier to read and what we are used to.

- *Using abbreviations.* An abbreviation is a code that must be translated. In order to translate it, operators must first learn it. If they have not done this, the code remains a mystery. Even if they have memorized it, translating it takes time. Solution: Do not use abbreviations.

- *Using jargon.* Jargon is a specialized vocabulary, like a foreign language. Again, if operators do not know it, you leave them out in the cold. Solution: Avoid using jargon.

- *Giving cryptic prompts, messages, and directions.* What do you do when the computer gives you a choice between "RESET THE FACILITATOR" and "BLOCK THE UNITIZER"? What do you do when this message appears: "SYSTEM ERROR 23"? For many operators, the response is a rise in blood pressure and the desire to wring the programmer's neck. Solution: Put the prompts in plain English and the error messages in a form that does not require program users, as a sort of penance, to look up their sins in the reference manual's catalog of errors.

Some Dos

Here are some general guidelines for the use of written language in your program:

- *Begin each sentence with its subject or main topic.*

- *Use short, simple sentences.* Long sentences—especially those with multiple clauses—are more difficult to understand.

- *Use simple, commonplace words.* Avoid complex words where simple ones will do. Use concrete rather than abstract language. Avoid abbreviations and jargon.

- *Make statements in a positive rather than a negative way.* For example, here are two ways to tell the operator how to prepare to print reports:
  (Positive) Load the file before printing reports.
  (Negative) Do not attempt to print reports until the file is loaded.

- *Make statements in the active rather than passive voice.* For example:
  (Active) Load the file before printing reports.
  (Passive) The file must be loaded before reports can be printed.

- *State actions in the order they must be performed.* For example:
  (Correct order) Load the file before printing reports.
  (Incorrect order) Before printing reports, load the file.

- *When listing multiple items or giving a set of directions, list each point on a separate line.* This makes the points easier to separate. For example:
  (List sequence) To load file,
    Call file directory
    Select file
    Type in file number
    Press Enter key
  (Nonlist sequence) To load file, call file directory, select file, type in number, press Enter key.

Making Text Readable

Text is easiest to read if it is left-justified—aligned on a common left margin, like the words on this page. Right-justification is nice for effect—for example, on title pages—but should be used very sparingly, since it is more difficult to read. Leave center justification to poets. (See Figure 4-1a, b, c.)

Avoid word wrap—allowing a word to be divided haphazardly between rows (Figure 4-2). Hyphenation is the technically correct way to divide a word between rows, but it is only a slight improvement in terms of readability. If possible, do not divide words between rows at all.

If you must present extended text on an 80-column display, either (1) use fewer than 80 columns (e.g., 60 columns), (2) divide the text into two columns, or (3) double-space between rows. Wide, 80-column lines are difficult to read.

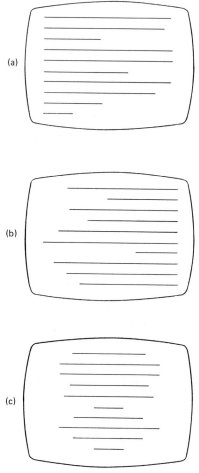

Figure 4-1 Three ways to justify text: (a) left, (b) right, and (c) center. Left-justification makes text the most readable.

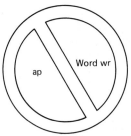

Figure 4-2 Avoid word wrap—breaking text haphazardly between successive rows.

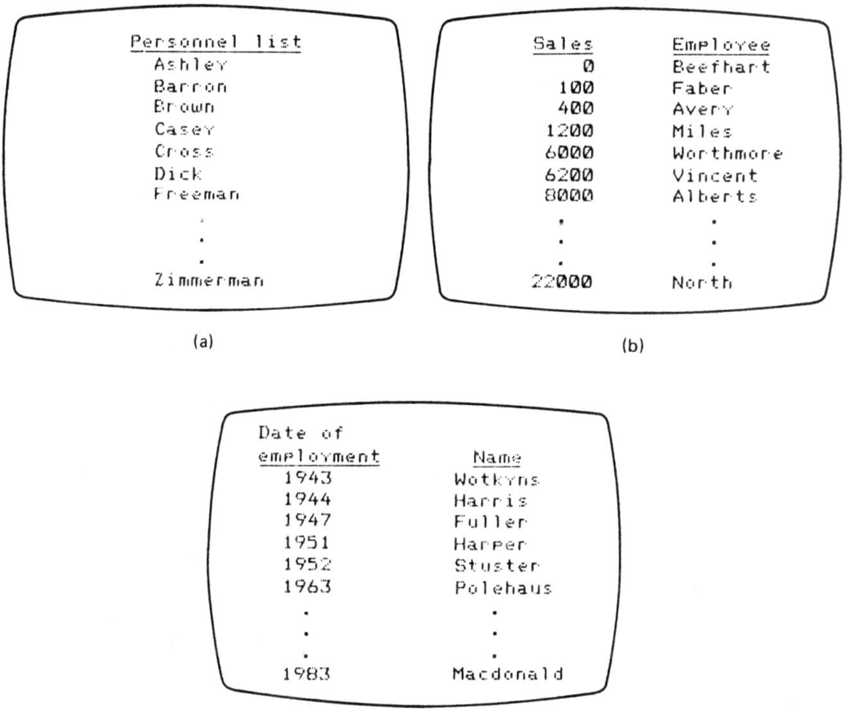

(a)

(b)

(c)

Figure 4-3 Three ordered lists: (*a*) alphabetic, (*b*) numeric, (*c*) chronologic. Ordering information in a logical way makes it easier for the operator to find things. (*From Simpson:* Design of User-Friendly Programs for Small Computers, *copyright 1985, by permission of McGraw-Hill Book Company.*)

Presentation of Lists and Directories

Many displays contain lists or directories. Examples are a list of documents, a list of part numbers, and a directory of names and telephone numbers. Present such lists in a recognizable order. For example, the list of documents should be presented in alphabetic order, the part numbers in numeric order, and the names in alphabetic order (Figure 4-3*a, b, c*).

By using an order, you give operators a key that allows them to relate any item on the list or directory to any other. This simplifies search and saves time. They do not have to search the entire list; they can quickly focus in on the part that should, by the ordering rule, contain what they are looking for.

It is possible to write BASIC code that will perform sorts, but such code is extremely slow and impractical for all but the shortest lists or directories. The typical BASIC bubble sort routine may take a minute or more to sort 100 items, with sorting time increasing exponentially as the size of the list or directory increases. Where BASIC sorting code is practical, the list or directory is so short that it can easily be searched by the operator. The solution to this problem is to use an assembly-language sorting utility. A number of these are available and can easily be used within a BASIC program.

Each time an element is added to the directory, the directory should be sorted. If several elements are added at once and the directory does not have to be referred to in the interim, you can wait until all items have been added before sorting. It is important to sort the directory after elements are added to it to keep the operator posted on the directory's current status. If an updated directory is not displayed, the operator may conclude that certain elements that should have been added were missed. This may lead to duplicate entries. (DOS 2.1 includes a SORT command, which can be used to sort an ASCII file, but this must be employed at the DOS level and is not practical for use within a BASIC program. If the directory is contained within a single file, the DOS SORT can be used to perform the sort at the beginning or end of the program, but this is not as good as sorting during the program to keep the directory constantly updated.)

Displaying a long list or directory on the PC poses some problems and requires some choices. As always, it is necessary to consider the needs of the operator. The headings on the directory should identify the information being displayed (see Figures 4-3a, b, c). Usually, a list or directory will be used to look up some item of information and take some action. For example, the operator may want to look up the name of a person and determine the corresponding telephone number. Consequently, the operator must be able to display different parts of the directory by (1) selecting the entry point to the directory and (2) moving forward or backward through the directory by scrolling or paging.

Display of different parts of the directory is one of the classic cases that requires partial paging, as described in the previous chapter—that is, typically, a display template is presented, and then different parts of the directory are presented within the same display area by alternately erasing the old information and then reprinting the new information. (The PgUp and PgDn keys are ideal for moving backward and forward through the directory, but they do not produce standard ASCII codes and require a special technique to read; for details, refer to the discussion in Chapter 8 concerning the cursor keys.)

Presenting Numeric Information

Many computer programs must display numeric information to the user, and there are several conventions for presenting such information. These conventions are both sensible—since they make the numeric information easier to read and interpret—and relatively easy to follow with PC BASIC.

Proper Number Formatting

An important convention in presenting numbers is to format all numbers within a program consistently. For example, if the program's output is dollars, display the output with a dollar sign and two decimal places—display 12 dollars as $12.00, 7.2 dollars as $7.20, 4.3741928 dollars as $4.37, and so on. If a program makes use of more than one type of numeric information, then numbers may need to be displayed in more than one way. For example, a stock market program might display portfolio information in the forms shown in Figure 4-4.

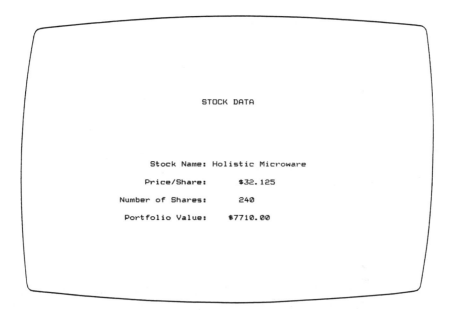

```
                        STOCK DATA




              Stock Name: Holistic Microware

                 Price/Share:        $32.125

            Number of Shares:          240

             Portfolio Value:       $7710.00
```

Figure 4-4 A hypothetical stock market program screen which presents information with several formatting requirements: stock name, a string which cannot exceed 20 characters; price per share, a dollar amount with three decimal places; number of shares, an integer; and portfolio value, a dollar amount with two decimal places.

Figure 4-4 contains three different types of quantities—Price/Share, Number of Shares, Portfolio Value—and the different types of numbers are formatted differently, depending upon type. Stock prices are reported to three decimal places. Number of shares is an integer and has no decimal. Portfolio value is a dollar amount and is displayed with a dollar sign and two decimal places. A particular program may use more than one display convention but should use the appropriate convention consistently for each type of quantity. This means avoiding displaying such quantities as a price of 2.4, 341.00 shares, or a portfolio value of $1531.5.

Using PRINT USING

The PRINT USING statement is the key to proper number formatting. It enables you to define a print formatting string which the PRINT statement then uses as a template in printing the number on the video display or printer. PRINT USING may also be used to format string quantities (see below).

The format of the PRINT USING statement is as follows:

```
PRINT USING format$; var 1, var 2, . . .
```

format$ is a string which defines the print format, and *var 1, var 2*, etc. are the numeric variables to be printed. *format$* may be defined in several ways. The simplest format consists of a set of number fields, which are defined with # signs.

Thus, to define a number as consisting of three digits, a PRINT USING statement of this form would be used:

```
PRINT USING "###"; var
```

When this statement is executed, three spaces will be allocated to the number, regardless of how many digits it contains. If it contains more, the format definition will be violated—a % sign will be printed to the left of the number and the entire number will be printed. In making format definitions, allocate sufficient space to numbers or they will not be printed properly. If a number contains fewer digits than the defined format, spaces will be inserted to the left of the number and the number will be right-justified within the print field. To illustrate, if the above statement is executed three times, with the variables 1.2345, 33397.1, and .0012, these results will be obtained:

```
   1
%33397
   0
```

A decimal point can be inserted into the format string to set the number of places to be displayed. For example,

```
PRINT USING "###.##"; var
```

will produce the following result on the numbers 1.2345, .789, and 456:

```
  1.23
  0.79
456.00
```

Note that leading and trailing zeros are added to fill out the number's format when printed.

Dollar signs can be added to the front of the number by including $$ at the beginning of the string. For example,

```
PRINT USING "$$###.##"; var
```

will produce this result on the numbers 1.2345, .789, and 456:

```
  $1.23
  $0.79
$456.00
```

These simple format strings will take care of most requirements in a typical business program. However, in addition to them, PRINT USING enables you to:

- Display a *plus* or *minus sign* at the beginning or end of a number.

```
PRINT USING "+###.##";1.2345 -->  +1.23
PRINT USING "###.##+";.789    -->  0.79+
PRINT USING "-###.##";456     --> -456.00
```

- Display *asterisks* instead of blanks as leading spaces in a number. The asterisks also define spaces for additional digits.

```
PRINT USING "**###.##";1.2345 --> ****1.23
PRINT USING "**###.##";.789    --> ****0.79
PRINT USING "**###.##";456     --> **456.00
```

- Display *commas* within the printed number. A comma must be inserted to the left of the decimal point within *format$*.

```
PRINT USING "######,.##";14568.71 --> 14,568.71
```

- Include *literal characters* in the printed number. To do this, use an underscore character to indicate that the following character is to be printed as a literal.

```
PRINT USING "_@##.#_%";76.52 --> @76.52%
```

- Format *string fields*. An ! indicates that only the first character of the field is to be printed.

```
PRINT USING "!";"FOUL IS FAIR" --> F
```

- Back slashes are used to control how many characters are printed. This is useful for truncating a string that may exceed a desired length. Two back slashes \\ indicate two characters, two backslashes separated by a space indicate three, etc.

```
PRINT USING "\\";"FOUL IS FAIR"   --> FO
PRINT USING "\ \";"FOUL IS FAIR"  --> FOU
PRINT USING "\  \";"FOUL IS FAIR" --> FOUL IS
```

These special formatting characters can be combined, and PRINT USING can also be used to format exponential numbers (refer to your BASIC manual for details).

Figure 4-5 contains a short program that can be used to type in various number formatting strings and numbers in order to see the results on your video display. Figure 4-6 contains a similar program for formatting and displaying strings. When these programs are run, they will first prompt you to enter a *format$* and then either a number or string. The result will then be displayed and the prompt will be presented beneath it. The program will continue cycling until you termi-

```
5 KEY OFF
10 CLS
20 INPUT "format$: ";FORMAT$
30 INPUT"Number: ";N
40 PRINT USING FORMAT$;N
50 PRINT
60 GOTO 20
```

Figure 4-5 Number formatting demonstration program.

```
5 KEY OFF
10 CLS
20 INPUT "format$: ";FORMAT$
30 INPUT"String: ";ST$
40 PRINT USING FORMAT$;ST$
50 PRINT
60 GOTO 20
```

Figure 4-6 Character string formatting demonstration program.

nate it with Ctrl-Break. It is suggested that you try out the various formats for yourself just to get a feeling for them.

PRINT USING makes it quite easy to format numeric output, even when you are not sure of the length or content of the information to be presented. In formatting numbers, you do not have to worry about the number of decimal places in the number or how many digits it contains. You need to determine only two things: (1) the *maximum size* of the number and (2) the *location of the print field.* You must determine the maximum size so that you do not produce an "overflow" situation when the number is printed—where the number, preceded by %, will run past the end of the defined print field (see above). Make a liberal estimate and then use it in defining the *format$* to use. If your program will format more than one type of number—for example, integer, single decimal place, two decimal place, exponential, etc.—you must define more than one *format$* for the formatting statements. Incidentally, since *format$* is a string, you can define it outside of the PRINT USING statement—for example, like this:

```
10 FORMAT$="##.#"
20 PRINT USING FORMAT$;74.8
```

If your program uses several different formats, it is wise to define all of the formats at the beginning of the program just as you would other constants that are used throughout the program (Figure 4-7). This enables you to change a particular *format$* by modifying a single assignment statement and makes the formats somewhat easier to keep track of.

The location of the print field is simply where on the display the number (or string) is to be printed. You can specify this on a screen design by using #s, Xs, or whatever other character suits your fancy (Figure 4-8). Then, when writing the code to generate the display, you can identify the horizontal and vertical coordinates at which the print field begins and position the cursor appropriately with LOCATE or TAB statements. Figure 4-9 is a listing of the code required to

```
10 REM--Define Format Strings--
20 FORM1$="##"
30 FORM2$="###.##"
40 FORM3$="####.###"
50 FORMS1$="\          \"
60 FORMS2$="\                    \"
```

Figure 4-7 This code illustrates the technique of defining formatting strings as string constants.

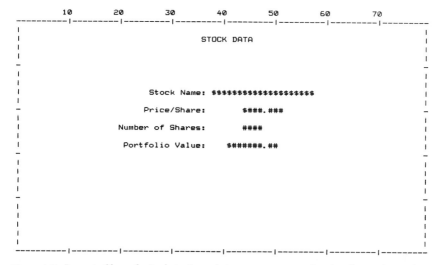

```
         10        20        30        40        50        60        70
----------|---------|---------|---------|---------|---------|---------|---------
|                              STOCK DATA                                      |
|                                                                              |
|                                                                              |
-                                                                              -
|                                                                              |
|                    Stock Name:  $$$$$$$$$$$$$$$$$$$$$                         |
|                    Price/Share:         $###.###                             -
-                                                                              
|                    Number of Shares:    ####                                 |
|                                                                              |
|                    Portfolio Value:     $######.##                           |
-                                                                              -
|                                                                              |
|                                                                              |
|                                                                              |
-                                                                              -
|                                                                              |
|                                                                              |
|                                                                              |
|                                                                              |
----------|---------|---------|---------|---------|---------|---------|---------
```

Figure 4-8 Layout of hypothetical stock market program screen showing formatting strings in locations of variables to be displayed.

```
5 KEY OFF
10 CLS
20 REM--Define Format Strings--
30 FORMST1$="\                     \":REM name=20 characters max.
40 FORM1$="$$###.###":REM stock price
50 FORM2$="####":REM number of shares
60 FORM3$="$$######.##":REM portfolio value
70 REM--Assign Values to Display--
80 NAM$="Holistic Microware"
90 PRSH=32.125
100 NUM=240
110 PORTVAL=PRSH*NUM
120 REM--Generate Headings--
130 LOCATE 2,36
140 PRINT"STOCK DATA"
150 LOCATE 8,26
160 PRINT"Stock Name:"
170 LOCATE 10,25
180 PRINT"Price/Share:"
190 LOCATE 12,20
200 PRINT"Number of Shares:"
210 LOCATE 14,21
220 PRINT"Portfolio Value:"
230 REM Generate Output--
240 LOCATE 8,38
250 PRINT USING FORMST1$;NAM$
260 LOCATE 10,44
270 PRINT USING FORM1$;PRSH
280 LOCATE 12,45
290 PRINT USING FORM2$;NUM
300 LOCATE 14,42
310 PRINT USING FORM3$;PORTVAL
```

Figure 4-9 Code required to generate screen shown in Figure 4-8.

generate the display shown in Figure 4-8. The LOCATE statement is used to position the cursor before printing each field.

In generating a printed report, you must use LPRINT USING. Its operation is identical to that of PRINT USING except that output is directed to the printer instead of the video display. LOCATE does not work with the printer, and so the print head must be positioned vertically with LPRINT and horizontally with TAB. TAB and PRINT USING cannot be combined in the same statement. Thus, the cursor must first be positioned horizontally with an LPRINT statement, and then the field printed with an LPRINT USING statement, like this:

```
10 LPRINT TAB (40)"";
20 LPRINT USING FORMAT1$;VARO
```

Line 10 positions the print head, and line 20 prints the number in the appropriate format, starting at column 40.

Guidelines for Presenting Numbers

There are two fairly common presentation situations: (1) displaying a few (usually) unrelated numbers and (2) displaying a set of related numbers.

In case 1, the convention is to print a descriptor for each number, followed by a separator (usually a colon), and then the number (Figure 4-10). Left-justify the descriptors. Descriptors and numbers in the same horizontal region of the report should be justified on common column numbers. If they change from row to row

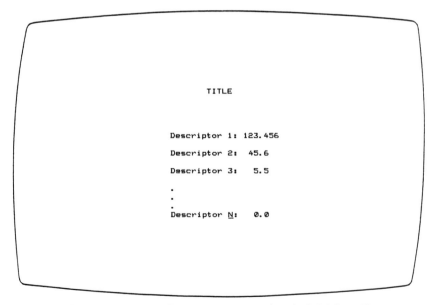

Figure 4-10   A case 1 type screen: Descriptors are printed on the left followed by a separator (:), and numbers are printed on the right.

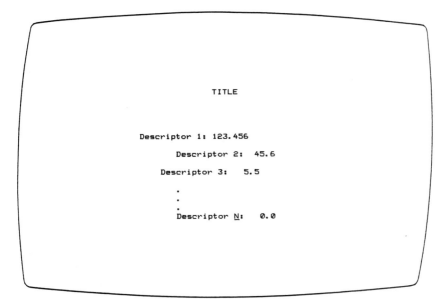

```
                        TITLE


            Descriptor 1: 123.456
                Descriptor 2:  45.6
              Descriptor 3:   5.5
                          .
                          .
                          .
                Descriptor N:   0.0
```

Figure 4-11 A poorly formatted case 1 type screen—the columns in which descriptors and numbers are presented vary from row to row. A better way to format the screen is shown in Figure 4-10.

of the screen, the screen is more difficult to read and looks sloppy. For comparison purposes, examine Figure 4-11, which contains the same information as Figure 4-10 but without common justification between rows.

In case 2, the convention is to present the numbers in a column beneath a descriptive heading (Figure 4-12). Columns of numeric information such as this should always be aligned on the decimal point. This permits the viewer to use a graphic cue—how far to the left of the decimal point the number extends—to estimate its magnitude. When numbers are aligned on a common left margin (Figure 4-13), you cannot use this cue and must read each number and keep score to determine which is biggest, smallest, or whatever. Incidentally, never, *ever* present a set of such numbers like text—printed out, one after the other, in rows. This makes the set very difficult to read and interpret.

The PRINT USING statement makes it very easy to format your screen in either of these two ways. Figure 4-9 (see above) contains the code required to generate a case 1 screen. It is even simpler to generate the numbers in the typical case 2 screen. Simply position the cursor, and then print each number on a successive row in the same format. Figure 4-14 contains some simple code that illustrates the technique for generating the screen shown in Figure 4-12.

Aiding Visual Search with Graphic Techniques

When a large data set is displayed (Figure 4-15), quite often the operator's task will involve searching through the numbers to identify those that meet certain

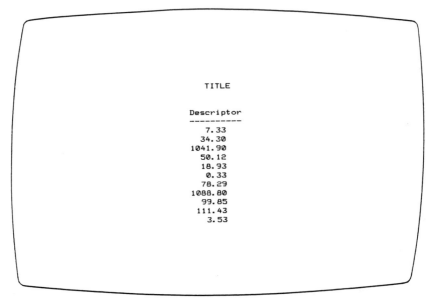

```
              TITLE

          Descriptor
          ----------
              7.33
             34.30
           1041.90
             50.12
             18.93
              0.33
             78.29
           1088.80
             99.85
            111.43
              3.53
```

Figure 4-12 A case 2 type screen: A column of numbers is presented beneath a heading, with all numbers aligned on the decimal point.

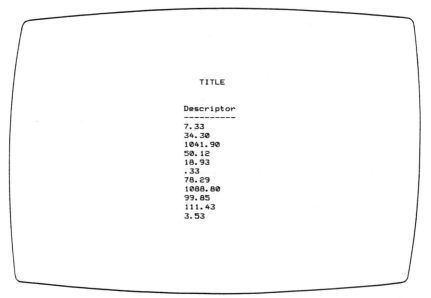

```
              TITLE

          Descriptor
          ----------
          7.33
          34.30
          1041.90
          50.12
          18.93
          .33
          78.29
          1088.80
          99.85
          111.43
          3.53
```

Figure 4-13 A poorly formatted case 2 type screen—the numbers are left-justified instead of aligned on the decimal point. A better way to format the screen is shown in Figure 4-12.

```
5 KEY OFF
10 CLS
20 LOCATE 2,39
30 PRINT "TITLE"
40 LOCATE 5,36
50 PRINT "Descriptor"
60 LOCATE 6,36
70 PRINT "----------"
80 FOR ROW=7 TO 17
90 LOCATE ROW,37
100 PRINT USING "###.##";ROW^1.7
110 NEXT
```

Figure 4-14   Code required to generate screen shown in Figure 4-12.

criteria. For example, the user may be looking for numbers that are low, high, fall within a particular range, or meet other definable criteria. If these criteria can be defined, it is often helpful to have the program highlight the numbers for the operator in order to aid visual search. For example, if the user is viewing the screen shown in Figure 4-15 and is searching for numbers above 50, then the search task would be considerably simplified by having the program highlight these numbers to make them stand out. The numbers may be presented in reverse, high-intensity, or blinking video.

If the highlighting criteria are straightforward, then it is fairly easy to write code to do the highlighting. Figure 4-16 contains code that will generate the screen shown in Figure 4-15. An IF-THEN test sets reverse video mode if a number exceeds 50. The number is then printed in reverse video. After it is printed, the display is set back to normal video.

SCORES

Subject	Score	Subject	Score	Subject	Score
1	43	16	28	31	29
2	41	17	0	32	46
3	29	18	50	33	6
4	60	19	2	34	33
5	39	20	22	35	53
6	8	21	30	36	49
7	22	22	33	37	11
8	35	23	7	38	32
9	8	24	22	39	11
10	56	25	49	40	12
11	13	26	52	41	19
12	19	27	25	42	22
13	14	28	43	43	55
14	54	29	0	44	12
15	35	30	36	45	35

Figure 4-15   A hypothetical screen in which a graphic technique—highlighting—is used to make the numbers above 50 easier to find.

```
5 KEY OFF
10 REM--Create Dummy Data Set--
20 DIM SCORE(45):REM data array
30 FOR N=1 TO 45
40 SCORE(N)=RND(1)*60
50 NEXT
60 REM--Generate Screen--
70 CLS
80 LOCATE 2,38
90 PRINT"SCORES"
100 LOCATE 5,12
110 PRINT"Subject   Score       Subject   Score       Subject   Score"
120 LOCATE 6,12
130 PRINT"-------  -----      -------  -----      -------  -----"
140 REM columns 1&2
150 FOR N=1 TO 45
160 IF N=1 OR N=16 OR N=31 THEN LOCATE 7:REM locate first score in row
170 IF N<=15 THEN COL=14:REM set column for scores 1-15
180 IF N>=16 AND N<=30 THEN COL=36:REM set column for scores 16-30
190 IF N>=31 THEN COL=58:REM set column for scores 31-45
200 GOSUB 230:REM call format & display subroutine
210 NEXT
220 END
230 REM--Format and Display Subroutine--
240 LOCATE,COL
250 PRINT USING"##";N;
260 LOCATE,COL+8
270 IF SCORE(N)>50 THEN COLOR 0,7
280 PRINT USING"###";SCORE(N)
290 COLOR 7,0:REM normal video
300 RETURN
```

Figure 4-16   Code required to generate screen shown in Figure 4-15.

It takes time for your PC to perform such tests, and the more complex the required tests, the more time it takes. The result is that the display will be generated more slowly. However, the PC is much faster at making these tests than an operator searching a display. Consequently, if a large data set must be searched, highlighting will save the operator considerable time in the long run.

Display Conventions

This section describes display conventions that should be followed in presenting dates, times, telephone numbers, colors, and "strings" on screens and reports. A basic principle of information display is to present information in as simple and obvious a form as possible. The conventions described below are all practical expressions of this basic principle. For example, since we habitually tend to write dates a certain way, usually month/day/year, it makes a certain amount of sense to present them that way on computer displays. The popularity of other, unnatural forms, such as 06081985, usually reflects a programmer's indifference to the program user, or the incorrect assumption that what suits the computer should suit the operator just fine. Such attitudes need some redirection, to put it mildly. Following the conventions outlined below will make things easier for the operator.

Presenting Dates

In normal written language, we tend to express dates in all of these forms:

Month/day/year: 4/9/48

Month-day-year: 4-9-48

Month (written) day, year: April 9, 1948

Day month (written) year: 9 April 1948

On the other hand, you seldom see dates written like this:

04091948

04,09,1948

04-09-1948

04/09/1948

While these last four forms are certainly decodable, they are not the form that we are used to. Each requires parsing and interpretation and is extra work for the operator to process. Yet, you will recognize that the first two forms are commonly used on computer displays, and the last two are both valid forms for typing in a date to the PC. When DOS 2.1 comes up, it will express the current date as 1-01-1980. DOS will then accept an entered date in several forms:

mm-dd-yy

mm/dd/yy

mm-dd-yyyy

mm/dd/yyyy

Leading zeros are not required during entry, and including the century digits of the year is optional. This makes entering a date fairly easy, although the date is not displayed in its most natural form. (Chapter 5 discusses date entry in detail.)

While the PC's normal way of presenting a date is not the best, it is not bad, and is better than some of the ways illustrated above. However, you can improve on the PC's default presentation mode without much difficulty. To begin, assume that you want to extract the system date and present that on one of your displays. The PC's *date* is stored in the system variable DATE$. The date is assigned when DOS is initialized and the user types in a date. DATE$ may be redefined during the program by setting it to a string that is properly formatted to represent the date.

The variable DATE$ is stored as a character string in the form *mm-dd-yyyy*. Hence, given a date of 1/5/86, if you print DATE$ in a BASIC statement, the 10-character string "01-05-1986" will be displayed. From this, you can extract the month, day, and year by taking substrings of DATE$, like this:

```
MONTH=VAL(LEFT$(DATE$,2))
DAY=VAL(MID$(DATE$,4,2))
YEAR=VAL(RIGHT$(DATE$,2))
```

Once you have extracted these quantities, you can display them in more natural form, without leading zeros and without showing all four digits of the year. For

```
10 DIM MONTH$(12)
20 DATA Jan,Feb,March,April,May,June,July,Aug,Sept,Oct,Nov,Dec
30 FOR MONTH=1 TO 12
40 READ MONTH$(MONTH)
50 NEXT
```

Figure 4-17 Code which loads the names of the months into the array MONTH$.

example, to use the *month/day/year* or *month-day-year* formats, simply print the dates like this:

```
PRINT MONTH;"/";DAY;"/";YEAR
```

or

```
PRINT MONTH;"-";DAY;"-";YEAR
```

Printing the actual month requires a little more code but is quite easy. Simply define an array to store the names of the months, load the array with month names, and then use the variable MONTH as the argument of the array to print the month's name. Figure 4-17 contains some simple code that will load the month names into the string array MONTH$. Once these names have been loaded, you can display a date of the form *month (written) day, year* like this:

```
PRINT MONTH$(MONTH);DAY;",";YEAR
```

Similarly, you can present a date of the form *day month (written) year* like this:

```
PRINT DAY;MONTH$(MONTH);YEAR
```

Note that in both of these cases, no spaces are printed in front of numbers, since BASIC automatically provides a separate space in front of a positive number.

Since the length of dates may vary, formatting them for printing requires a conversion to string form rather than direct printing. Figure 4-18 is the listing of four simple subroutines that can be used to convert the date to string form for

```
7000 REM--Date-Formatting Subroutines--
7010 REM-Format month/day/year-
7020 LOCATE ROW,COL
7030 PRINT MONTH;"/";DAY;"/";YEAR
7040 RETURN
7050 REM-Format month-day-year-
7060 LOCATE ROW,COL
7070 PRINT MONTH;"-";DAY;"-";YEAR
7080 REM-Format month (written) day, year-
7090 LOCATE ROW,COL
7100 PRINT MONTH$(MONTH);DAY",";YEAR
7110 RETURN
7120 REM-Format day month (written) year-
7130 LOCATE ROW,COL
7140 PRINT DAY;MONTH$(MONTH);YEAR
7150 RETURN
```

Figure 4-18 Four subroutines to position and print the date in different formats.

printing. Each of these subroutines generates a date string and then prints the date at the row and column specified in the arguments ROW and COL.

Naturally, you can use any MONTH, DAY, and YEAR in printing a date and are not bound by the system date.

Presenting Times

The correct format for presenting a time is *hour:minute:second*. For example, 15 minutes and 59 seconds past noon would be displayed as 12:15:59. Time, like date, is set in DOS and assigned to a system variable. The time variable is TIME$, which, nicely, stores the time in the format just described. This format, showing number of characters, is as follows: *hh:mm:ss*. The *hh* is a two-digit hour, the *mm* is a two-digit minute, and the *ss* is a two-digit second. The *hh* runs from 0 to 23 and the *mm* and *ss* run from 0 to 59. Thus, if a PC is running 24 hours a day, the hour will increase above 12 after 12 o'clock noon, in the manner of military time.

You can use the substring parsing technique described above to extract *hh*, *mm*, and *ss* from TIME$.

Similarly, you can use a subroutine to format and display a time of your own, if necessary. Note that, in displaying time, leading zeros *are* quite natural and acceptable in the minute and second, but not in the hour.

Presenting Telephone Numbers

The correct format for presenting a telephone number is *area code-prefix-number*. For example, 123-456-7890. Leading and trailing zeros are acceptable in all three number groups, since they are significant to the user. No surprises here.

Using Colors

Certain colors are used in conventional ways. For example, the red-orange-green triad, like traffic lights, often signify stop or danger, caution, and go, respectively. The red and blue pair often represent hot and cold, respectively. The context of the screen may totally alter the meaning of the colors used—on a topographic display, for example, green may represent earth and red an architectural feature. Before you use a color, make sure that you do not violate the usual convention for using the color. Do not, for example, use green to signify stop or danger.

Presenting "Strings"

One of the reasons to avoid presenting a date as a sequence of run-on numbers— 04091943—is that such numbers are more difficult to read. The separate parts of the number are pushed together. This requires the operator to separate them visually and mentally. Hence, the convention of separating month, day, and year by hyphens or slashes.

A similar requirement exists for any set of characters—numbers, letters, graphic characters—which the programmer might, for whatever reason, want to display. Such character sequences, or *strings,* may be used in various ways in a program—for example, as passwords, codes, or the content of a database. You cannot read a string like a word. To make sense of it, you must take it apart. It is best not to display strings at all but to present the information represented by the string in more natural form. However, if displaying the string is unavoidable, break it up by inserting spaces between every four or five characters, e.g., display the string RT67%KL9+WW45:99 like this: RT67 %KL9 +WW4 5:99. This gives the operator a little breathing room to separate the different parts of the string and make sense of them.

Special Video Modes

If you have an IBM PC with the Monochrome/Printer adapter, then several video modes are available to you. These include standard (light on dark) video, reverse (dark on light) video, blinking, high intensity, underlining, and various combinations of the foregoing. If you have the Color/Graphics adapter, or a PC*jr*, then you cannot display underlining, but most of the other video modes and their combinations are still available. The present discussion assumes the use of the Monochrome/Printer adapter and tells how to produce the video modes and their combinations. The section is divided into two parts. The first describes the special video modes available to the IBM PC and covers the mechanics of setting them with the COLOR statement. The second part covers the use of these modes within a program—the why and when of using them. Though the first part of the section concerns readers with the Monochrome/Printer adapter, the second part applies to all readers, regardless of their hardware.

The Mechanics of Special Video Modes

Video modes are activated with the first two arguments of the COLOR statement. The syntax of this statement is as follows:

```
COLOR character, background
```

The *character* argument sets the character color, and video mode, as follows:

0 = black character

1 = underlined character

2 to 7 = white character

The background argument sets the background color, as follows:

0 to 6 = black background

7 = white background

Thus, these three COLOR statements will produce the video modes indicated:

COLOR 0,0 = black characters on black background (invisible)

COLOR 1,0 = underlined (white characters on black background only)

COLOR 2,0 through COLOR 7,0 = normal video

COLOR 7,7 = white characters on white background (invisible)

COLOR 7,0 = white characters on black background

High-intensity characters are produced by adding 8 to *character*. Thus,

COLOR 9,0 = high-intensity + underlined

COLOR 10,0 through COLOR 15,0 = high-intensity

Blinking characters are produced by adding 16 to *character*. Thus,

COLOR 17,0 = blinking + underlined

COLOR 18,0 through COLOR 23,0 = blinking

COLOR 25,0 = blinking + high-intensity + underlined

COLOR 26,0 = blinking + high-intensity

Setting the video mode is simple but keeping track of the arguments is enough to give you a headache. Life can be simplified by deciding what modes you will need and then creating a little table that lists the modes and the arguments required to get the desired results. Note that since *character* arguments 2 to 7 all produce the same results you need only one of them; the same is true of *background* arguments 0 to 6. You do not need six or seven ways to do the same thing; you need only *one*. Table 4-1 summarizes the COLOR argument combinations used in this book. Video mode is identified in the left column, and *character* and *background* arguments for the COLOR statement are given in the right. For example, "normal" (white on black) video is produced with the statement COLOR 7,0. Combinations of video modes are indicated by indentation and + signs. For example, normal video and blinking are produced with COLOR 23,0; underlining is added by using COLOR 17,0. Note that there are four video options under normal and high-intensity video but only two under reverse video. This is because underlining requires white characters against a dark background, and is incompatible with reverse video.

TABLE 4-1   Video Mode Selection Arguments (Simplified)

Video mode	Character	Background
Normal	7	0
+ Blinking	23	0
+ Underlined	17	0
+ Underlined	1	0
High-intensity	15	0
+ Blinking	31	0
+ Underlined	25	0
+ Underlined	9	0
Reverse	0	7
+ Blinking	16	7

```
 5 KEY OFF
10 CLS
20 X=7:Y=0:GOSUB 140
30 X=23:Y=0:GOSUB 140
40 X=17:Y=0:GOSUB 140
50 X=1:Y=0:GOSUB 140
60 X=15:Y=9:GOSUB 140
70 X=31:Y=0:GOSUB 140
80 X=25:Y=0:GOSUB 140
90 X=9:Y=0:GOSUB 140
100 X=0:Y=7:GOSUB 140
110 X=16:Y=7:GOSUB 140
120 COLOR 7,0
130 END
140 COLOR X,Y
150 PRINT X,Y,"abcdefghijklmnopqrstuvwxyz01234567890"
160 PRINT
170 RETURN
```

Figure 4-19 This program, for PC with Monochrome/ Printer adapter, displays all possible special video modes.

If you have not explored all of these video modes before, it is well to display them all simultaneously to compare them. In fact, this is true even if you are familiar with them all, since direct comparisons can be quite revealing. Figure 4-19 contains the listing of a little program that prints a different row of characters in each of the video modes. Type this in, run it, and compare the video modes.

Guidelines for Using Special Video Modes

Use *normal* video for creating your displays. The special modes should be used to highlight or attract attention. If used too liberally, they lose their impact or simply confuse.

Use *blinking* to attract attention to something that the operator should know about immediately (Figure 4-20). For example, use it to warn of danger (such as the possibility of overwriting a file), to inform the operator of an error state (a data-entry error or a program error condition), and to indicate an action that must be taken immediately (the need to write a file before exiting the program). As Table 4-1 shows, blinking can be done in various ways—normal, high-intensity, reverse, combined with underlining—yet most programs only need *one* way to attract attention. If you are using the Monochrome/Printer adapter and normal video, it is suggested that you use high intensity, blinking video for such messages (COLOR 31,0). Try not to have more than one blinking message on the screen at a time. Blinking means that the operator must act and usually the operator can act to resolve only one problem at a time. If your program does require more than one level of attention-getting, use normal, blinking video for the second level of messages (COLOR 23,0). Avoid the other blinking variations (combined with underlining, reverse, etc.). If more levels than this are required—in a nuclear power plant simulation, with everything going wrong at once—then it is probably a good idea to take a different approach to attracting the operator's attention. Instead of using different types of blinking to code the messages in terms of importance, you might display a status panel which rank-orders the problems so that the operator can act on them in the most effective order (Figure 4-21).

If you are using the Color/Graphics adapter or a PC*jr*, then the same principle

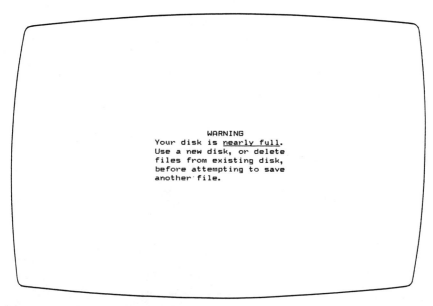

```
                  WARNING
         Your disk is nearly full.
         Use a new disk, or delete
         files from existing disk,
         before attempting to save
         another file.
```

Figure 4-20 Blinking should be used to attract the operator's attention to a condition that requires immediate action, as in this screen, which is presented following an attempt to save a file to a disk that is full.

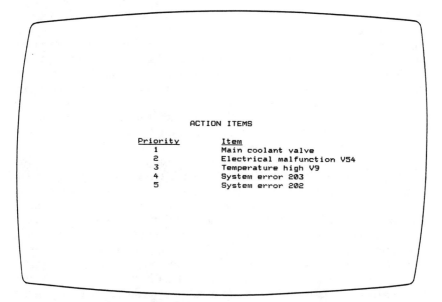

```
                  ACTION ITEMS

         Priority        Item
            1            Main coolant valve
            2            Electrical malfunction V54
            3            Temperature high V9
            4            System error 203
            5            System error 202
```

Figure 4-21 When the operator must act on several items, it is best to present them in prioritized list format, as shown here, rather than as individual blinking messages.

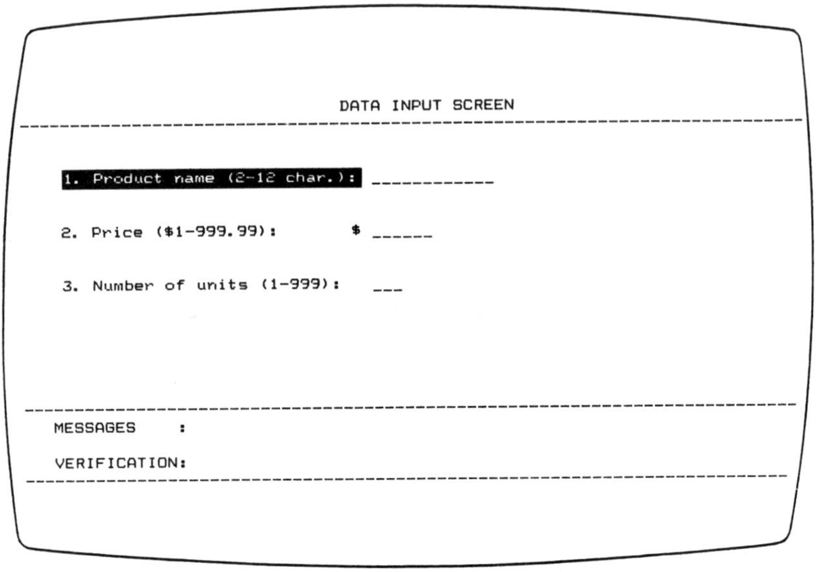

```
┌─────────────────────────────────────────────────────────────┐
│                                                               │
│                    DATA INPUT SCREEN                          │
│  ---------------------------------------------------------    │
│                                                               │
│  ┌1. Product name (2-12 char.):┐ _____                │
│                                                               │
│  2. Price ($1-999.99):        $ _____                        │
│                                                               │
│  3. Number of units (1-999):   ___                            │
│                                                               │
│                                                               │
│                                                               │
│  ----------------------------------------------------------   │
│  MESSAGES   :                                                 │
│                                                               │
│  VERIFICATION:                                                │
│  ----------------------------------------------------------   │
│                                                               │
└─────────────────────────────────────────────────────────────┘
```

Figure 4-22 Highlighting is used on this data-input screen to indicate which of several prompts is currently active.

applies—limit the types of blinking used to one or, at the most, two. Use a bright color—white or yellow—in the blinking message. Avoid the use of blue or red since the eye is less sensitive to these colors, especially at the periphery of the visual field.

Reverse or high-intensity video are both ways to *highlight* information on the display. Of these two, reverse stands out more from a normal video background and is the preferred method of highlighting. Highlighting may be used for several different purposes—to indicate the system state, operating mode, the item being worked on, the file name, and so forth. Highlighting informs the operator of a condition that exists. Unlike blinking, it does not demand immediate action. (Figure 3-46 showed a portion of a word-processing screen with several state indicators highlighted with reverse video.)

Though high-intensity video can be used in the same manner as reverse video, it is suggested that you use it to *focus attention on the user's current action*. For example, you might use it to highlight the option on a program selection menu that the user has just selected; this allows the user to verify the menu choice before proceeding. (Menu highlighting is discussed in Chapter 8; see example in Figure 8-4.) High-intensity video is also useful to identify which prompt on a data-input screen is currently active; as the user fills in the screen, the active prompt brightens, and after the entry has been made, it returns to normal video (Figure 4-22). (Prompt highlighting is discussed in Chapters 5 and 6.) In both of these examples, high-intensity video is used to highlight just one item on the screen—the one that the user's attention is currently focused on.

What about underlining? Underlining is like italics in writing, and it is sug-

```
                    DIRECTIONS

To save file, type in file name and press Enter key.
File name must contain 1 to 8 characters, and may be
followed by a period (.) and a 1 to 3 character suffix.

     Examples:
          LO
          OUC.H
       DETEST.IT
       TOLSTOY.LEO


File name: _____
```

Figure 4-23 Use of underlining to emphasize key words on a text display.

gested that you use it in its traditional role in the text you present on your video screens. Use it to emphasize words that you want to make stand out (Figure 4-23).

You can combine underlining with blinking and high-intensity video, or even have all three together if you like. The author's opinion is that this is overkill and can seldom be justified. Most programs can get by nicely with just four video modes:

Normal	(COLOR 7,0)
High-intensity blinking	(COLOR 31,0)
High intensity	(COLOR 15,0)
Reverse	(COLOR 0,7)

If your program uses extensive text, and certain words need emphasis, add underlining (COLOR 1,0) to the list.

Chapter

5

User Input

This chapter is divided into three sections. The first section gives an overview of data-input statements. It tells, among other things, what is wrong with INPUT, what is better about LINE INPUT, and what must be done to INKEY$ to make it useful. The second section describes the input-validation sequence—the actions that occur prior to, during, and following user input. The third section shows how to handle simple syntax-dependent entries such as dates and times.

BASIC Data-Input Statements

This section discusses three BASIC data-input statements: INPUT, LINE IN-PUT, and INKEY$. Each of these has certain qualities that affect its utility in data-input routines. In the following, each statement is discussed, in turn, to put it in perspective. Code examples will be given to illustrate its application.

INPUT

The INPUT statement is the easiest way to collect keyboard entries. The syntax of this statement in its simplest form is as follows:

```
INPUT var 1, var 2, . . .
```

var may be a string or numeric variable, and the only limit to the number of *var*s is how many can be typed into a program line. In general, it is best to use one variable per INPUT statement, so that the user does not have to type in commas; this makes it both easier for the operator, and reduces the chance of screen disruption (see below).

When the INPUT statement is executed, it prints a question mark and blinking cursor on the screen like this and waits for the user to type something in:

```
?_
```

As entries are typed in, the user can back up and modify previous keystrokes to make changes. The entry does not become final until the Enter key is pressed.

The operator can type in as long an entry as desired—up to 254 characters. If the typed entry is too long, the screen may scroll or portions of it may be overwritten.

Commas *cannot* be used as entries, since BASIC interprets them as separating entry variables.

If the assignment variable is a real variable, and the user types in a string variable in response to a prompt, the message "Redo from start" is printed on the screen and scrolling occurs. This will also occur if the user includes an extra comma in an entry or makes fewer entries than the statement requires. The appearance of the screen is disrupted when such scrolling occurs. (Incidentally, it is always best to use string variables as assignment variables, as explained below.)

A prompt string can be included in the INPUT statement by using a more elaborate syntax:

```
INPUT "prompt"; var 1, var 2, . . .
```

For example,

```
INPUT "Please type in your surname: ";SURNAME$
```

When this line is executed, it will print the prompt on the screen, followed by a question mark and blinking cursor, like this:

```
Please type in your surname: ?_
```

INPUT will not display the **?** if a comma instead of a semicolon is used before the variable. For example, this form of the INPUT statement

```
INPUT "Please type in your surname: ",SURNAME$
```

will produce this prompt:

```
Please type in your surname: _
```

The **?** is appropriate in prompts that pose questions, but not elsewhere. Thus, when INPUT is used, it is best to suppress the **?** by using a comma instead of a semicolon.

You can, of course, also print the prompt with a PRINT statement, followed by a semicolon, instead of including it in the INPUT statement:

```
10 PRINT "Please type in your surname: ";
20 INPUT "",SURNAME$
```

This will produce the prompt as shown immediately above. Note that the null string, "", is included as a prompt string in the INPUT statement to suppress the question mark.

That pretty much covers INPUT. If you have been programming for more than a few weeks. there were probably no surprises here. What does it all add up to?

First, INPUT is very easy to use.

Second, it has weak points that a careless, inept, or mischievous operator will find: typing in too long an entry, or an entry with the wrong number of separating commas, will disrupt the screen. In addition, a comma cannot be used as a data-entry character. These flaws make INPUT unsatisfactory for most professional-level programs since it is important to maintain the integrity of screens. At the same time, INPUT is very handy for use in simple programs, while prototyping a preliminary version of a sophisticated program, and for a variety of "quick and dirty" data-input applications.

Incidentally, while a real or integer variable can be used with the INPUT or INKEY$ statements (LINE INPUT requires a string variable), it is always safest to use a string variable instead. When a string variable is used, anything can be typed in with no adverse effects on the screen or program. If the required entry is a number, the string variable can be converted to its equivalent numeric form with the VAL statement, like this:

```
10 INPUT NUMBER$
20 NUMBER = VAL(NUMBER$)
```

This procedure also permits you to test the value of an integer variable within program code, instead of permitting BASIC to do so in the INPUT statement. To illustrate, code like this is very dangerous and should be avoided:

```
10 INPUT INTEGER%
```

If the user types in a number outside the legal limits, an overflow error occurs. However, if the code is modified as shown below, you can perform a conversion first to a real variable (line 20), conduct a range test (line 30), and assure that INTEGER% is only assigned an acceptable value.

```
10 INPUT INTEGER$
20 INTEGER = VAL(INTEGER$)
30 IF INTEGER < −32768 OR INTEGER > 32767 GOTO 10
40 INTEGER% = INTEGER
```

LINE INPUT

The mechanics of using LINE INPUT are the same as those of using INPUT. Three important differences are (1) LINE INPUT accepts any character in an entry, including commas; (2) only one assignment variable may be used per LINE INPUT statement; and (3) the assignment variable must be a string. These differences correct some of the real and potential problems of INPUT (see above).

To illustrate the difference, type in the following lines, run them, and then attempt to type in an entry with a comma in it, such as "Chandler, Raymond."

```
10 INPUT "Prompt: ";A$
20 PRINT A$
```

(You should get the "Redo from start" error message.) Change INPUT to LINE INPUT and try again. This time your entry should be displayed.

LINE INPUT is far from perfect. It shares with INPUT the drawback that it does not control the *length* of what the user enters. If the user types in too long an entry, the screen will be disrupted. Nonetheless, LINE INPUT is generally safer and better for use in data input. While not perfect, it is satisfactory for the majority of data-input tasks.

The only way to prevent the user from holding down a key, generating a string of characters, and sending the screen scrolling is to monitor the length of the current entry and to prevent that entry from extending beyond a predefined maximum length. Neither INPUT nor LINE INPUT can do this job since they do not assign the user's keystrokes to a variable until after the Enter key has been pressed—when it is too late to test the entry's length to prevent damage to the screen. In order to protect the screen, the keystrokes must be monitored, one by one, as they are typed in, and a running score must be kept of the length of the total entry. This requires using the INKEY$ statement, as described below.

INKEY$

Though this chapter has been referring to INKEY$ as a "statement," technically it is a variable whose content is the single character currently being read by the PC from its keyboard buffer. If no key has been pressed, then INKEY$ = "", the null string. To illustrate, type in the following line, run it, and press various keys on your keyboard.

```
10 PRINT INKEY$:GOTO 10
```

As you type a key, the letter goes sailing up your video display (Figure 5-1). Hold down the key for a while and the character will form a column up the screen as

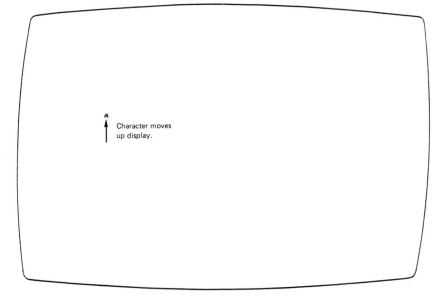

Figure 5-1 The typed-in character moves up the screen when the INKEY$ variable is printed.

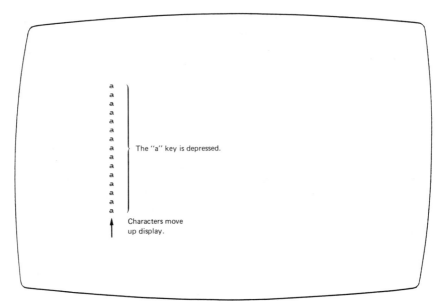

Figure 5-2 Holding a key down causes a string of characters to move up the screen when the INKEY$ variable is printed.

the keyboard's repeat feature causes the key to be repeated (Figure 5-2). As soon as you let up on the key, the screen goes blank again, since INKEY$ once again becomes the null string.

Because INKEY$ is so volatile, it is seldom used directly as a variable. Instead, a program variable is set equal to it, like this:

```
10 CHAR$=INKEY$:IF CHAR$="" GOTO 10
20 PRINT CHAR$
30 GOTO 10
```

The IF-GOTO clause on line 10 will keep the line looping endlessly until INKEY$ reports a character other than the null string. At that point, control drops to line 20 and CHAR$ is printed. If you run this little program, you will see that the only time the column of characters moves up the screen is when you type something in (Figure 5-3).

Aha!—but so what? Is this useful for data input? In this form, not really. First, INKEY$ displays no blinking cursor. Second, what is typed is not displayed on the screen. Third, once the user types something in, there is no going back to change it before verifying it with the Enter key. Fourth, INKEY$ reports one character, and very few inputs are that short. Fortunately, with a little ingenuity, all of these shortcomings can be resolved. Let us take them one at a time.

Blinking the cursor. Let us start by showing how INKEY$ might be used in a simple input situation to collect a verification prompt. Suppose that your program requires the user to verify something on the screen by typing in either "y" for yes

Figure 5-3 By printing only values of INKEY$ which are unequal to the null string, the column of typed-in characters will move up the screen only when a character is typed in.

or "n" for no. The lines shown in Figure 5-4 will print an appropriate prompt on the screen, collect a single keystroke, and make sure that the key pressed is one of the valid ones.

Type in and run these lines, and this prompt will appear on your screen:

```
Is this correct? (y/n)
```

But that is all. No blinking cursor. However, the problem is easy to correct. You will recall these special video modes from Chapter 4, no doubt:

Normal	COLOR 7,0
High-intensity blinking	COLOR 31,0
High intensity	COLOR 15,0
Reverse	COLOR 0,7

A blinking cursor can be created by setting the video mode to high-intensity blinking and then printing a character to simulate a cursor. This brings us to two important points about prompts. First, the active prompt (assuming more than one appears on the screen) should be highlighted to draw attention to itself; it is suggested that this be done with high-intensity video (COLOR 15,0). Second, the

```
10 REM--INKEY$ Verification Routine--
20 PRINT"Is this correct? (y/n)"
30 VER$=INKEY$:IF VER$="y" OR VER$="n" GOTO 40 ELSE 30
40 END
```

Figure 5-4 Simple INKEY$-based verification routine.

```
10 REM--INKEY$ Verification Routine--
15 COLOR 15,0:REM high-intensity video
20 PRINT"Is this correct? (y/n): ";
21 COLOR 31,0:REM high intensity blinking
22 PRINT CHR$(219)
23 COLOR 7,0:REM normal
30 VER$=INKEY$:IF VER$="y" OR VER$="n" GOTO 40 ELSE 30
40 PRINT VER$
```

Figure 5-5 An improved INKEY$-based verification routine—with highlighted prompt and blinking cursor.

prompt's cursor should blink and be highly visible. This may be accomplished by selecting a cursor character such as CHR$(219) or CHR$(220), both of which are much more apparent than the usual nearly invisible underline cursor. Appendix G of the IBM PC and PCjr BASIC manuals* shows the ASCII characters available. All of these will work, and which one you choose is to some degree a matter of personal preference. The key consideration is *visibility*. (Good taste is also a concern—not every program user likes a cursor that looks like a smiling face.)

Let us modify the input routine by printing the prompt in high-intensity video and by adding a blinking cursor. Since a cursor will now follow the prompt, it should end with a colon and an extra space; these changes must be made to line 20. The modified version of the routine is shown in Figure 5-5. The modifications are as follows: Line 15 sets high-intensity video and a semicolon has been added to the end of the prompt so that the "cursor" will be printed at the end of it; line 21 sets high-intensity blinking video; line 22 prints a cursor character; and line 23 sets normal video. Type this in and run it, and you should get a prompt that looks like this, with a blinking cursor:

```
Is this correct? (y/n): ■
```

Displaying the entry. Line 40 of the routine is already displaying the entry but in the wrong place. It should be displayed at the location of the cursor. You can position the printed character there with a LOCATE statement. Since a routine such as this may be used to print the verification prompt in various places on the screen, the cursor will not always appear in the same place. Thus, it is best to determine the cursor's current position within the routine itself, rather than assign specific coordinates to a LOCATE statement. The modified routine is shown in Figure 5-6.

A semicolon has been added to the end of line 22 to suppress the carriage return. After line 22 executes and prints the cursor, the actual cursor's position is one character to the right. The typed entry must be printed one space to the left of this. A POS statement will return the cursor's current column number, so the position at which the character should be printed is POS(0)-1. Therefore, line 35 has been added to calculate the column number and position the cursor. Adding line 35 requires changing the line number following the GOTO in line 30 from 40

---

*BASIC by Microsoft Corporation, IBM Corporation, 1982, and BASIC (PCjr) by Microsoft Corporation, IBM Corporation, 1984.

```
10 REM--INKEY$ Verification Routine--
15 COLOR 15,0:REM high-intensity video
20 PRINT"Is this correct? (y/n): ";
21 COLOR 31,0:REM high intensity blinking
22 PRINT CHR$(219);
23 COLOR 7,0:REM normal
30 VER$=INKEY$:IF VER$="y" OR VER$="n" GOTO 35 ELSE 30
35 LOCATE ,POS(0)-1:REM position real cursor
40 PRINT VER$
```

Figure 5-6 A better INKEY$-based verification routine—
this displays the operator's entry, if valid.

to 35. In addition, a semicolon was added at the end of line 22 to prevent a
carriage return.

Type in the changes, run the routine, and see what happens. First, this prompt
appears:

```
Is this correct? (y/n): ■
```

Nothing happens unless you type in a "y" or an "n"—in which case the cursor
disappears and the typed-in character appears in its place, in normal video, like
this:

```
Is this correct? (y/n): y
```

Although this routine accepts only a single keystroke and does not permit Enter
key verification, it could be quite useful in certain situations. This type of prompt
is often used to verify something else that is on the screen. For example, during
data input, after a series of entries have been made, it is common to present a
prompt such as this to allow the user to verify previous entries.

Such prompts are used to permit the user to indicate a decision one way or
another, usually to verify some action that is about to occur. The following are
representative prompts:

```
Do you want to continue? (y/n):
Do you want to make any changes? (y/n):
Your previous action will erase file. Proceed? (y/n):
Is printer ready and on line? (y/n):
```

This type of prompt should *not* be used to collect data from a user. In the
applications just illustrated, the prompts are used for program control, that is, to
decide what course the program should sail.

Enter key verification.   Enter key verification of an INKEY$ entry can be provided
by adding a second INKEY$ loop which tests for CHR$(13)—the ASCII code of
the Enter key. The additions required to provide this feature are shown in Figure
5-7.

A semicolon has been added to the end of line 40 to suppress the carriage
return. Line 50, containing a second INKEY$ loop, has been added. The current
value of INKEY$ is assigned to the variable VER$. Line 60, also new, tests
whether VER$=CHAR$. If so, then the Enter key has been pressed, the test has
been passed, and control drops to line 70. If the test is failed, then the statements

```
10 REM--INKEY$ Verification Routine--
15 COLOR 15,0:REM high-intensity video
20 PRINT"Is this correct? (y/n): ";
21 COLOR 31,0:REM high intensity blinking
22 PRINT CHR$(219);
23 COLOR 7,0:REM normal
30 CHAR$=INKEY$:IF CHAR$="y" OR CHAR$="n" GOTO 35 ELSE 30
35 LOCATE ,POS(0)-1:REM position real cursor
40 PRINT CHAR$;
50 VER$=INKEY$:IF VER$="" GOTO 50
60 IF VER$=CHR$(13) GOTO 70 ELSE LOCATE ,POS(0)-1:GOTO 21
70 END
```

Figure 5-7 A still better INKEY$-based verification routine—
this one requires Enter key verification of the entry.

following ELSE become active; these reposition the cursor one space to the left
and send control back to line 21. The result is that the cursor overprints the
previous entry and the user can make another.

Type in and try these lines. First, the old prompt will appear, like this:

```
Is this correct? (y/n): ∎
```

When you type in a "y," you will get this:

```
Is this correct? (y/n): y
```

Press any key other than the Enter key and the original prompt will reappear:

```
Is this correct? (y/n): ∎
```

Type in a "y" or "n," and then press the Enter key. Now the routine ends, and
BASIC's familiar "OK" appears on the next line:

```
Is this correct? (y/n): n
OK
```

That is all there is to Enter key verification. Next, we get into something more
fascinating—multiple-keystroke entries.

Multiple-keystroke entries. The INKEY$ routines described above can be ex-
tended to accept multiple entries by concatenating individual keystrokes into a
longer entry. The core logic of a very simple multiple-keystroke routine is shown
in Figure 5-8.

Step 1 is to print the prompt, current entry, and cursor. In Step 2, a single
character (CHAR$) is INKEY$ed. In Step 3, the character is tested to see if the
Enter key has been pressed. If so, the typed-in entry is complete and the routine
terminates. If CHAR$ <> CHR$(13), then control drops to step 4, in which
CHAR$ is concatenated with a longer entry (ENTRY$). ENTRY$ will grow as
additional characters are INKEY$ed and concatenated with it.

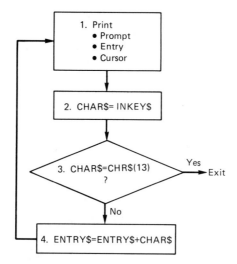

Figure 5-8 Core logic in a very simple INKEY$-based multiple-keystroke input routine.

The BASIC code required to perform these steps is shown in Figure 5-9. The program lines corresponding to each step are as follows:

20 to 90	Step 1
100	Step 2
110	Step 3
120 to 130	Step 4

While this routine illustrates the general technique for collecting multiple keystrokes with the INKEY$ variable, in this form it is certainly no rival to the LINE INPUT (or even the INPUT) statement. Among other shortcomings, this routine does not permit the user to back up and make corrections, and there is nothing to limit the length of a multiple-keystroke entry. However, building on this model, it is possible to create a truly powerful data-input routine, as described below.

```
10 REM--INKEY$ Multiple-Keystroke Input Routine--
20 COLOR 15,0:REM high-intensity video
30 PRINT"Prompt: ";
40 COLOR 7,0:REM normal
50 LOCATE ,9:REM position cursor to print current entry
60 PRINT ENTRY$;:REM cumulative entry
70 COLOR 31,0:REM high intensity blinking
80 PRINT CHR$(219);:REM print cursor
90 COLOR 7,0:REM normal
100 CHAR$=INKEY$:IF CHAR$="" GOTO 100
110 IF CHAR$=CHR$(13) THEN LOCATE ,POS(0)-1:PRINT " ":GOTO 140
120 ENTRY$=ENTRY$+CHAR$
130 GOTO 50
140 END
```

Figure 5-9 Code of very simple INKEY$-based multiple-keystroke input routine based on Figure 5-8.

Building a powerful INKEY$-based data-input routine. Let us build a general INKEY$-based data-input routine. To make it easier to talk about, we will call it the "KEYS" routine. Our objective is to make KEYS a useful and practical alternative to the LINE INPUT statement. Since we may want to employ it many times in a program, we should build it as a subroutine that can be called from anywhere in a program and be used to fulfill *any* data-input needs.

Here are some requirements that KEYS must meet:

- Permit multiple-keystroke entries.

- Print a prompt that is provided to it as an argument—the string variable PROMPT$. The prompt is to be displayed at a row and column defined in the arguments ROW and COL.

- The prompt is to be highlighted during data input, but it should return to normal video after the input has been made.

- Test entries for a minimum and maximum length based on the arguments SHORT (minimum) and LONG (maximum).

- Print a maximum length indicator following the prompt, based on the LONG argument, like this:

Please type in your surname: _____

- Permit backspacing to change previously entered keystrokes.

- Permit an immediate exit from data input by pressing the Escape (ESC) key.

- Filter or trap unwanted keystrokes—only standard keyboard characters are to be accepted in the entry.

- Permit the programmer to define a default entry for input that the user can verify by pressing the Enter key.

Here is how this subroutine would work. The programmer decides the location of the printed prompt, its content, and minimum and maximum acceptable length. These quantities are then provided as arguments to KEYS in code like this:

```
10 ROW=10:REM define row
20 COL=10:REM define column
30 PROMPT$="Please type in your surname":REM define prompt
40 SHORT=2:REM minimum acceptable length
50 LONG=24:REM maximum acceptable length
60 GOSUB 2000:REM call KEYS data-input subroutine
70 SURNAME$=ENTRY$:REM assign entry to program variable
```

Line 60 calls KEYS, which is located at line 2000. Line 70 then assigns the variable returned (ENTRY$) to the program variable SURNAME$. All cursor positioning, highlighting, prompt printing, length testing, and so forth is to occur in the subroutine itself. This is how KEYS would work from the programmer's point of view.

Now let us consider how the data-input process would work from the user's point of view. First, assume that the user will be working with a data-input screen with several prompts on it and that only one will be active at one time; the active prompt will be highlighted. The user will type in entries normally, with the Backspace key used for making corrections. Only standard character keys will be accepted in the entry; other keys—such as Control key combinations—will be ignored. If the user attempts to type in too short or too long an entry, the program will not permit it. If the user decides to abandon the input process, typing the ESC key will clear whatever has been typed in so far and data input will cease. After making an entry, the user will press the Enter key and the prompt will return to normal (nonhighlighted) video.

The logic of KEYS is shown in Figure 5-10. Step 1 is to print the prompt, current entry (ENTRY$), and cursor on the screen.

In step 2, a single character is INKEY$ed and then assigned to the variable CHAR$.

In step 3, CHAR$ is tested to determine if the Enter key has been pressed. If so, then control goes to step 3a, which performs a minimum length test on ENTRY$. If ENTRY$ is too short (shorter than the argument SHORT), then control returns to step 2 to INKEY$ another character. If LEN(ENTRY$)≥ SHORT, then the subroutine is exited.

In step 4, CHAR$ is tested to determine if the Escape key has been pressed. If so, the subroutine is exited.

In step 5, CHAR$ is tested to determine if the Backspace key has been pressed. If so, then control goes to step 5a, which performs a minimum length test on ENTRY$. If ENTRY$ = "", then attempting to take a substring of it (in step 5b) will produce an error condition. Thus, if the test in step 5a is failed, control returns to step 2 to INKEY$ another character. If the test is passed, then control goes to step 5c and the last character concatenated with ENTRY$ is removed by taking a substring of ENTRY$ consisting of LEFT$(ENTRY$(LEN(EN-TRY$) − 1)); the revised ENTRY$ is then displayed.

In step 6, a maximum length test is performed. If LEN(ENTRY$) = LONG then no additional character can be concatenated with it, and so control is sent back to step 2 to INKEY$ an acceptable terminating character (Enter key or Escape key). If LEN(ENTRY$) is acceptable, then control flows to step 7.

In step 7, the entry is tested for an ASCII value between 32 and 126—the standard keyboard characters. If the ASCII value of the entry is within this range, then the character is acceptable and control flows to step 8. If the ASCII value is outside of this range, then control is sent back to step 2 to INKEY$ another character.

In step 8, ENTRY$ is concatenated with CHAR$, and then control is sent to step 2 to INKEY$ the next character.

This logic is fairly straightforward. Essentially, it consists of INKEY$ing a character, running a series of tests on the character, and, if all the test results are satisfactory, concatenating the character with ENTRY$. It is important to keep this simple framework in mind, for we are about to discuss the BASIC code required to perform these steps. While the flowchart consists of eight steps and three substeps, the code takes nearly 50 lines. Thus, it is easy to get lost in the forest if one concentrates too closely on the trees, that is, the individual lines of code.

The BASIC code required to perform the data-input functions is shown in Figure 5-11. This consists of three subroutines. Lines 2000 to 2340 are the main subroutine. Lines 2350 to 2380 print a prompt. And lines 2390 to 2470 erase the

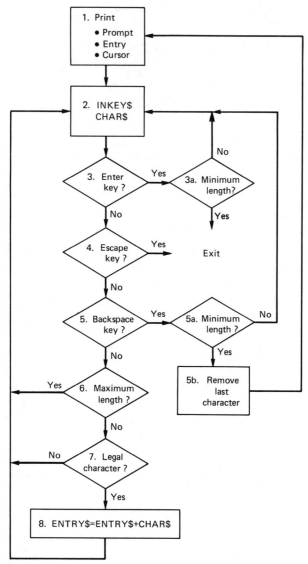

Figure 5-10 Logic of KEYS, a sophisticated INKEY$-based data-input subroutine.

data-input field and print a maximum entry length marker (i.e., an underline). The main subroutine calls the second and third subroutines at the beginning and end of data input, and whenever the data-input field must be erased. At the beginning of data input, the prompt is highlighted; at the end, it is in normal video. Table 5-1 is a line-by-line summary of the function performed by each line or connected group of lines. The summary is brief, since the listing in Figure 5-11 contains many remarks to explain what is going on.

```
2000 REM--Multiple-Keystroke INKEY$ Subroutine--
2010 ENTRY$="":REM initialize entry
2020 LENGTH=LEN(ENTRY$)
2030 COLOR 15,0:REM high intensity
2040 GOSUB 2350:REM print prompt
2050 GOSUB 2390:REM print length marker
2060 LOCATE ROW,COL2:REM position cursor to data-input field
2070 PRINT ENTRY$;:REM display current entry
2080 COLOR 31,0:REM high-intensity blinking
2090 PRINT CHR$(219);:REM print cursor
2100 COLOR 7,0:REM normal
2110 CHAR$=INKEY$:IF CHAR$="" GOTO 2110:REM collect keystroke
2120 REM-Test for Enter Key-
2130 IF CHAR$=CHR$(13) GOTO 2140 ELSE 2190
2140 IF LENGTH )= SHORT GOTO 2150 ELSE BEEP:GOTO 2110:REM minimum length test
2150 GOSUB 2350:REM print prompt
2160 GOSUB 2390:REM print length marker
2170 PRINT ENTRY$+" ":REM print entry & erase cursor
2180 GOTO 2340:REM exit subroutine
2190 REM-Test for ESC Key-
2200 IF ASC(CHAR$)=27 THEN GOSUB 2350:GOSUB 2390:ENTRY$="":GOTO 2340:ELSE 2210:R
EM exit subroutine
2210 REM-Test for Backspace Key-
2220 IF ASC(CHAR$)=8 GOTO 2230 ELSE 2270
2230 IF LENGTH )= 1 GOTO 2240 ELSE BEEP:GOTO 2110:REM minimum length test
2240 LENGTH=LENGTH-1
2250 ENTRY$=LEFT$(ENTRY$,LENGTH):REM remove last keystroke
2260 GOTO 2030
2270 REM-Maximum Length Test-
2280 IF LENGTH=LONG GOTO 2110
2290 REM-Filter non-Standard Characters-
2300 IF ASC(CHAR$))=32 AND ASC(CHAR$)(= 126 GOTO 2310 ELSE BEEP:GOTO 2110
2310 ENTRY$=ENTRY$+CHAR$:REM concatenate old and new entries
2320 LENGTH=LEN(ENTRY$)
2330 GOTO 2060
2340 RETURN:REM exit point from subroutine
2350 REM-Print Prompt-
2360 LOCATE ROW,COL
2370 PRINT PROMPT$;
2380 RETURN
2390 REM-Erase Field, Print Length Marker-
2400 COLOR 7,0:REM normal
2410 COL2=COL+LEN(PROMPT$)+1
2420 LOCATE ROW,COL2
2430 PRINT SPACE$(LONG)
2440 LOCATE ROW,COL2
2450 PRINT STRING$(LONG,"_")+" "
2460 LOCATE ROW,COL2
2470 RETURN
```

Figure 5-11 Listing of KEYS, a sophisticated INKEY$-based data-input subroutine.

Keystroke filtering.

One way to look at the data-input subroutine shown in Figure 5-11 is as a keystroke filter. Several of its steps (see Figure 5-10) use IF-THEN logic to test the identity of a keystroke and take a particular action based on that identity. Steps 3, 4, and 5 look for specific keys—Enter, Escape, or Backspace, respectively. However, the main keyboard filter is in step 7. This filter tests whether the typed-in character has an ASCII value between 32 and 126, the range of values of the standard keyboard characters.

It may have occurred to you in reviewing this code that this range could be changed quite easily. The effect of changing the range is to alter which keys the subroutine accepts and which it simply ignores. Note that, if the test in step 7 is failed, whatever key was pressed is never printed on the data-input line. Appendix G of the IBM PC and PCjr BASIC manuals* lists the ASCII character codes

*BASIC by Microsoft Corporation, May 1982, IBM Corporation; BASIC (PCjr) by Microsoft Corporation, 1984, IBM Corporation.

TABLE 5-1   Line-by-Line Summary of the Listing in Figure 5-11

Lines	Function performed
2010 to 2020	Initialize ENTRY$ and LENGTH. (Note that ENTRY$ can be provided as a default entry by defining it as a subroutine argument and calling the subroutine at line 2020.)
2030 to 2100	Call subroutines to print prompt and length marker; position cursor to start of data-input field; print ENTRY$ and cursor.
2110	INKEY$ CHAR$.
2120 to 2180	Test if CHAR$ is Enter key press. If it is, test whether minimum length test is satisfied; if it is, reprint prompt, length marker, and entry in normal video and exit subroutine.
2190 to 2200	Test if CHAR$ is Escape key press. If it is, reprint prompt and length marker in normal video, erase input field, and set ENTRY$ = "".
2210 to 2260	Test if CHAR$ is Backspace key press. If it is, test whether minimum length test is satisfied; if it is, remove the last character concatenated with it.
2270 to 2280	Perform maximum length test on ENTRY$. If ENTRY$ has reached maximum length, do not allow concatenation with CHAR$.
2290 to 2300	Test whether CHAR$ is a standard keyboard character. If it is, permit concatenation with ENTRY$.
2310 to 2330	Concatenate ENTRY$ and CHAR$, and recalculate length of ENTRY$.
2340	RETURN—exit point from subroutine.
2350 to 2380	Subroutine to print prompt.
2390 to 2470	Subroutine to erase field and print length marker.

available on these machines. The ASCII value ranges and types of characters (excluding symbols) are as follows:

ASCII value	Type character
32	Space
48–57	Numbers
65–90	Capital letters
97–122	Lowercase letters

It would make sense to modify this range to suit the application of the subroutine. For example, if you were using the subroutine to collect numeric input, you could use the range 48 to 57 and also include 46 (.).

To collect only capital letters use the range 65 to 90.

And so on.

LINE INPUT Reprise

KEYS is very powerful and useful for the most demanding data-input requirements. It is also somewhat more than is needed in simple programs where there is no great concern about the user typing in too long an entry or the other problems that the subroutine is designed to correct.

Where that much data-input power is not needed, LINE INPUT will work just fine. Let us build a general LINE INPUT–based data-input subroutine. Our objective, as with KEYS, is to make it as flexible as possible and to perform as many of the functions of KEYS as possible. Not all of the functions can be performed with a LINE INPUT–based subroutine, but many can. The following are the functions that we used as a specification in developing KEYS. To illustrate what can and cannot be done with LINE INPUT, let us make a function-by-function comparison.

- Permit multiple-keystroke entries. OK—no problem for LINE INPUT.

- Print a prompt at a row and column specified by the arguments PROMPT$, ROW, and COL. OK.

- Highlight prompt during data input but return to normal video afterward. OK.

- Test entries for minimum and maximum length based on arguments SHORT and LONG. Not OK—length can only be tested after the input has been typed in, not on a keystroke-by-keystroke basis.

- Print a maximum length indicator, like this:

```
Please type in your surname: _ _ _ _ _ _ _ _ _ _ _ _ _ _ _ _ _ _ _ _ _ _ _ _ _ _ _ _ _ _ _ _ _ _ _ _ _
```

It is no problem to *print* the underline, but a problem occurs if the Backspace or Delete key is pressed—these subtract underline characters and move the line to the left. Thus, the length of the underline can change during data input. The purpose of the underline—as a length cue—is thereby compromised. In short, not OK.

- Backspacing is permitted, as noted above. OK.

- An immediate exit from the subroutine via the Escape key route is not possible. Not OK.

- Unwanted keystrokes cannot be filtered. Not OK.

- Permit a default entry. Not OK.

Final score: OK 4, not OK 5. But if the not OKs do not matter in your particular application, then LINE INPUT may be perfectly fine. And it is certainly a lot simpler.

After digesting the code in Figure 5-11, the LINE INPUT data-input subroutine (Figure 5-12) is a cinch.

A line-by-line summary of the subroutine is shown in Table 5-2.

```
10 CLS
20 ROW=10
30 COL=10
40 PROMPT$="Prompt:"
45 LONG=24
50 GOSUB 2500
60 END
2500 REM--LINE INPUT Subroutine--
2510 COLOR 15,0:REM high intensity
2520 GOSUB 2570:REM print prompt
2530 COLOR 7,0:REM normal
2540 LINE INPUT ENTRY$
2550 GOSUB 2570:REM print prompt
2560 RETURN:REM exit point from subroutine
2570 REM-Print Prompt-
2580 LOCATE ROW,COL
2590 PRINT PROMPT$ SPC(1)
2600 RETURN
```

Figure 5-12 Listing of a LINE INPUT–based data-input subroutine.

TABLE 5-2   Line-by-Line Summary of the Listing in Figure 5-12

Lines	Function performed
2500 to 2520	Set high-intensity video; call subroutine to print prompt; reset normal video.
2540	LINE INPUT ENTRY$
2550	Call subroutine to print prompt (normal video).
2560	RETURN—exit point from subroutine.
2570 to 2600	Subroutine to print prompt.

This subroutine and KEYS are more or less interchangeable, although KEYS performs length tests and the LINE INPUT subroutine does not. However, it is a simple matter to convert code showing one subroutine to work with the other. These modifications will be left to the reader.

The Input-Validation Sequence

The input-validation sequence is the process by which inputs are taken from the operator, tested, and eventually accepted (or rejected) by the computer. There are five steps in this process:

1. *Prompting.* The operator is prompted to make the input.

2. *Data input.* The operator makes the input to the computer.

3. *Error testing.* The computer tests the operator's input for errors. If an error is found, the process returns to step 1, prompting. If not, the process moves to step 4, editing.

4. *Editing.* The operator is given a chance to modify the input.

5. *Data acceptance.* The computer accepts the data for use.

The logic of these five steps is shown in Figure 5-13.

The input-validation sequence is, literally, a *dialog*. It starts with a question, or prompt, from the computer. The operator answers the question by making an input. The computer next performs an error test to decide whether the entry is acceptable. It lets the operator reconsider his or her side of the dialog and change (edit) it, if necessary. Finally, the computer accepts the data as legitimate and stores them away in memory somewhere.

Prompting

The prompt is a question. It must meet all the information requirements of what we would consider a reasonable question in normal human dialog. Some things which are often used as prompts, and which obviously do not meet this requirement, are the following:

- A blinking cursor
- A blinking question mark
- A prompt which says "Entry"

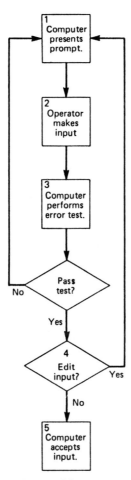

Figure 5-13 Input-validation sequence logic.
(*From Simpson:* Design of User-Friendly
Programs for Small Computers, *copyright
1985, by permission of McGraw-Hill Book
Company.*)

Such prompts fail to meet the basic information requirements, which are (1) to
draw attention, (2) to tell what input is required, (3) to tell what format the input
should have, and (4) to show the default value, if there is one.

Draw attention.   A prompt must draw attention to itself to prevent it from being
lost in the rest of the screen. If it is not conspicuous, the operator must search for
it, which is extra work. Search is reduced by placing prompts consistently from
screen to screen. Many programs use data-input screens which present prompts
at several locations (Figure 5-14), and here search is unavoidable unless the
prompt attracts attention in some other way, such as highlighting and displaying
a blinking cursor.

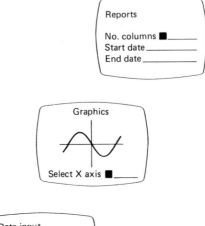

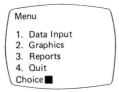

Figure 5-14 A prompt must draw attention with a blinking cursor, since the input field may vary from screen to screen, as shown here.

Regardless of the data-input situation, make the prompt stand out by (1) highlighting it when it is active and (2) displaying a prominent blinking cursor. Highlighting may be done with reverse or high-intensity video or with color. (Use color cautiously, following the guidelines in Chapter 4.) The KEYS subroutine (Figure 5-11) discussed in the previous section highlights the prompt with high-intensity video but can easily be modified to use reverse video. It also presents a very prominent blinking cursor.

Tell what input is required.   The prompt must be descriptive enough to leave no doubt about what information is being asked for. A blinking cursor, or a prompt that says "Enter data," is too vague. The prompt must be more explicit. For example:

```
Please type in the price of corn: $ _ _ _ _ _ _ _ _ _
```

This prompt is polite. It asks "please." This is nice in some cases but unnecessary in others. A descriptive prompt such as this is desirable if the program will be used infrequently or by inexperienced operators. More sophisticated operators generally prefer more succinct prompts, for example:

```
Price of corn: $ _ _ _ _ _ _ _ _
```

This prompt still contains the essential information—but skips the "please" and telling the operator to type in the entry. In general, the more inputs required, the more succinct the prompts should be.

The first prompt tells the operator to "type in" the entry. Sometimes prompts tell the operator to "enter" something, which is less explicit; unsophisticated operators may not know that a keyboard entry is required and may attempt to load data from a disk, read a file, or "enter" data in some other way. The more explicit the prompt the better.

Finally, the prompt indicates that the price of a particular commodity (corn) is required and displays a $ in the data-input field. KEYS permits you to include a dollar sign or other special symbol as part of the prompt. For example, to present the prompt shown above, define the PROMPT$ argument like this:

```
10 PROMPT$="Please type in the price of corn: $"
```

The prompt will then be displayed with the $ sign, as shown above.

Tell the input format.   If data must be entered in a particular format, show the format in the prompt. For example:

```
Date (month/day/year): _ _ _ _ _ _ _ _ _ _ _ _ _
```

If there is a length limit to the entry, show graphically in the prompt what the limit is. The best way to do this is with an underline. For example:

```
Please type in your last name: _ _ _ _ _ _ _ _
```

KEYS automatically generates a length-delimiting underline. For reasons described in the previous section, length delimiters are not feasible with LINE INPUT–based data-input routines. The length limit may also be shown with brackets:

```
Please type in your last name: [                    ]
```

(KEYS can be easily modified to generate brackets instead of an underline.)

Show the default value.   If an entry has a default value, display the default in the data-input field. For example:

```
Enter the file name: SYS.DOC
```

Permit operators to verify and enter this value by simply pressing the Enter key, without retyping the entry itself. KEYS can be used to enter a default value, as noted in the previous section. The procedure is to define ENTRY$ (the operator entry) in program code as a subroutine argument and then to call the subroutine at line 2020 (see Figure 5-11). By doing this, the subroutine will be made to display ENTRY$ in the data-input field, followed by a blinking cursor. For example, to generate the above prompt, include lines such as these in your program:

```
10 PROMPT$="Enter the price of corn: $"
20 ENTRY$="SYS.DOC"
30 GOSUB 2020
```

The foregoing guidelines all say the same thing: *Make sure the operator knows what you want.* This is what we expect when another person comes up to us and asks a question. If the question is phrased properly, it tells us what we need to know to answer properly. If the question is vaguely worded or incomplete, or if it allows several interpretations, we cannot answer properly.

Data Input

Most of the rules to follow during data input emerge from common sense. Nonetheless, since the rules are often broken, well, you draw the conclusion about certain programmers' common sense.

Display the entry.   Display (or "echo") the operator entry back on the screen. This provides the feedback that the operator needs to be sure that an entry has been accepted by the computer. Without such feedback, the operator cannot be sure. Uncertain operators tend to make duplicate entries, often producing unintended results. If you have ever attempted to operate a computer without a functioning visual display, you understand the problem.

Permit error correction during data input.   The previous section described various INKEY$-based verification routines, and made much of displaying the verification keystroke—usually a "y" or "n"—back to the operator. Such routines should always echo back what they get and never let the operator's input simply disappear into the black hole of the computer.

A second reason to display the entry is to permit the operator to identify errors. Skilled keyboard operators will detect many of their errors through their hands; they usually know when they have made an error without looking at the screen. However, many errors will go undetected unless they are observed. You must therefore make it possible for them to observe and correct an entry before it becomes final. The operator must be able to back up and make changes.

The entry should not be accepted by the computer until the operator verifies it by pressing the Enter key. This assures that the program will not proceed until the operator has had a chance to reconsider and cancel the entry. The INKEY$-based verification routines in the previous section illustrated how to permit Enter key verification of single-keystroke entries. Data-input code that uses the INPUT or LINE INPUT statements, or the KEYS subroutine, has automatic Enter key verification.

There are occasions when single-keystroke entry, without Enter key verification, is acceptable. The test is whether the entry is itself a verification of some previous action. For example, if this prompt appears at the bottom of a data-input screen that has just been filled out by the operator.

```
Do you have any changes? (y/n): ■
```

the operator's entry is a verification of what has been entered. Typing in a "y" says that the content of the screen is acceptable; an "n" says it is not. In this case, Enter key verification is unnecessary.

Keep the operator in control.   A specific example of the more general principle of operator control of the input process is the operator's ability to correct previous entries. The operator should never be locked into a situation from which there is no escape other than the rigidly defined one controlled by the computer. Thus, not only should the operator be able to correct previous entries, but he or she should also be able to abandon the input altogether and go have lunch or do some other more important thing. This is one of the reasons that KEYS provides an Escape key exit from data input. This gives the operator an out and the needed control.

There should always be an easy way to exit the data-input process without being forced to carry on mechanically to the end. This is an operator convenience. It is also a way out for inexperienced users who cannot figure out what to do. Without it, such operators may find themselves trapped so that the only escape is to exit from the program by brute force—by interrupting and restarting the program. Interrupting and restarting can have disastrous consequences, and the temptation to employ such measures should be minimized. Provide a standard escape procedure, such as pressing the Escape key, that will return the operator to a safe harbor (e.g., the last menu).

Keep entries short.   Keep operator entries as short as possible. Entries that are made repeatedly should be a maximum of five to seven characters long—the shorter, the better.

Permit entries in their natural form.   Permit operators to make entries in the form that is most natural for them. This applies to dates, units of measure, quantities, names, or anything else that might be represented differently within the computer than in normal, written communication. For example, do not require an operator to enter leading zeros unless the zeros are truly significant, e.g., do not require operators to enter a date in a format such as 04/02/85. Let operators enter the date as they would write it and have the computer add the leading zeros or make whatever other transformation is necessary for internal use.

Keep the operator posted on delays.   If an operator entry will cause an extended delay—5 seconds or more—then display a message (or other sign) such as the following to show that the program has not stopped:

```
Processing data. Please stand by.
```

As operators gain experience, they will worry less about delays. However, even experienced operators worry when a program takes too long to do something, thinking that the delay means a problem with processing, memory, or something else.

Error Test

Data-input errors are inevitable, and the program and operator must be protected from their consequences. Without error protection, a program may crash when certain entries occur, and the operator's previous work may be lost. Moreover, once this happens to an operator, he or she seldom trusts the program in the future and is often unwilling to use it to its full potential. This is not news to an experienced programmer or designer who spends a fair amount of time anticipating data-input errors and building software to handle them safely.

Error-testing involves several different issues. The first of these is an error-testing *philosophy*—a sort of attitude that the designer must adopt in deciding what to expect from the operators who use the program. Philosophy does not have much to do with program code directly—but it suggests what type of code is required in the first place. Thus, an error-testing philosophy is the first topic covered in this subsection.

A second important issue is the error tests themselves. Once you have designed an input routine and have decided that certain types of errors are likely to occur, you must write code to test for them. This is the second topic covered.

After an error has been discovered, what do you do about it? This is where the error message comes in. A good error message does more than identify an error in the rather mindless "SYSTEM ERROR" fashion so common in many programs. Rather than slap the operator's hand, it helps the operator fix the thing that went wrong.

Error-testing philosophy.   You must assume that any error, however improbable, will in fact occur. This is admittedly a pessimistic philosophy, based on the premise that one ought to expect the worst in order to guard against it. For example, assume that operators will make errors such as the following:

- Enter numbers where letters are requested, and vice versa.
- Exceed length limits.
- Enter nothing.
- Enter inappropriate punctuation.
- Enter control characters.
- Do exactly what you tell them not to do.
- Etc.

An assumption that operators will not do these and similar things implies that they will act responsibly—and this assumption is folly. This is not meant as an insult to the fine, intelligent people who use microcomputer programs. Rather, it is based on the desire to spare you the anguish of the telephone call in which an operator describes to you the bizarre sequence of keystrokes that permitted all the valuable files to be purged, that made the program disk unreadable, and that sent the disk drives into a self-destructive frenzy.

You must anticipate what errors *can* occur, devise error tests to trap them, and write error messages to tell the operator what went wrong and what to do about it. The first part—anticipating errors—requires you to use your crystal ball or, if you do not have one, to consider the possibilities. The second and third parts are more straightforward, since they amount to the solution of a problem that has previously been defined. As is often said, the most difficult part of solving a problem is to define it. In the realm of error-testing, defining the problem is anticipating what errors may occur. Enough philosophy.

Error-testing.   An error test consists of code designed to handle certain specific types of errors. For example, the following lines contain a type of test referred to as a *range* test:

```
10 INPUT "Number (1-5): "; NUMBER$
20 NUMBER = VAL(NUMBER$)
30 IF NUMBER> =1 AND NUMBER< =5 GOTO 40 ELSE PRINT "Number must be
between 1 and 5":GOTO 10
40 PRINT NUMBER
```

The prompt tells the operator to type in a number between 1 and 5. Line 30 contains IF-GOTO logic that tests whether the number is within the acceptable range. If so, control flows to line 40 and the number is printed. If the test is failed, then control is sent back to line 10, requiring the operator to reenter the number. This is an *active* error test in the sense that specific code (line 30) has been written to test for a specific, anticipated error.

A *filter* can also be used to test for certain more general types of errors. For example, KEYS (Figure 5-11) contains these lines:

```
2290 REM-Filter Non-Standard Characters-
2300 IF ASC(CHAR$)> =32 AND ASC(CHAR$)< =126 GOTO 2310 ELSE
BEEP:GOTO 2110
2310 ENTRY$ =ENTRY$ +CHAR$:REM concatenate old and new entries
```

Line 2300 acts as a filter to prevent nonstandard characters from becoming part of ENTRY$. For example, if someone types in a Ctrl or Alt key combination, it is simply ignored. A filter like this can be used to trap many errors at the point at which they are being typed in and can reduce the amount of separate testing that must be done in program code. KEYS also contains a built-in length test that disallows ENTRY$ if it is shorter than SHORT (minimum length argument) or longer than LONG (maximum length argument).

Certain types of errors will cause a system interrupt and cannot be tested for with either an active test or a filter. For example, if the operator types in the Ctrl-C, Ctrl-Break, or Ctrl-Alt-Del combination, an interrupt is sent through the PC that has the same effect on its sensibility as a punch to the nose of its operator. These types of errors—if they are "errors" and not intentional—must be handled differently and are taken up in Chapter 7, "Error Management."

Finally, certain types of entry errors are recognizable and can be corrected by the system itself. For example, if a prompt requests a name that the system knows—for example, the name of a file or a name in a directory—and the operator mistypes it, it may be possible to compare the operator's entry with the system vocabulary and make a correction. This type of error correction is, unfortunately, beyond the scope of the present book, although a simple example of it is given below.

In summary, you need to be concerned with (1) active tests, (2) filters, (3) error management, and, perhaps, (4) error correction. These test components and their relationships are illustrated in Figure 5-15. Filters have already been discussed, and error management is discussed in Chapter 8. Hence, the following discussion focuses mainly on active tests.

Three simple and widely used error tests are the range test, identity test, and length test.

The *range* test, described above, looks for an input that falls within a particular range. Range tests are important to prevent unacceptable values of numeric or string variables from entering the working database of the program. An unacceptable value is one that is nonsensical, may lead to an error condition, or should be rejected for other reasons. For example, in a simple program like this,

```
10 INPUT A
20 PRINT "99/A=";99/A
```

if the user enters 0, an error condition will occur when line 20 attempts to divide 99 by 0. Similar problems can occur when invalid numbers are used to perform other types of mathematical operations. In such cases, tests must be conducted to assure that only valid entries are used. Analogous problems can occur with strings.

Though we tend to think of ranges as applying exclusively to numbers, they apply to all characters which have standard ASCII values. (The ASCII values of characters recognized by the IBM PC and PC*jr* are given in Appendix G of their respective BASIC manuals.*) Thus, it is just as reasonable to conduct a range test on a typed-in name or symbol as on a number. Here is an example:

```
10 INPUT "Letter (A-G): ";LETTER$
20 IF LETTER$>="A" AND LETTER$<="G" GOTO 30 ELSE PRINT "Letter
must be between A and G":GOTO 10
30 PRINT LETTER$
```

Type in and run this little program, and it will accept only the letters A, B, C, D, E, F, or G. Since lowercase letters have different ASCII values than capital letters, the test will not accept a, b, c, d, e, f, or g. However, line 20 can be

---

BASIC by Microsoft Corporation, IBM Corporation, 1982, and *BASIC (PCjr) by Microsoft Corporation*, IBM Corporation, 1984.

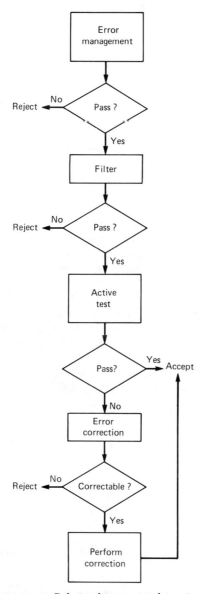

Figure 5-15 Relationships among the various error-control mechanisms: error management, filters, active tests, and error correction.

modified to allow lowercase as well as capital letters. Change line 20 to read as follows, and then run the program again:

```
20 IF (LETTER$>="A" AND LETTER$<="G" OR LETTER$>="a" AND
LETTER$<="g") GOTO 30 ELSE PRINT "Letter must be between A and G"
GOTO 10
```

Now it will accept either capital or lowercase letters. (Note that the error message was not changed, since people do not, generally, distinguish between capital and lowercase letters.)

Try typing in names beginning with letters both within and outside the range, such as "Cheever" and "Paton."

Cheever passes the test. Paton does not. This demonstrates that you can use a single test character to test for a multiple-character entry. When the test (such as the one in line 20) contains a single letter, BASIC compares only the first letter of the entered variable with it. The longer the string used in the test, the more characters will be compared. In fact, BASIC will compare as many characters as you provide in the test—up to an upper limit of 40, which is far more than will ever be needed. To illustrate, change line 20 to this:

```
20 IF LETTER$>="Able" AND LETTER$<="Adam" GOTO 30 ELSE PRINT "Name
must be between Able and Adam":GOTO 10
```

Run the program and type in some names beginning with A, such as Abrams, Ace, Ada, Arthur, and so on. Only names whose collective characters fall within the acceptable range are accepted.

Naturally, range tests can also be used to test for certain symbols, as well. To illustrate, the following symbols have the ASCII values indicated:

Symbol	ASCII value
!	33
"	34
#	35
$	36
%	37
&	38

Hence, this test will exclude anything other than the characters $ and %:

```
20 IF LETTER$>="$" AND LETTER$<="%" GOTO 30 ELSE PRINT "Character
must be either $ or %":GOTO 10
```

Range tests can be used to test for virtually any combination of characters, including those with nonsuccessive ASCII codes. Recall the ASCII value ranges and types of characters (excluding symbols) given earlier in this chapter:

ASCII value	Type character
32	Space
48 to 57	Numbers
65 to 90	Capital letters
97 to 122	Lowercase letters

This test will allow either capital or lowercase letters:

```
20 IF (ASC(LETTER$)>=65 AND ASC(LETTER$)<=90 OR ASC(LETTER$)>=97 AND
ASC(LETTER$)<=122) GOTO 30 ELSE PRINT "Entry must be a letter":GOTO 10
```

This test will allow either capital letters or numbers:

```
20 IF (ASC(LETTER$)>=48 AND ASC(LETTER$)<=57 OR ASC(LETTER$)>=65 AND
ASC(LETTER$)<=90) GOTO 30 ELSE PRINT "Entry must be a capital letter or
number":GOTO 10
```

Incidentally, if you are testing for individual characters or ranges of characters which do not possess adjacent ASCII codes, be careful how you construct the logic of your tests. Expressions with relational and logical expressions like these can become complex very quickly. Construct them carefully, and keep the order of operations in mind. In such expressions, the order of operations is:

1. Function calls
2. Arithmetic operations
3. Relational operators
4. Logical operations, in this order:
   NOT
   AND
   OR
   XOR
   EQV
   IMP

Since ANDing is done before ORing, the first comparison and second comparison in this expression will occur before the OR test is made.

```
20 IF (ASC(LETTER$)>=48 AND ASC(LETTER$)<=57 or ASC(LETTER$)>=65 AND
ASC(LETTER$)<=90) GOTO 30 ELSE PRINT "Entry must be a capital letter or
number":GOTO 10
```

However, if the first and second comparisons require ORing, and these are then ANDed, parentheses are required to assure that the operations are performed in the intended order. For example, this expression looks for a combination of number and letter variables.

```
20 IF ((ASC(NUMBER$)=48 OR ASC(NUMBER$)=57) AND (ASC(LETTER$)=65 OR
ASC(LETTER$)=90)) GOTO 30 ELSE PRINT "Entry must be a combination of
number 0 or 9 and letter A or Z"
```

The parentheses are required in the above expression to force ORing to be performed before ANDing. While parentheses are not always required, using them can often make your expressions easier to understand and lessen the likelihood of mistakes.

```
5 KEY OFF
10 CLS
20 DIM OK$(20)
30 OK$(1)="strawberry"
40 OK$(2)="chocolate"
50 OK$(3)="vanilla"
60 OK$(4)="peach"
70 OK$(5)="tutti frutti"
80 OK$(6)="coconut"
90 INPUT"Flavor: ";FLAVOR$
100 GOSUB 140
110 IF IDENTITY$="ok" GOTO 120 ELSE PRINT "That flavor is unacceptable":GOTO 90
120 PRINT FLAVOR$
130 END
140 REM--identity tester--
150 IDENTITY$="":REM initialize identity flag
160 FOR A=1 TO 20
170 IF OK$(A)="" GOTO 190
180 IF FLAVOR$=OK$(A) THEN IDENTITY$="ok": A=20
190 NEXT
200 RETURN
```

Figure 5-16   A simple program which is used to perform an identity test against the program's vocabulary of six ice cream flavors.

The *identity* test is a special case of the range test. It tests whether the entered variable is identical to a number or character string within the program's vocabulary of acceptable variables. Here is an example of a program that performs an identity test:

```
10 INPUT "Type in an expletive beginning with 'd': ";SWEAR$
20 IF SWEAR$="darn" or SWEAR$="dang" GOTO 30 ELSE PRINT "That
expletive is unacceptable":GOTO 10
30 PRINT SWEAR$
```

The operation of this little program should be self-explanatory. This type of test is useful when the operator's entry must be a specific, predefined number or string. In many cases, what is acceptable may not be a single thing, but several different things that may not be easy or convenient to test for in a single line of code such as line 20 above. For example, if 20 or 100 different entries are acceptable, a different strategy must be used for testing.

One approach to testing for many entries is illustrated by the short program shown in Figure 5-16. This program uses a FOR-NEXT loop to compare an entered value with the program's "vocabulary" of acceptable answers. The vocabulary, which is defined in lines 30 to 80, consists of the names of six ice cream flavors, which are assigned to the first six elements of the array OK$. Line 90 obtains an input from the operator and assigns it to the variable FLAVOR$. Line 100 then calls an identity testing subroutine at line 140. This subroutine uses a flag, the variable IDENTITY$, to communicate with the input routine. Line 150 initializes the flag to the null string. Lines 160 to 190 then use a FOR-NEXT loop to search through the elements of the vocabulary array, comparing each element with the entered variable FLAVOR$. If a match is made in line 180, IDENTITY$ is set to "ok" and the search through the array ceases. If no match is made, then IDENTITY$ remains set to the null string. After the subroutine is finished, control returns to line 110 of the input routine, which examines IDENTITY$. If IDENTITY$ = "ok" then the entered flavor is acceptable; if not, an error message is printed and another input is required.

```
5 KEY OFF
10 CLS
20 INPUT"string: ";WORD$
30 GOSUB 3000
40 PRINT NORM$
50 GOTO 20
3000 REM--Upper- Lowercase Normalizer--
3010 NORM$=""
3020 IF WORD$="" GOTO 3090
3030 FOR A=1 TO LEN (WORD$)
3040 CHAR$=MID$(WORD$,A,1)
3050 ASCII=ASC(CHAR$)
3060 IF ASCII)=65 AND ASCII(=90 THEN CHAR$=CHR$(ASCII+32)
3070 NORM$=NORM$+CHAR$
3080 NEXT
3090 RETURN
```

Figure 5-17 Subroutine (lines 3000 to 3090) which converts any mixed-case input string to all lowercase characters.

One complication in range and identity testing is the distinction BASIC makes between capital and lowercase letters. While this difference is important in some applications, more often than not the operator will not pay much attention to it. Thus, if an identity test demands that a name be typed in with all capital letters and the operator uses all lowercase, the entry will be rejected. Rejection will also occur if the operator types in all capital letters or some inappropriate combination of capital and lowercase letters. Unless the distinction between capital and lowercase letters is important to the program, input routines should accept any combination of capital and lowercase letters and restrict their testing to the semantic content of the entry. Since many combinations will probably be possible, the best way to handle the inputs is to filter them through a subroutine that converts all letters to lowercase. Range and identity tests can then be performed on the converted entries.

Figure 5-17 is the listing of a simple subroutine that converts any capital letter in a string to lowercase but leaves other characters in the string alone. The word to be converted is provided to the subroutine in the argument WORD$. The subroutine then goes through the string, character by character, converts it, and returns the converted string in the variable NORM$ (for normalized). NORM$ is initialized in line 3010 to the null string. Line 3020 tests whether WORD$ is the null string and, if so, skips the analysis and goes straight to the RETURN in line 3090. The working part of the subroutine consists of lines 3030 to 3080. A FOR-NEXT loop is used to take one-character substrings of WORD$ from the first character through to the last. The ASCII value of each character is taken in line 3050. Line 3060 then tests whether this value is within the ASCII range of capital letters (65 to 90). If so, the letter (CHAR$) is redefined as its lowercase equivalent. Line 3070 then uses these characters to construct a new, "normalized" string called NORM$, which has no capital letters.

This subroutine is used to normalize the user's entry before testing it. Here is a simple example of how it might be applied:

```
10 INPUT "Type in 'Y' or 'N': ";WORD$
20 GOSUB 3000
30 IF NORM$="y" OR NORM$="n" GOTO 40 ELSE PRINT "Entry must be
either 'Y' or 'N'":GOTO 10
40 PRINT WORD$
```

The prompt directs the operator to type in a capital Y or N. The operator may do this, or type in a lowercase "y" or "n," or type in something incorrect. Line 3000 normalizes the entry, converting it to lowercase, and returning the entry in the variable NORM$. NORM$ is tested in line 30 as a lowercase letter. If it is a "y" or "n," the test is passed; if not, then reentry is required. The operator may use capital or lowercase letters, since all entries are converted to lowercase anyway. If the test is passed, then WORD$ is an acceptable entry and is printed by line 40.

You will note that a normalizing subroutine such as that shown in Figure 5-17 does a simple type of *error correction* by converting mixed-case entries to a common, lowercase form. Such a subroutine can be extended to do other types of error correction, if you know what to expect. For example, it could be used to filter out spaces, symbols, inappropriate punctuation, and the like. The error corrections that are feasible are very much a function of the types of inputs required. However, the model just given provides an example of one type of simple error correction that can be extended to many BASIC programs.

A third type of test is the length test. Here is an example:

```
10 INPUT "Please type in your first name (12 char max) :";SURNAME$
20 IF LEN(SURNAME$)>=1 AND LEN(SURNAME$)<=12 GOTO 30 ELSE PRINT "Name
must be between 1 and 12 characters long":GOTO 10
30 PRINT SURNAME$
```

A length test such as this is necessary whenever you must impose limits on the length of an entry. The limits may emerge from common sense or from the memory or file requirements of your program. Imposing length limits is especially important if you are using random-access files, since overlength entries may exceed the field-length limits of the file.

Note that KEYS allows you to set a lower and upper length limit, and it automatically conducts a length test on entries. This means that an external (i.e., outside the subroutine) length test is unnecessary. If you use a different data-input routine, then you must do your own external length testing.

Error messages.   This subsection begins by presenting some general guidelines for writing and displaying error messages. Later, BASIC code examples will be given to show how to integrate error-messaging with data-input routines. You should write error messages that apply to each error your program tests for and detects and display the appropriate message when an error occurs. Guidelines for writing and displaying error messages are given below.

Display the message as close to the offending entry as possible. During data input, the logical place for the operator to look for feedback information is just after the entry has been typed in. The message might be displayed temporarily in place of the prompt (Figure 5-18*a*), below it (Figure 5-18*b*), or in another place nearby. It is generally best to leave the prompt and incorrect entry on the screen while the message is being displayed, and to erase the error message and data-input field afterward to allow reentry. This sequence is illustrated in Figure 5-19. On a crowded display, it may not be feasible to present the error message close to the prompt for space reasons. In this case, the message should be presented on an error-message line, a location used to display all error messages (Figure 5-18*c*). If

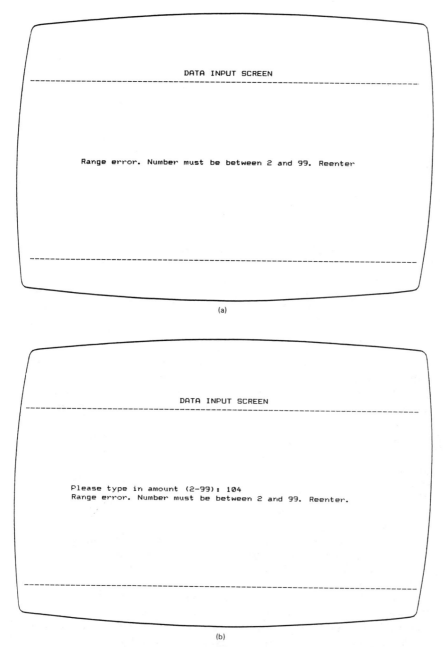

Figure 5-18 Three ways to present error messages: (*a*) temporarily in place of the prompt, (*b*) below the prompt, or (*c*) in a central message area.

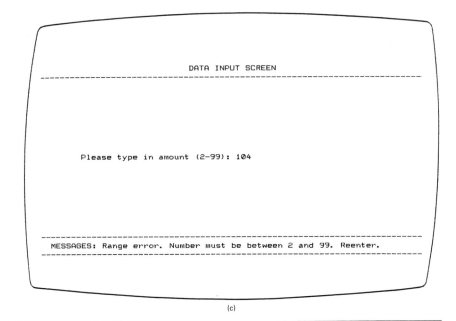

```
                        DATA INPUT SCREEN
   ----------------------------------------------------------------------



          Please type in amount (2-99): 104




   ----------------------------------------------------------------------
   MESSAGES: Range error. Number must be between 2 and 99. Reenter.
   ----------------------------------------------------------------------
```

(c)

Figure 5-18 (continued)

you do not put the message beside the offending entry, select a part of the display and use the same location for presenting all such messages. (Keep in mind the principle of consistency.) The error message should do three things: (1) alert the operator that an error has occurred, (2) identify the error, and (3) tell the operator how to recover (Figure 5-20).

To *alert* the operator, use an audio signal (a beep) and a blinking message. Even if the operator is not paying close attention to the display, he or she will be alerted by an audio signal. And, since the error message will not be displayed forever—usually for only a few seconds—it is important to draw the operator's attention to it before it disappears. High-intensity blinking will draw the operator's eyes to the written message. Incidentally, audio signals and blinking messages are alerting to the extent that they are novel. If your program is emitting a continuous stream of beeps and uses many blinking messages, the novelty of the error message is diluted. This is one reason to be conservative in the use of these alerting techniques. Do not use them unless they are really necessary.

The error message must *identify* what is wrong. If identification of the error will permit the operator to figure out what to do next, that is all that is needed. However, if the nature of the error is still ambiguous, more information must be provided. For example, it is not enough to tell the operator that a data-input error has just occurred. The type of error must be identified. For example:

```
Entry must be between 1 and 24 characters in length.
Number must be between 100 and 1000.
Only options 1 through 4 are acceptable.
```

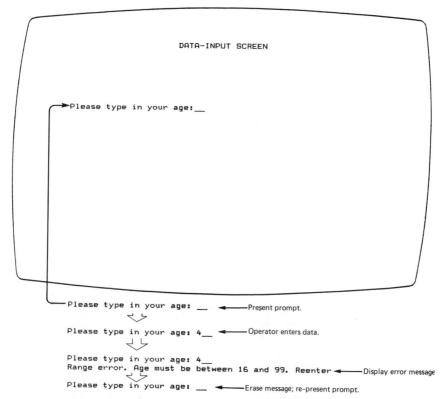

DATA-INPUT SCREEN

Please type in your age:__

Please type in your age: __ ◄———Present prompt.

Please type in your age: 4__ ◄———Operator enters data.

Please type in your age: 4__
Range error. Age must be between 16 and 99. Reenter ◄———Display error message

Please type in your age: __ ◄———Erase message; re-present prompt.

Figure 5-19 Sequence in presenting an error message following incorrect entry: Prompt is presented, incorrect entry is typed in, error message is displayed for a few seconds, and then message is erased and prompt re-presented.

Whatever you do, avoid messages that tell nothing or that insult the operator. For example:

```
Invalid entry
Error 51
Reenter
```

The final part of the message is the *recovery* action. This tells the operator what to do to get out of a fix. The recovery action may be to reenter data, to select a legal program option, to restart the program, or to take some other action. Whatever it is, do not assume that the operator will automatically know. Define the action, even if it is obvious. For example, the recovery action following an invalid data input is to reenter data, and the error message should contain these words:

```
Reenter data
```

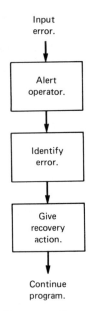

Input
error.

Alert
operator.

Identify
error.

Give
recovery
action.

Continue
program.

Figure 5-20   Functions of an error message:
alert the operator, identify the error, give the
recovery action.

If most or all of the entries made by the operator have the same recovery action,
then the "Reenter data" part of the message may be considered optional. If in
doubt, include it.

Figure 5-21 shows several acceptable error messages to illustrate the points
discussed above. In each of these examples, the error message appears beneath
the prompt and data-input field.

Make your error messages *brief, factual, and explicit.* Do not attempt to punish
the operator for mistakes. Avoid sarcasm. Punishment or sarcasm from a computer is offensive and inexcusable. Such behavior is not polite from a human, and
the computer, being less than human, has no right to it at all. Give your program
the personality of a very helpful but rather dull and literal-minded friend who
wants to make sure the operator understands the error and knows what to do
about it.

Now let us consider the mechanics of presenting error messages. An error
message can be generated directly in program code, as was done in some of the
simple examples earlier in this chapter. If the program involves a small amount of
data input and few error messages are required, then direct generation is probably the best approach. If the program involves several inputs and requires many
error messages, then it is much better to write a subroutine to do the work. In
fact, it makes a good deal of sense to use a subroutine in either case, since
presenting the message properly involves (or should involve) more than simply

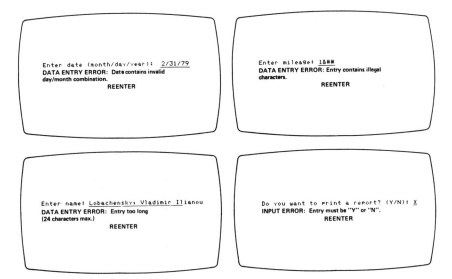

Figure 5-21 Examples of four error messages, following incorrect data input. Each message contains three parts: (*a*) alert, (*b*) identification, and (*c*) recovery action. (*From Simpson:* Design of User-Friendly Programs for Small Computers, *copyright 1985, by permission of McGraw-Hill Book Company.*)

printing it and then returning to data input. Here is what should happen when an error has been detected and a message must be displayed:

1. Position the cursor to print the message

2. Beep to alert the operator

3. Turn on high-intensity blinking video

4. Print the message

5. Switch back to normal video

6. Insert a time delay of 5 to 10 seconds

7. Erase the message

You can do all this directly in program code, but it is easier and more efficient to use a subroutine. So let us write a little error-message generator in the form of a subroutine. Let us assume that the error message will be printed below the prompt and that the prompt itself will be generated by either the KEYS or the LINE INPUT data-input subroutines. You will recall that both of these subroutines position the prompt with the LOCATE statement, using the arguments ROW and COL. Since the error message will be printed below the prompt, it can be positioned by using the arguments ROW + 1 and COL. Figure 5-22 is the listing of a subroutine that will generate a blinking error message (defined by the argument MESSAGE$) below the prompt, and display it for approximately 6

```
4000 REM--Error Message Generator--
4100 LOCATE ROW+1,COL
4110 BEEP
4120 COLOR 31,0:REM high-intensity blinking
4130 PRINT MESSAGE$
4140 COLOR 7,0:REM normal
4150 FOR TIME=1 TO 6000:NEXT:REM 6-second delay
4160 LOCATE ROW+1,COL
4170 PRINT SPACE$(LEN(MESSAGE$))
4180 RETURN
```

Figure 5-22 An error-message–generation subroutine.

seconds. (Line 4150 is a time delay loop; each 1000 represents approximately 1 second.)

Let us see how the subroutine might be used during data input. Here is a little program that collects an input directly and then uses the subroutine to display a message. (The subroutine is not shown in the following lines, but assumed to be part of the program.)

```
10 ROW=10
20 COL=1
30 LOCATE ROW,COL
40 LINE INPUT "Please type in your surname (2-24 char): ";SURNAME$
50 IF LEN(SURNAME$)>=2 AND LEN(SURNAME$)<=24 GOTO 90 ELSE 60
60 MESSAGE$="Length error. Entry must contain 2 to 24 characters"
70 GOSUB 4000:REM call error-message generator
80 GOTO 30
90 PRINT SURNAME$
```

Line 30 positions the cursor, and line 40 collects the input from the operator. Line 50 then performs a length test, sending control to line 90 if the test is passed or to line 60 if it is failed. If the test is failed, line 60 defines the error message and line 70 calls the error-message–generating subroutine, which displays the error message on the row below the prompt. Afterward, control is sent back to line 30 to collect another input. While this little program is not a good model of how to collect a data input, it does illustrate the general technique for generating an error message.

Now let us look at a more realistic example, this one using KEYS for performing data input. [Though not shown, both KEYS (Figure 5-11) and the error-message–generator subroutine (Figure 5-20) are part of the following program.]

```
10 ROW=10
20 COL=1
30 PROMPT$="Please type in your age (12-99): "
40 SHORT=2
50 LONG=2
60 GOSUB 2000:REM call KEYS data-input subroutine
70 AGE=VAL(ENTRY$):REM evaluate input from KEYS
80 IF AGE>=12 and AGE<=99 GOTO 120 ELSE 90
90 MESSAGE$="Length error. Entry must contain 2 to 24 characters"
100 GOSUB 4000:REM call error message generator
110 GOTO 60
120 PRINT AGE
```

This program resembles the previous one, but here the input is collected by KEYS, which is called at line 60. KEYS returns its input as the variable ENTRY$, which is evaluated in line 70 and assigned to the variable AGE. Line 80 then conducts a length test, whose outcome decides whether an error message is displayed or AGE is printed.

Use of the error-message generator is fairly straightforward, and we need not dwell on it much further, except to offer some ideas on how it might be modified for use in particular programs.

First, consider error-message placement. As the subroutine is now written, it will display the error message on the row below the prompt. If you do not want to display it there, modify the row and column arguments in line 4160 so that you can place it somewhere else. For example, if you want to display all error messages in the same location (e.g., row 23, column 1), change line 4160 to read as follows:

```
4160 LOCATE 23,1
```

If your error messages are too long to fit on a single line, use more than one string variable to represent the message, and print different parts of the message on different rows. For example, suppose that you want to present the message on two separate lines. Use the variables LINE1$ and LINE2$ to represent the message, and change line 4130 and add line 4135 to the program like this:

```
4130 PRINT LINE1$
4135 PRINT LINE2$
```

And if you want a three-line message, well, you get the idea.

Now, if your program tends to make the same sorts of tests repeatedly—range, identity, length, or whatever—then it may pay to "can" some of the error messages in the error-message subroutine itself, rather than defining them with each data-input routine. To illustrate, Figure 5-23 is a modified version of the error-message generator with three "canned" error messages shown on lines 4010, 4020, and 4030. Line 4010 contains a standard range error message, line 4020 contains a standard identity error message, and line 4030 contains a standard length error message. Each of these messages contains variable arguments which can be assigned within the program. For example, the range error message in line 4010 has the arguments LOW and HIGH, which correspond to the lower

```
4000 REM--Error Message Generator--
4010 MESSAGE$="Range error. Value must be between"+STR$(LOW)+" and"+STR$(HIGH)+"
. Reenter.":GOTO 4040
4020 MESSAGE$="Identity error. Acceptable entries: "+ACCEPT$+". Reenter":GOTO 40
40
4030 MESSAGE$="Length error. Entry must contain"+STR$(SHORT)+" to"+STR$(LONG)+"
characters. Reenter"
4040 LOCATE ROW+1,COL
4050 BEEP
4060 COLOR 31,0:REM high-intensity blinking
4070 PRINT MESSAGE$
4080 COLOR 7,0:REM normal
4090 FOR TIME=1 TO 6000:NEXT:REM 6-second delay
4100 LOCATE ROW+1,COL
4110 PRINT SPACE$(LEN(MESSAGE$))
4120 RETURN
```

Figure 5-23 Error-message–generation subroutine containing three "canned" messages.

and upper limits of the acceptable range. If these arguments are provided and the subroutine is called at line 4010, then it will print a standard error message. This saves the bother of providing the text of the error message within the program.

For example, to print a message showing an entry outside the acceptable range 12 to 99, include code such as this:

```
10 LOW = 12
20 HIGH = 99
30 GOSUB 4010:REM generate canned error message
```

Subroutines come in very handy when your program must do the same sort of thing repeatedly, and they are certainly useful in generating error messages. In some cases it pays to "can" the error tests themselves and build them into a standard testing module similar to the error-message generator (Figure 5-22). That is, you could build a subroutine that both performed the error tests and generated an appropriate error message, if the test was failed. Doing this becomes practical when the program performs many highly uniform and similar tests.

Editing

Permit the operator to edit entries before they become permanent. Operators often change their minds or recognize data-input errors after the fact. Therefore, it is important for them to be able to change earlier entries. In any program that builds a database through keyboard entries, editing should be possible during both initial entry and afterward.

During *initial entry,* as data are being typed in, the operator should be able to back up, make changes, or rewrite the entire field if desired. This requirement is met by the INPUT and LINE INPUT statements but not by the INKEY$ statement. KEYS does permit editing, however. Editing is possible with INPUT, LINE INPUT, and KEYS up until the time the Enter key is pressed.

Editing should also be possible *after* initial entry, that is, after the Enter key has been pressed to verify the entry. One approach is to provide a block or page editing capability. This type of editing occurs after a series (i.e., a block or page) of entries has been made (Figure 5-24). After making the entries, the operator is prompted to indicate whether any editing is to be done, using a prompt like this:

```
Do you want to edit? (y/n)
```

If the operator types in "y," then a new prompt asks for the number of the item to change. The operator is then permitted to reenter the selected item, just as during initial data input. That is, the data-input prompt is presented as before— on the screen or in the designated input area of the screen—and all the same error tests are made. After the entry is completed, the operator is again prompted to indicate whether editing is required. If so, the process just described recurs. If not, the program moves to the next phase. Figure 5-25 is a little program that illustrates editing of a single earlier entry. The general technique is extended to data-input screens with several entries in the next chapter.

If the program builds a database, then it should be possible to edit any element in that database, using a technique similar to block or page editing, as described

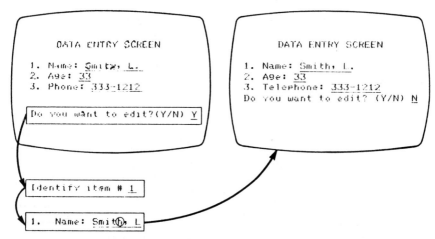

Figure 5-24 An example of page editing. After entries have been made, a prompt asks whether the operator wants to edit (bottom row of screen). After entering Y for yes, the operator is prompted to identify the item number to change. The program then permits reentry of data, producing the corrected screen on the right. (*From Simpson:* Design of User-Friendly Programs for Small Computers, *copyright 1985, by permission of McGraw-Hill Book Company.*)

above. Data-input and database editing are not directly related. However, it is often advisable to integrate them together. That is, use the same screens for accessing and editing the database that are used for entering the data in the first place. This is, in fact, an application of our old friend, the consistency principle, since it means that the data set is presented to the operator in the same form during both data input and subsequent database editing.

Data Acceptance

The data, having been entered, verified, tested, and edited, become part of the temporary or permanent data set of the program.

Handling Syntax-Dependent Entries— Dates, Times, Phone Numbers

This section covers two subjects. The first is a simple way to collect dates and times from an operator, using the PC's built-in DATE$ and TIME$ variables. The

```
5 KEY OFF
10 CLS
20 INPUT"Enter number (1-10): ";A$
30 N=VAL(A$)
40 IF N)=1 AND N(=10 GOTO 50 ELSE BEEP: PRINT"Number must be between 1 and 10":G
OTO 10
50 PRINT "Okay? (y/n)"
60 CHAR$=INKEY$:IF CHAR$="" GOTO 60
70 IF CHAR$="N" OR CHAR$="n" GOTO 10:REM back up and reenter
80 IF CHAR$="Y" OR CHAR$="y" GOTO 90 ELSE 60
90 END
```

Figure 5-25 A short program which permits the operator to verify the previous entry.

second subject is a strategy for dealing with such entries more generally, that is, when built-in variables (such as DATE$ and TIME$) are not available, and you must develop BASIC code to parse and analyze the entry character by character.

Using DATE$ and TIME$ in BASIC Programs

The DOS commands DATE and TIME can be used in BATCH files (see Chapter 7) to present the familiar Date and Time prompts to the operator and thereby collect a system date and time. When the operator types in the entry, invalid entries are detected and bring back the prompt, forcing the operator to reenter the requested information until an entry of valid syntax and content is made.

BASIC does not have a DATE and TIME command, but it does have the DATE$ and TIME$ variables and statements. These can be used to define the system date and time within a BASIC program. For example, you can insert a line of code such as this in your program to collect the system date:

```
10 INPUT "Date (mm/dd/yy): ";DATE$
```

This *will* work, at least in the sense that it allows the operator to redefine the system date (or time, if the TIME$ variable is used). However, if the operator types in an invalid entry, an error condition will occur and the program will crash. For this reason, a routine such as the one shown above should *not* be used without error trapping.

A simple solution to the problem is to activate an error-trapping routine with the ON ERROR GOTO statement before redefining DATE$ or TIME$. The ON ERROR GOTO statement allows you to send program control to a particular line in the program when an error condition occurs, rather than having the program crash. Thus, you can use it to trap the error condition that may occur if the operator types in an invalid date or time. Figure 5-26 is the listing of a subroutine that can be used to collect the date in a BASIC program. This subroutine generates a prompt with KEYS (which starts at line 2000) and an error message with the error-message–generator subroutine (starts at line 4000). Both of these subroutines must be present to use the date collector itself.

Lines 5010 to 5030 set prompting arguments for KEYS. SHORT and LONG are the minimum and maximum length of an acceptable date entry. The shortest possible entry would consist of a one-digit month, one-digit day, and two-digit year, such as this:

```
1/1/88
```

This consists of six characters; thus SHORT is 6. The longest possible entry would consist of a two-digit month, two-digit day, and four digit year, such as this:

```
12/12/1988
```

This consists of ten digits; thus LONG is 10. Line 5030 defines the date prompt, and line 5040 calls KEYS to generate the prompt. Line 5050 sets up an error trap

```
5000 REM--Date Collector--
5010 SHORT=6
5020 LONG=10
5030 PROMPT$="Date (mm/dd/yy): "
5040 GOSUB 2000
5050 ON ERROR GOTO 5080
5060 DATE$=ENTRY$
5070 RETURN
5080 MESSAGE$="Entry has unacceptable format or content"
5090 GOSUB 4000
5100 RESUME 5040
```

Figure 5-20 Subroutine to collect date, using BASIC's
DATE$ variable.

with the ON ERROR GOTO statement, which will send control to line 5090 in
the event of an error condition. If no error occurs, then control will flow to line
5060, which redefines DATE$ as ENTRY$—the value returned by KEYS—and
the date subroutine terminates with a RETURN statement in line 5080. However, if an error does occur, then line 5090 defines an error message, which is
displayed when the error-message subroutine is called at line 5100. Line 5110
then sends control back to line 5040 to prompt the operator to make another
entry.

There are three important things to keep in mind about the subroutine just
described. First, the subroutine can only be used to collect dates that are acceptable according to PC BASIC's internal criteria. Hence, if your program is being
used to keep track of dates in Nero's or Chaucer's lifetime, you are out of luck,
since dates that old are verboten. Second, redefining DATE$ will alter the system
date. If that is your objective or if you do not mind altering the system date, fine.
However, if you want to collect dates for some other purpose—for example,
entering the dates off invoices or other historical records, then you may not want
to change the system date while so doing. (One solution to this problem is to
collect the system date at the beginning of the program, assign it to a variable,
and reassign the system date later.) Third, the error-trapping routine activated by
line 5050 will send control to line 5050 after *any* error occurs in the program.
Thus the program's general error-trapping routine must be reactivated following
this subroutine. (Refer to Chapter 7 for a detailed discussion of program error-
trapping routines.)

To illustrate the subroutine's use, suppose that you want to collect a date from
the user. This date will be assigned to the program variable DA$. The date
prompt is to be displayed at row 4, column 10. The following code will collect the

```
5110 REM--Time Collector--
5120 SHORT=4
5130 LONG=8
5140 PROMPT$="Time (hh:mm:ss): "
5150 GOSUB 2000
5160 ON ERROR GOTO 5190
5170 TIME$=ENTRY$
5180 RETURN
5190 MESSAGE$="Entry has unacceptable format or content"
5200 GOSUB 4000
5210 RESUME 5150
```

Figure 5-27 Subroutine to collect time, using BASIC's TIME$
variable.

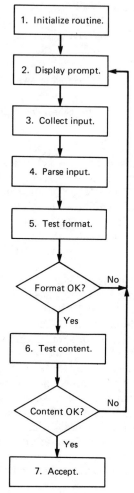

Figure 5-28 Logical flow in a routine that tests input syntax and content.

date, assign it to the program variable DA$, and reactivate the program's general error-handling routine (located at line 1000) afterward.

```
10 ROW=4
20 COL=10
30 GOSUB 5000:REM call date collector subroutine
40 DA$=DATE$:REM assign date to program variable
50 ON ERROR GOTO 10000:REM reset ON ERROR GOTO routine
```

This subroutine is easy to use and leaves the messy part—testing the validity of the entry—to BASIC. A similar routine can be developed for collecting a time,

```
5 KEY OFF
6 CLS
10 DIM DAYS(12)
20 DATA 31,28,31,30,31,30,31,31,30,31,30,31
30 FOR MONTH=1 .TO 12
40 READ DAYS(MONTH)
50 NEXT
60 CLS
70 ROW=10
80 COL=10
90 REM--Date Collector--
100 SHORT=6
110 LONG=10
120 PROMPT$="Date (mm/dd/yy): "
130 GOSUB 2000
140 SEP1=0
150 SEP2=0
160 LAST=LEN(ENTRY$)
170 FOR CHAR=1 TO LAST
180 CHAR$=MID$(ENTRY$,CHAR,1)
190 IF SEP1=0 THEN IF (CHAR$="/" OR CHAR$="-") THEN SEP1=CHAR:GOTO 210:REM locat
e first / or -
200 IF SEP2=0 THEN IF (CHAR$="/" OR CHAR$="-") THEN SEP2=CHAR:REM locate first /
 or -
210 NEXT
220 IF (SEP1=0 OR SEP2=0 OR SEP2=LAST) THEN MESSAGE$="Improper format":GOSUB 400
0:GOTO 130
230 MONTH=VAL(MID$(ENTRY$,1,SEP1-1))
240 DAY=VAL(MID$(ENTRY$,SEP1+1,SEP2-1))
250 YEAR=VAL(MID$(ENTRY$,SEP2+1,LAST))
260 REM-Validity Tests-
270 IF (DAY=0 OR MONTH=0 OR YEAR=0) THEN MESSAGE$="Improper format":GOSUB 4000:
GOTO 130
280 DAYS(2)=28
290 IF MONTH=2 AND YEAR/4=INT(YEAR/4) THEN DAYS(2)=29:REM leap year
300 IF MONTH)=1 AND MONTH(=12 GOTO 310 ELSE MESSAGE$="Invalid month":GOSUB 4000:
GOTO 130
310 IF DAY)=1 AND DAY(=DAYS(MONTH) GOTO 320 ELSE MESSAGE$="Invalid day":GOSUB 40
00:GOTO 130
320 IF YEAR)=1900 THEN YEAR=YEAR-1900
330 IF YEAR)=80 AND YEAR(=99 GOTO 340 ELSE MESSAGE$="Invalid year":GOSUB 4000:GO
TO 130
340 PRINT"Date: "; MONTH;"/";DAY;"/";YEAR
350 GOTO 130
```

Figure 5-29 Program to collect date without using BASIC's DATE$ variable.

using the system variable TIME$. A subroutine for doing this is shown in Figure 5-27.

While it is handy to let BASIC do the dirty work—assess the validity of the input—the side effects of using DATE$ and TIME$, and the constraints of being bound by BASIC's validity criteria make this approach unsatisfactory in some applications. Then you must devise an input routine that collects the variable of interest and performs its own validity tests. A strategy for doing this is given below.

Parsing and Analyzing Compound Entries

Dates, times, and telephone numbers share the property of being *compound* entries. That is, their content consists not of a single number but of several, divided by separators. In order to assess the validity of such an entry, it must first be parsed (taken apart), and then its parts must be analyzed separately. If the entry is not constructed properly, then its *syntax* is incorrect. Thus, error-testing such an entry involves the additional dimension of assessing the entry's syntax.

TABLE 5-3   Line-by-Line Summary of the Listing in Figure 5-29

Lines	Function performed
10 to 50	Read days of month into array DAYS%.
60 to 130	Clear screen and assign arguments for KEYS subroutine. Call subroutine to display prompt.
140 to 150	Initialize arguments SEP1 and SEP2. SEP1 is the character position of the first separator (/ or -) in the entry; SEP2 is the character position of the second separator.
160	Measure length of entry, and assign it to the variable LAST.
170 to 210	Examine each character of entry and determine if it is a separator. Line 190 looks for the first separator. When it finds it, it sets SEP1 to CHAR, the character position of the separator. After finding the separator, SEP1 will no longer be 0 and will be skipped on subsequent passes through the FOR-NEXT loop. Line 200 looks for the second separator, and sets SEP2 to its character position.
220	Perform a simple syntax test. If SEP1 = 0 then the first separator is missing. If SEP2 = 0 then the second separator is missing. If SEP2 = LAST then the last character is a separator. In any of these cases, the syntax or format of the entry is incorrect. The error message generator is then called and a new input must be made.
230 to 250	Extract MONTH%, DAY%, and YEAR% by taking substrings of EN-TRY$ and evaluating their contents. The limits of the substrings are determined by the locations of SEP1 and SEP2, which were extracted during parsing (lines 170 to 210).
260 to 330	Perform validity tests. Line 270 looks for three content errors that probably indicate improper format—values of 0 for month, day, or year. Line 280 sets the number of days in February to 28—this value may be changed to 29 by line 290, if the year is a leap year. Line 300 performs a range test on MONTH%, and line 310 performs a range test on DAY%. Line 320 tests whether the year was entered with the century as well as decade digits; if so, 1900 is subtracted so that YEAR% is normalized to contain only decade digits. Line 330 performs a range test on YEAR%.
340	The entered date is printed.

The standard formats for presenting dates, times, and telephone numbers are as follows:

Date: *month/day/year* or *month-day-year*. For example, 7/7/87 or 8-8-88.

Time: *hour:minute:second*. For example, 12:15:57.

Telephone number: *area code-prefix-digits*. For example, 123-456-7890.

In addition to these three commonplace examples, a given program may make use of other compound entries. Thus, the problem of parsing and analyzing such entries is not limited to these three cases. What is needed, therefore, is a general approach to handling such entries—one that can be modified and extended to suit the requirements of specific situations. Figure 5-28 is a block diagram showing the steps in such a routine. Step 1 is to initialize the data-collection routine—assign subroutine arguments and other variables relevant during data input. Step 2 is to display a prompt to the operator. Step 3 is to collect the input via the keyboard. Step 4 is to parse the entry—take it apart to separate the different elements of its content (such as month, day, and year in a date). Step 5 is to test the format or syntax of the entry; if format is bad, reentry is required. If format is good, then the sequence flows to step 6, during which the content of the entry is tested. If content is bad, reentry is required; if good, then the entry is accepted.

To illustrate these steps more concretely, let us develop a BASIC routine for collecting a date and assessing its validity in terms of both syntax and content. The example can be extended to other applications—for example, to collecting a time, telephone number, or other compound entry. The code for collecting a date is shown in Figure 5-29. A line-by-line summary of the functions performed in Figure 5-29 is given in Table 5-3.

There is a good—though imperfect—match between the code blocks in Figure 5-29 and the more general input model shown in Figure 5-28. The differences are mainly in steps 5 (Test Format) and 6 (Test Content). These two steps are not cleanly separated. In fact, some content testing—length and acceptable character testing—is built into KEYS and occurs before any entry is returned for testing by steps 5 and 6. Format testing occurs in lines 220 and 270—and both of these are heuristic (common sense, or rule of thumb) tests rather than rigorous tests. There are many different ways to make an entry with incorrect format, and it is difficult to predict and test for all of these in advance. Thus, it is generally better to develop simple tests that will catch most format errors. The format tests used here look for missing separators, or for DAY%, MONTH%, or YEAR% values of zero. The first is clearly a format error, but the second is actually a content error that suggests a format error—namely, typing in a letter in place of a number, or using too many separators, or leaving one or more entries out. To decide what types of format tests are necessary, you must simply use common sense. Construction of a content test is much more straightforward and usually involves using some combination of range, identity, and length testing.

Chapter

6

Data-Input Screens

This chapter shows how to design simple data-input screens. The first section discusses data-input forms, data-input screens, and database-review screens— and the importance of consistency among them. The sections following describe and illustrate three different types of data-input screens: (1) scrolling prompt screen, (2) single-row input, and (3) full-screen input.

Data-Input Screens, Data-Input Forms, and Database-Review Screens

Programs which build databases usually require the operator to enter data through the keyboard while viewing a *data-input screen*. Often, a set of related entries will be entered together. If many entries are required, then it is common to collect the data on a paper *data-input form,* and to use this form when typing in the data at the keyboard. After the data have been entered, the operator may review them on a *database-review screen*. In this scenario, the data have three different manifestations:

1. Data-input form
2. Data-input screen
3. Database-review screen

These three manifestations of the data (Figure 6-1) should be as much alike, or consistent, as possible, since operators will make comparisons among them. They will enter data from form to screen or from form to database-review screen. They will compare information in the database screen against the input form. The more the three are alike, the easier it is for the operator.

In many programs, the operator will enter data on the spot, without a form, basing the entries on knowledge or the requirements of an ongoing analysis. However, it is still a good idea to keep the notion of the data-input form in mind, for the data-input screen will be easier to use if it resembles such a form. When the screen resembles a form, it allows the operator to view the entire set of

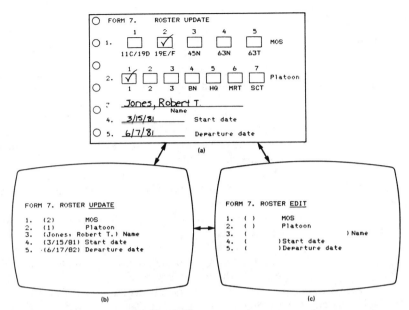

Figure 6-1   There should be a high degree of consistency among (a) the data-input form, (b) the data-input screen, and (c) the database-review screen, as shown here. This makes it easier for the operator to relate the three to one another. (*From Simpson,* Design of User-Friendly Programs for Small Computers, *copyright 1985, by permission of McGraw-Hill Book Company.*)

required inputs at once. The alternative approach is to present one input prompt at a time—which tends to reduce the relationship among inputs. When you design a data-input screen that resembles a form, your program permits *full-screen input.*

Though full-screen input is generally desirable, there are cases when it does not make sense or may actually be undesirable. First, if only one entry is required, the issue evaporates. Second, if the operator's task is very repetitive—for example, entering hundreds of price–product-name pairs—then it may be better to avoid full-screen input. In this case, the operator will probably pay very little attention to the data-input screen but will simply type the data in while viewing the hard copy.

The following sections show three common ways to design data-input screens.

Scrolling Prompt Screen

Description

A scrolling prompt screen presents prompts at the bottom of the screen. After the operator types in the entry and presses the Enter key, the prompt and its content scroll up the screen and the next prompt is presented at the bottom of the screen. The screen in effect moves up each time an entry is made. A scrolling prompt screen is shown in Figure 6-3 (see below).

Required BASIC Code

The scrolling prompt screen is the easiest type of data-input screen to design since it is not actually designed at all—its appearance is simply the consequence of what happens naturally when prompts are presented, data are typed in, and the Enter key is pressed. The code required to generate such a screen usually consists of a series of INPUT or LINE INPUT statements, without any attempt to position the prompt with the LOCATE statement before presenting it. Figure 6-2 contains a simple program for collecting a series of fifty related entries, which are stored in the array DATUM$. Lines 20 to 40 consist of a FOR-NEXT loop which calls a data-input subroutine fifty times. This subroutine, consisting of lines 100 to 170, presents a prompt, permits the operator to back up and reenter, and performs an error test. After all fifty elements of the array have been entered, lines 50 to 80 display them on the screen.

Figure 6-3 shows what the screen looks like as the first nine prompts are presented and data are entered. Each new prompt appears below the previous prompt. If a data-input error is detected, as after entry number 6, the error message is displayed beneath the prompt and the prompt is presented again. To back up, as after entry number 7, the operator types in a *, and this causes the previous prompt to reappear, allowing reentry. This is but one of many ways to write such code but is fairly representative.

Scrolling prompt screens are not necessarily bad. If many repetitive entries are required, then they are often recommended, since the code is simple and fast, and the operator will not be paying much attention to the screen anyway.

Single-Row Input

Description

In single-row input, all data-input prompts are displayed in the same position on the screen, one at a time. The operator responds to the first prompt by typing in

```
5 KEY OFF
6 CLS
7 LOCATE 24,1
10 DIM DATUM$(50)
20 FOR ELEMENT=1 TO 50
30 GOSUB 100:REM call data input routine
40 NEXT
50 REM--Display Entries--
60 FOR ELEMENT=1 TO 50
70 PRINT DATUM$(ELEMENT)
80 NEXT
90 END
100 REM--Data Input Subroutine--
110 PRINT"Entry";ELEMENT;": ";
120 LINE INPUT DATUM$(ELEMENT)
130 IF DATUM$(ELEMENT)="*" THEN IF ELEMENT)= 2 THEN ELEMENT=ELEMENT-1:GOTO 110:R
EM back up
140 IF DATUM$(ELEMENT))="A" AND DATUM$(ELEMENT)(="z" GOTO 160 ELSE 150:REM range
 test
150 BEEP:PRINT"Range error. Entry must be between 'A' and 'z'":GOTO 100
160 PRINT
170 RETURN
```

Figure 6-2 Demonstration program which generates a scrolling prompt screen.

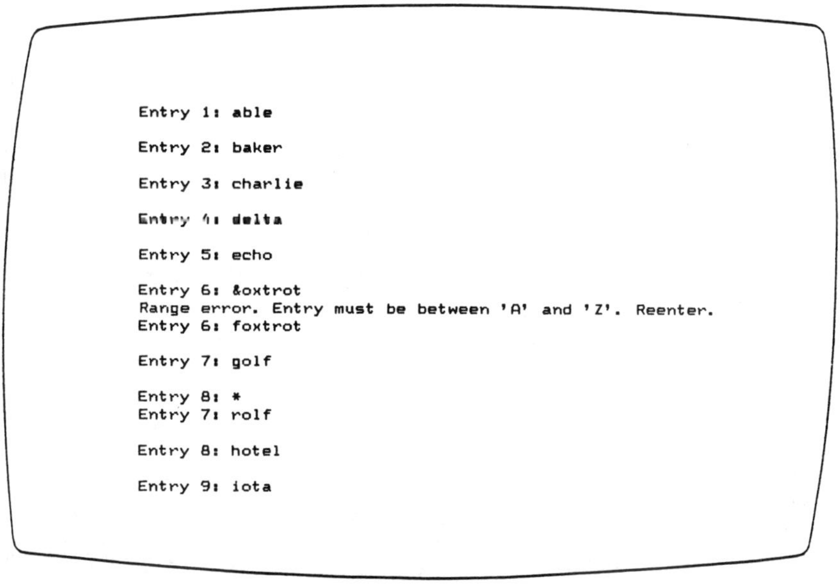

```
     Entry 1: able

     Entry 2: baker

     Entry 3: charlie

     Entry 4: delta

     Entry 5: echo

     Entry 6: &oxtrot
     Range error. Entry must be between 'A' and 'Z'. Reenter.
     Entry 6: foxtrot

     Entry 7: golf

     Entry 8: *
     Entry 7: rolf

     Entry 8: hotel

     Entry 9: iota
```

Figure 6-3 Appearance of data-input screen generated by program shown in Figure 6-2 after nine entries. An error was made in entry 6 and then corrected. The operator decided to revise entry 7 after making it.

an entry and verifying it. That prompt then disappears and is replaced by the second prompt. This process continues until the operator has typed in and verified all entries. The appearance of a single-row input screen across two inputs is shown in Figure 6-4.

The drawback of single-row input is that each prompt is presented separately and requires separate verification. This has two consequences. First, the connection between prompts, if there is one, is diminished. Second, separate verification—presenting a prompt which permits the operator to edit the previous entry—following each entry slows data input. It is much more efficient to make a series of entries before performing separate verification, since this takes less time. In some cases, separate verification can be foregone. However, if it is, then some other convenient means must be made available that permits the operator to edit previous entries.

Single-row input is most often used when the data inputs are made while information is being displayed on the screen. The inputs may be influenced by the displayed information or may be merely incidental. For example, the main part of the screen may be displaying stock data, and the operator reviews these data in order to make inputs into an analysis routine. It is quite reasonable to use single-row input when either of two conditions (or both) applies:

1. The operator must refer to displayed information to make the inputs.

2. Only a few entries are required.

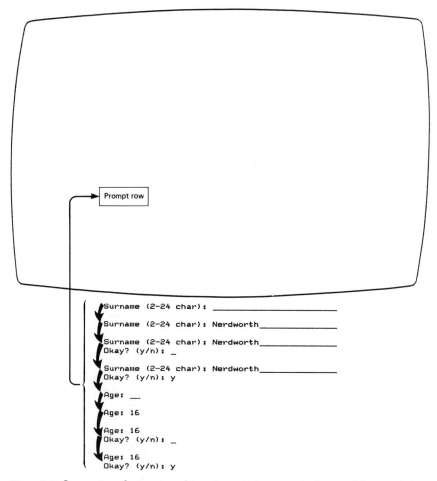

Figure 6-4 Succession of prompts and inputs appearing on a single row of the screen in a program that requires single-row input: A prompt is presented, and then the operator makes an entry and verifies it before proceeding to the next prompt.

If neither of these conditions is met, then full-screen input (see below) should be used.

Required BASIC Code

The code required to perform single-row input is fairly straightforward. Figure 6-5 is a block diagram showing the major steps and decisions that must be performed with such screens.

Step 1 is to generate the data-input screen, the backdrop against which data entries are made. Step 2 is to call the data-input subroutine; this code consists of nothing more than a subroutine call. Data input is done within a subroutine because it may have to be performed more than once, and it is more efficient to

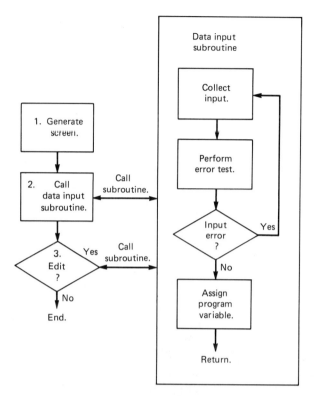

Figure 6-5 Major steps and decision points in code that performs single-row input as shown in Figure 6-4.

use a subroutine than to duplicate the data-input code within the program. Step 3 is the verification or editing step. After the operator makes the entry, a prompt is presented asking whether editing is required. If the answer is yes, then the data-input subroutine is called a second time and a new entry is made. The key part of the program is the data-input subroutine. This subroutine (right) collects the input, performs an error test, presents an error message if applicable, and eventually assigns a program variable based on what the operator types in. Control then returns to the program.

Now let us consider the way these steps can be performed with BASIC code. Since step 1 is to generate a data-input screen, that screen must be designed. The screen that will be used is shown in Figure 6-6. This screen is very simple, consisting of a title ("DATA INPUT SCREEN"), a central information display area (which will be left blank), and a prompt and message area at the bottom. The two main areas of the screen will be separated by horizontal lines.

The code itself will make use of various subroutines presented earlier in this book, as well as one new one. The subroutines that will be used are shown in Figure 6-7. The starting line number of these subroutines, and their purposes, are shown in Table 6-1.

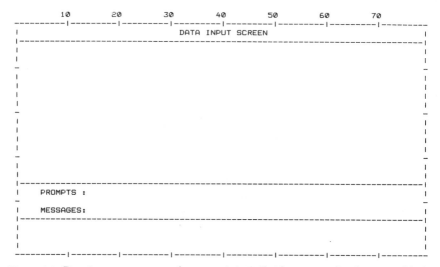

Figure 6-6 Data-input screen template, consisting of title, a central information block (blank), and a prompt and message area at the bottom.

```
1000 REM--Clear Part of One Row--
1010 LOCATE ROW,COL:REM position cursor
1020 PRINT SPACE$(LENGTH):REM clear part of row
1030 LOCATE ROW,COL:REM reposition cursor
1040 RETURN
1300 REM--Center & Print Title (video display)--
1310 COL=(81-LEN(TITLE$))/2:REM (use 40 for 40-column display)
1320 LOCATE ,COL
1330 PRINT TITLE$
1340 RETURN
1430 REM--Print Line--
1440 CHAR$=CHR$(CHAR)
1450 LOCATE ROW,COL
1460 PRINT STRING$(LENGTH,CHAR$)
1470 RETURN
2000 REM--Multiple-Keystroke INKEY$ Subroutine--
2010 ENTRY$="":REM initialize entry
2020 LENGTH=LEN(ENTRY$)
2030 COLOR 15,0:REM high intensity
2040 GOSUB 2350:REM print prompt
2050 GOSUB 2390:REM print length marker
2060 LOCATE ROW,COL2:REM position cursor to data-input field
2070 PRINT ENTRY$;:REM display current entry
2080 COLOR 31,0:REM high-intensity blinking
2090 PRINT CHR$(219);:REM print cursor
2100 COLOR 7,0:REM normal
2110 CHAR$=INKEY$:IF CHAR$="" GOTO 2110:REM collect keystroke
2120 REM-Test for Enter Key-
2130 IF CHAR$=CHR$(13) GOTO 2140 ELSE 2190
2140 IF LENGTH )= SHORT GOTO 2150 ELSE BEEP:GOTO 2110:REM minimum length test
2150 GOSUB 2350:REM print prompt
2160 GOSUB 2390:REM print length marker
2170 PRINT ENTRY$+" ":REM print entry & erase cursor
2180 GOTO 2340:REM exit subroutine
2190 REM-Test for ESC Key-
2200 IF ASC(CHAR$)=27 THEN GOSUB 2350:GOSUB 2390:ENTRY$="":GOTO 2340:ELSE 2210:R
EM exit subroutine
2210 REM-Test for Backspace Key-
2220 IF ASC(CHAR$)=8 GOTO 2230 ELSE 2270
2230 IF LENGTH )= 1 GOTO 2240 ELSE BEEP:GOTO 2110:REM minimum length test
2240 LENGTH=LENGTH-1
2250 ENTRY$=LEFT$(ENTRY$,LENGTH):REM remove last keystroke
2260 GOTO 2030
2270 REM-Maximum Length Test-
```

```
2280 IF LENGTH=LONG GOTO 2110
2290 REM-Filter non-Standard Characters-
2300 IF ASC(CHAR$))=32 AND ASC(CHAR$)(= 126 GOTO 2310 ELSE BEEP:GOTO 2110
2310 ENTRY$=ENTRY$+CHAR$:REM concatenate old and new entries
2320 LENGTH=LEN(ENTRY$)
2330 GOTO 2060
2340 RETURN:REM exit point from subroutine
2350 REM-Print Prompt-
2360 LOCATE ROW,COL
2370 PRINT PROMPT$;
2380 RETURN
2390 REM Erase Field, Print Length Marker
2400 COLOR 7,0:REM normal
2410 COL2=COL+LEN(PROMPT$)+1
2420 LOCATE ROW,COL2
2430 PRINT SPACE$(LONG)
2440 LOCATE ROW,COL2
2450 PRINT STRING$(LONG, "_")+" "
2460 LOCATE ROW,COL2
2470 RETURN
4000 REM--Error Message Generator--
4100 LOCATE ROW,COL
4110 BEEP
4120 COLOR 31,0:REM high-intensity blinking
4130 PRINT MESSAGE$
4140 COLOR 7,0:REM normal
4150 FOR TIME=1 TO 6000:NEXT:REM 6-second delay
4160 LOCATE ROW+1,COL
4170 PRINT SPACE$(LEN(MESSAGE$))
4180 RETURN
4500 REM--Verification Prompt--
4510 COLOR 15,0:REM high-intensity video
4520 LENGTH=28
4530 GOSUB 1000:REM erase row, position cursor
4540 PRINT"Do you want to edit? (y/n) ";
4550 COLOR 31,0:REM high-intensity blinking
4560 PRINT CHR$(219)
4570 COLOR 7,0:REM normal
4580 VER$=INKEY$:IF VER$="" GOTO 4580
4590 IF VER$="Y" OR VER$="y" OR VER$="N" OR VER$="n" GOTO 4600 ELSE BEEP:GOTO 45
80
4600 GOSUB 1000:REM erase prompt
4610 RETURN
```

Figure 6-7 Subroutines used in data-input programs in this chapter. Subroutines and starting lines are: Clear Part of One Row (1000), Center & Print Title (1300), Print Line (1430), KEYS (2000), Error-Message Generator (4000), Verification Prompt (4500).

TABLE 6-1 Starting Line Numbers of Routines Shown in Figure 6-7

Line	Purpose
1000	Clear part of one row—used to erase part of a row before displaying new information.
1300	Center and print title—used to center and print a title on the video display.
1430	Print line—used to print the horizontal lines that separate the screen.
2000	KEYS—a general-purpose INKEY$-based data-input subroutine. (Incidentally, this is *not* the data-input subroutine shown on the right in Figure 6-5, although it is used by that subroutine.)
4000	Error-message generator—used to display a blinking error message. Note that lines 4100 and 4160 contain LOCATE statements that will print all error messages at row 21, column 14—opposite the "MESSAGE:" indicator.
4500	Verification prompt—this subroutine will present the prompt "Do you want to edit? (y/n)" on the screen, and return either a y, n, Y, or N, based on the operator's response.

```
10000 REM--Data Input Routine--
10010 KEY OFF
10020 REM-Generate Screen-
10030 CLS
10040 TITLE$="Data Input Screen"
10050 GOSUB 1300:REM print title
10060 CHAR=196:REM line char
10070 LENGTH=79:REM line length
10080 COL=1
10090 ROW=2
10100 GOSUB 1430:REM print line
10110 ROW=18
10120 GOSUB 1430:REM print line
10130 ROW=22
10140 GOSUB 1430:REM print line
10150 LOCATE 19,4
10160 PRINT"PROMPTS :"
10170 LOCATE 21,4
10180 PRINT"MESSAGES:"
10190 REM-Data Input-
10200 GOSUB 10280:REM data input subroutine
10210 IF ENTRY$="" GOTO 10370:REM ESC key pressed
10220 REM-Verification-
10230 ROW=21
10240 GOSUB 4500
10250 IF VER$="Y" OR VER$="y" GOTO 10260 ELSE 10370
10260 GOSUB 10280:REM recall data input subroutine
10270 GOTO 10230
10280 REM-Data Input Subroutine-
10290 ROW=19
10300 COL=14
10310 PROMPT$="Product name (2-12 char.):"
10320 SHORT=2
10330 LONG=12
10340 GOSUB 2000
10350 PRODNAME$=ENTRY$
10360 RETURN
10370 END:REM end of data input routine
```

Figure 6-8   Demonstration program that performs single-row input to collect a single entry. (Requires subroutines shown in Figure 6-7.)

These subroutines will be used to build the data-input code. Since all but the last one have been described earlier in this book, the following discussion assumes that you are familiar with them and it will not go into their internal workings. (If you are not familiar with them, you may want to review their descriptions—particularly KEYS and ERROR MESSAGE—in Chapters 3 to 5.)

Now let us write the code to generate the screen, collect a single input—Product Name—and permit operator verification. Figure 6-8 is the listing of the program (excluding the subroutines described above, which are part of the program). Table 6-2 shows a line-by-line summary of the functions performed by the program.

This program illustrates the type of code required to perform effective single-row data input. This example was very simple—it collected a single input and had no error testing or messages (excepting the usual length and acceptable character testing performed within KEYS). To make the problem more interesting, let us change it to collect three inputs and do some error-testing. The three inputs and their acceptable ranges are as follows:

Product name (2 to 12 char.)

Price ($1 to 999.99)

Number of units (1 to 999)

TABLE 6-2   Line-by-Line Summary of the Listing in Figure 6-8

Lines	Function performed
10010	Turn off function key display.
10020 to 10180	Generate screen.
10190 to 10210	Call data-input subroutine and test for a null input—what will be returned if the operator exits KEYS by pressing the Escape key.
10220 to 10260	Call verification subroutine, which displays the prompt "Do you want to edit? (y/n)." If the operator responds y or Y, then line 10260 calls the data-input subroutine, allowing editing of the earlier entry. Otherwise, line 10250 sends control to line 10370, which terminates data input.
10280 to 10360	Data-input subroutine. This subroutine is accessed during initial data entry and may be accessed during editing. Lines 10290 to 10330 define the prompting arguments, and line 10340 calls the KEYS subroutine. Line 10350 assigns a program variable based on the input returned by KEYS.

Figure 6-9 is a block diagram showing the major steps and decisions that must be performed with the three-input version of the program. This diagram is similar to Figure 6-5, but it includes three data-input subroutines (right) and three editing decisions (steps 3, 5, and 7). Step 1 is the same—the screen is generated. Step 2 is to call the first data-input subroutine. In step 3 the first editing decision is made: if the operator decides to edit, then the first data-input subroutine is called again; if not, control flows to step 4. Steps 4 and 5, and steps 6 and 7, are identical to steps 2 and 3—a data-input subroutine is called, and then editing is made possible. After entering and possibly editing all three inputs, the sequence ends.

What will happen on the screen is that the first prompt will appear on the PROMPTS row (Figure 6-10), and the operator will make the first entry. The verification or editing prompt will then appear on the MESSAGES row (Figure 6-11), and the operator will respond to it. After completing the first entry and possibly editing, the prompt for the second input will appear on the PROMPTS row. If an error occurs, an error message will appear on the MESSAGES row (Figure 6-12). Each new prompt will, in effect, replace the previous one.

The code to generate the screen and collect and verify the three inputs is shown in Figure 6-13. (This program includes the subroutines in Figure 6-7, although they are not shown.) A line-by-line summary of the functions performed by the program is given in Table 6-3.

Full-Screen Input

Description

In full-screen input, all prompts are presented on the screen simultaneously and remain there during data entry. Figure 6-14 is an example of such a screen, with three prompts (an actual screen may contain a dozen or more such prompts). Adequate separation must be provided between prompts, and the prompts must

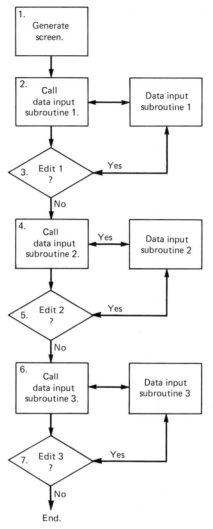

Figure 6-9   Major steps and decision points in code that performs single-row input with three separate entries.

be numbered for reference during editing, which occurs after all entries have been made. Error messages may be presented over the prompt (temporarily replacing it), below it, or in a central message area; in Figure 6-14, all error messages will be printed in the message area, opposite the word MESSAGES, at the bottom of the screen. The verification prompt will appear opposite the word VERIFICATION, also at the bottom of the screen.

When data entry starts, the first prompt is highlighted. The operator types in the first entry and then presses the Enter key. The first prompt then returns to

```
                           DATA INPUT SCREEN
-----------------------------------------------------------------------------



-----------------------------------------------------------------------------
PROMPTS : Product name (2-12 char.): _____
MESSAGES:
-----------------------------------------------------------------------------
```

Figure 6-10 Appearance of single-row input screen when first prompt is displayed.

```
                           DATA INPUT SCREEN
-----------------------------------------------------------------------------




-----------------------------------------------------------------------------
PROMPTS : Product name (2-12 char.): Foxgloves __
MESSAGES: Do you want to edit? (y/n) _
-----------------------------------------------------------------------------
```

Figure 6-11 Single-row input screen after operator has made first entry, pressed Enter key, and verification prompt has been displayed.

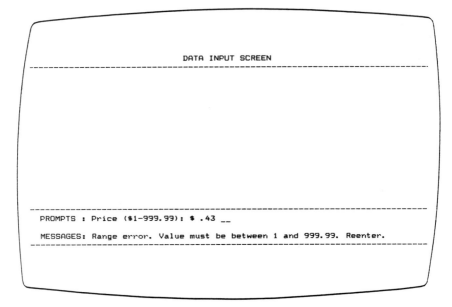

Figure 6-12 Single-row input screen when a data-input error has been made—error message is displayed on MESSAGES row.

```
10000 REM--Data Input Routine--
10010 KEY OFF
10020 REM-Generate Screen-
10030 CLS
10040 TITLE$="DATA INPUT SCREEN"
10050 GOSUB 1300:REM print title
10060 CHAR=196:REM line char
10070 LENGTH=79:REM line length
10080 COL=1
10090 ROW=2
10100 GOSUB 1430:REM print line
10110 ROW=18
10120 GOSUB 1430:REM print line
10130 ROW=22
10140 GOSUB 1430:REM print line
10150 LOCATE 19,4
10160 PRINT"PROMPTS :"
10170 LOCATE 21,4
10180 PRINT"MESSAGES:"
10190 REM-Data Input & Verification #1-
10200 REM Input
10210 GOSUB 10490:REM data input subroutine
10220 IF ENTRY$="" GOTO 10900:REM ESC key pressed
10230 REM Verify
10240 ROW=21
10250 GOSUB 4500
10260 IF VER$="Y" OR VER$="y" GOTO 10270 ELSE 10290
10270 GOSUB 10490:REM recall data input subroutine
10280 GOTO 10240
10290 REM-Data Input & Verification #2-
10300 REM Input
10310 GOSUB 10610:REM data input subroutine
10320 IF ENTRY$="" GOTO 10900:REM ESC key pressed
10330 REM Verify
10340 ROW=21
10350 GOSUB 4500
10360 IF VER$="Y" OR VER$="y" GOTO 10370 ELSE 10390
10370 GOSUB 10610:REM recall data input subroutine
10380 GOTO 10340
```

```
10390 REM-Data Input & Verification #3-
10400 REM Input
10410 GOSUB 10760:REM data input subroutine
10420 IF ENTRY$="" GOTO 10900:REM ESC key pressed
10430 REM Verify
10440 ROW=21
10450 GOSUB 4500
10460 IF VER$="Y" OR VER$="y" GOTO 10470 ELSE 10900
10470 GOSUB 10760:REM recall data input subroutine
10480 GOTO 10440
10490 REM-Data Input Subroutine-
10500 REM product name-
10510 ROW=19
10520 COL=14
10530 LENGTH=40
10540 GOSUB 1000:REM erase previous prompt
10550 PROMPT$="Product name (2-12 char.):"
10560 SHORT=2
10570 LONG=12
10580 GOSUB 2000
10590 PRODNAME$=ENTRY$
10600 RETURN
10610 REM-price-
10620 ROW=19
10630 LENGTH=40
10640 GOSUB 1000:REM erase previous prompt
10650 PROMPT$="Price ($1-999.99): $"
10660 SHORT=1
10670 LONG=6
10680 GOSUB 2000
10690 PRICE=VAL(ENTRY$)
10700 IF PRICE)=1 AND PRICE<=999.99 GOTO 10750 ELSE 10710
10710 MESSAGE$="Range error. Value must be between 1 and 999.99. Reenter."
10720 ROW=21
10730 GOSUB 4000
10740 GOTO 10620
10750 RETURN
10760 REM-no. units-
10770 ROW=19
10780 GOSUB 1000:REM erase previous prompt
10790 PROMPT$="Number of units (1-999):"
10800 SHORT=1
10810 LONG=3
10820 GOSUB 2000
10830 UNITS=VAL(ENTRY$)
10840 IF UNITS)=1 AND UNITS<=999 GOTO 10890 ELSE 10850
10850 MESSAGE$="Range error. Value must be between 1 and 999. Reenter."
10860 ROW=21
10870 GOSUB 4000
10880 GOTO 10770
10890 RETURN
10900 END:REM end of data input routine
```

Figure 6-13 Demonstration program that performs single-row input and collects three entries. (Requires subroutines shown in Figure 6-7.)

normal video, and the second prompt is highlighted, becomes active, and permits the second entry. Figure 6-15 shows the appearance of the screen after the first two entries have been made; the second entry is in error, and an error message appears at the bottom of the screen.

After successfully completing all entries, the verification prompt appears at the bottom of the screen, as shown in Figure 6-16. If the operator types in y or Y, then a second verification prompt appears, requesting the number of the prompt whose entry is to be edited (Figure 6-17).

Since the operator may inadvertently type in an invalid prompt number, the value typed in must be range-tested. Figure 6-18 shows the error-message consequence of typing in an invalid prompt number entry—an error message appearing in the MESSAGES row.

TABLE 6-3   Line-by-Line Summary of the Listing in Figure 6-13

Lines	Function performed
10010	Turn off function key display.
10020 to 10180	Generate screen.
10190 to 10220	Call data-input subroutine 1 and test for a null input—what will be returned if the operator exits KEYS by pressing the Escape key.
10230 to 10280	Call verification subroutine, which displays the prompt "Do you want to edit? (y/n)." If the operator responds y or Y, then line 10270 calls data-input subroutine 1, allowing editing of the earlier entry. Otherwise, line 10260 sends control to line 10290, which permits entry and verification of input 2.
10290 to 10380	See discussion of lines 10190 to 10280.
10390 to 10480	See discussion of lines 10190 to 10280.
10490 to 10600	Data-input subroutine 1. This subroutine is accessed during initial data entry and may be accessed during editing. Lines 10510 to 10530 define arguments for the subroutine called by line 10540 which erases the previous prompt. (Since several prompts of varying lengths may be presented, the prompt row must be erased before printing a new prompt on it to assure that none of the previous prompt remains. Strictly speaking, this is not necessary with the first prompt, but it is required for all later prompts.) Lines 10550 to 10570 define additional prompting arguments, and line 10580 calls the KEYS subroutine. Line 10590 assigns a program variable based on the input returned by KEYS. This subroutine does not include separate error testing, although KEYS performs the usual length and acceptable character testing.
10610 to 10750	Data-input subroutine 2. See discussion of lines 10490 to 10600, and note the error test in line 10700.
10760 to 10890	Data-input subroutine 3. See discussion of lines 10490 to 10600, and note the error test in line 10840.

Once a valid prompt number has been identified, that prompt again becomes active, permitting reentry of the information that the operator wants to change. Figure 6-19 shows how the screen looks after the operator has selected prompt 3 and changed its entry from 5 to 4.

Following reentry, the verification prompt reappears, permitting further changes, if desired. The data-input and verification sequence terminates when the operator types in n or N in response to the verification prompt.

Full-screen input has several advantages. It permits the operator to view all prompts simultaneously, reinforcing any relationships among them. Prompts and inputs remain on the screen throughout data input and do not require the operator to recall previous entries. Editing is done once per screen, rather than after each entry, as with single-row input (see previous section). If data-input forms are used, then the screen can be designed to resemble them, thereby making the screen a concrete analog of the form itself, rather than a more abstract, time-varying segment of the form.

Required BASIC Code

Figure 6-20 is a block diagram showing the major steps and decisions required with full-screen input.

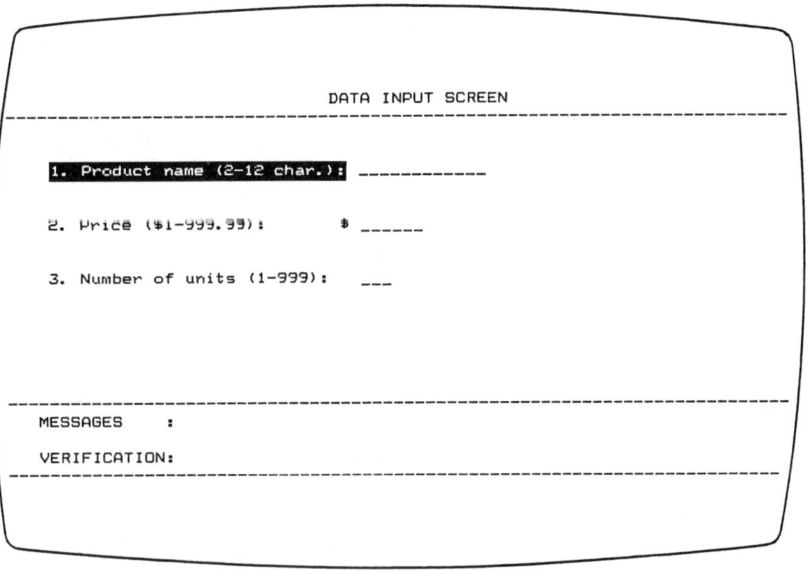

```
                          DATA INPUT SCREEN
------------------------------------------------------------------------

  █1. Product name (2-12 char.):█  _____

  2. Price ($1-999.99):          $ _____

  3. Number of units (1-999):    ___




------------------------------------------------------------------------
  MESSAGES    :

  VERIFICATION:
------------------------------------------------------------------------
```

Figure 6-14 Appearance of a full-screen input screen.

```
                          DATA INPUT SCREEN
------------------------------------------------------------------------

  1. Product name (2-12 char.): Nachos _____

  █2. Price ($1-999.99):█        $ .95 __

  3. Number of units (1-999):    ___




------------------------------------------------------------------------
  MESSAGES    : Range error. Value must be between 1 and 999.99. Reenter.

  VERIFICATION:
------------------------------------------------------------------------
```

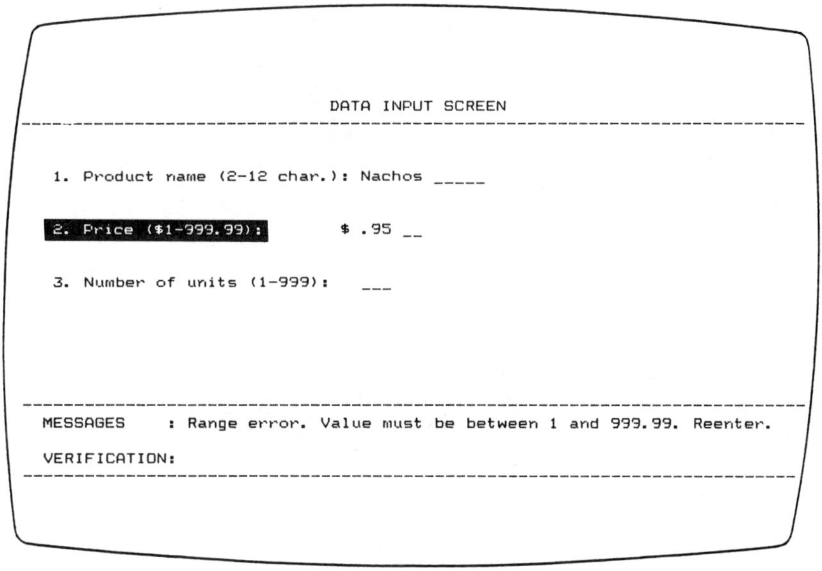

Figure 6-15 Full-screen input screen after two entries have been made—the second entry
is in error, and an error message is displayed on the MESSAGES row.

```
                           DATA INPUT SCREEN
-----------------------------------------------------------------------

    1. Product name (2-12 char.): Nachos _____

    2. Price ($1-999.99):        $ 1.25 _

    3. Number of units (1-999):    5 _



-----------------------------------------------------------------------
    MESSAGES   :

    VERIFICATION: Do you want to edit? (y/n) _
-----------------------------------------------------------------------
```

Figure 6-16 Full-screen input screen after all entries have been made, and verification prompt has appeared on VERIFICATION row.

```
                           DATA INPUT SCREEN
-----------------------------------------------------------------------

    1. Product name (2-12 char.): Nachos _____

    2. Price ($1-999.99):        $ 1.25 _

    3. Number of units (1-999):    5 _



-----------------------------------------------------------------------
    MESSAGES   :

    VERIFICATION: Prompt number: _
-----------------------------------------------------------------------
```

Figure 6-17 Full-screen input screen after operator has indicated that editing is required— prompt number is requested on VERIFICATION row.

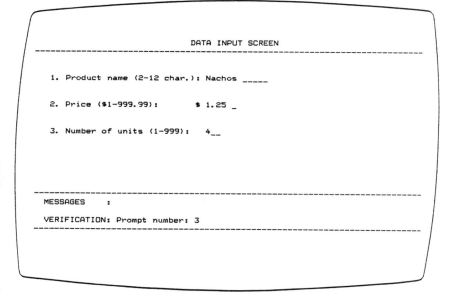

```
                        DATA INPUT SCREEN
-------------------------------------------------------------------------

  1.  Product name  (2-12 char.):  Nachos _____

  2.  Price  ($1-999.99):          $ 1.25 _

  3.  Number of units  (1-999):     5 _




-------------------------------------------------------------------------
  MESSAGES       : Range error.  Value must be between 1 and 3.  Reenter.

  VERIFICATION: Prompt number: 4
-------------------------------------------------------------------------
```

Figure 6-18 Full-screen input screen after operator has entered an invalid prompt number—error message appears on MESSAGES row.

```
                        DATA INPUT SCREEN
-------------------------------------------------------------------------

  1.  Product name  (2-12 char.):  Nachos _____

  2.  Price  ($1-999.99):          $ 1.25 _

  3.  Number of units  (1-999):     4__




-------------------------------------------------------------------------
  MESSAGES       :

  VERIFICATION: Prompt number: 3
-------------------------------------------------------------------------
```

Figure 6-19 Full-screen input screen after operator has entered correct prompt number and changed input 3 from 5 to 4.

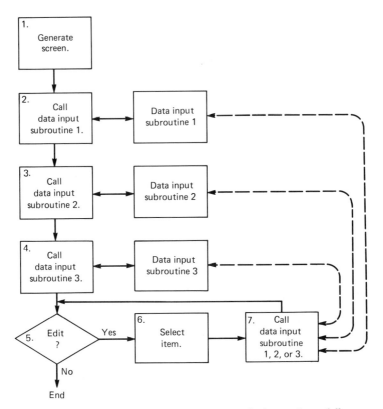

Figure 6-20 Major steps and decision points in code that performs full-screen input as illustrated in Figures 6-14 through 6-19.

Step 1 is to generate the data-input screen. This is also the first step with single-row input, but a difference here is that the prompts are part of the screen and must be presented with the rest of the screen. Step 2 is to call the first data-input subroutine. Step 3 is to call the second data-input subroutine, and step 4 the third. (If more than three inputs were required, additional data-input subroutines would be called, as required.) Step 5 is the verification or editing step. A prompt appears asking whether the operator wants to edit. If the operator types in y or Y, then control flows to step 6, which requires the operator to type in the number of the prompt whose entry is to be edited. Step 7 then calls the indicated data-input subroutine, allowing reentry. After editing, control returns to step 5, permitting further editing or termination of data input, if no editing is required.

Before going into program code, let us take a brief detour and talk about two subroutines. The first of these is KEYS (Figure 5-11). This subroutine, you will recall, actually consists of three separate subroutines. The main subroutine calls secondary subroutines at lines 2350 and 2390 to print the prompt and length marker, respectively. Up to now, all program code in this book has accessed KEYS either at line 2000 or 2020 (if a default entry was to be presented). However, the subroutines at lines 2350 and 2390 can be used separately to print the

```
4500 REM--Verification Prompt--
4510 COLOR 15,0:REM high-intensity video
4520 LENGTH=28
4530 GOSUB 1000:REM erase row, position cursor
4540 PRINT"Do you want to edit? (y/n) ";
4550 COLOR 31,0:REM high-intensity blinking
4560 PRINT CHR$(219)
4570 COLOR 7,0:REM normal
4580 VER$=INKEY$:IF VER$="" GOTO 4580
4590 IF VER$="Y" OR VER$="y" OR VER$="N" OR VER$="n" GOTO 4600 ELSE BEEP:GOTO 45
80
4600 GOSUB 1000:REM erase prompt
4610 IF VER$="N" OR VER$="n" GOTO 4710:REM no edits
4620 PROMPT$="Prompt number:"
4630 SHORT=1
4640 LONG=1
4650 GOSUB 2000
4660 N0=VAL(ENTRY$)
4670 IF N0)=1 AND N0<=N GOTO 4710 ELSE 4680
4680 MESSAGE$="Range error. Value must be between 1 and"+STR$(N)+". Reenter.
4690 GOSUB 4000
4700 GOTO 4650
4710 RETURN
```

Figure 6-21 This subroutine permits the operator to indicate whether editing is required and, if so, to identify the relevant prompt by number.

```
10000 REM--Data Input Routine--
10010 KEY OFF
10020 REM-Generate Screen-
10030 CLS
10040 TITLE$="DATA INPUT SCREEN"
10050 GOSUB 1300:REM print title
10060 CHAR=196:REM line char
10070 LENGTH=79:REM line length
10080 COL=1
10090 ROW=2
10100 GOSUB 1430:REM print line
10110 ROW=18
10120 GOSUB 1430:REM print line
10130 ROW=22
10140 GOSUB 1430:REM print line
10150 LOCATE 19,4
10160 PRINT"MESSAGES    :"
10170 LOCATE 21,4
10180 PRINT"VERIFICATION:"
10190 REM-Generate Prompts-
10200 GOSUB 10660:REM display Prompt 1
10210 GOSUB 10750:REM display Prompt 2
10220 GOSUB 10840:REM display Prompt 3
10230 REM-Data Input-
10240 REM Input #1
10250 GOSUB 10420:REM call data input subroutine
10260 IF ENTRY$="" GOTO 10930:REM ESC key pressed
10270 REM Input #2
10280 GOSUB 10470:REM call data input subroutine
10290 IF ENTRY$="" GOTO 10900:REM ESC key pressed
10300 REM Input #3
10310 GOSUB 10560:REM call data input subroutine
10320 IF ENTRY$="" GOTO 10930:REM ESC key pressed
10330 REM-Verification-
10340 ROW=21
10350 COL=18
10360 N=3:REM number of prompts
10370 GOSUB 4500
10380 IF VER$="n" OR VER$="N" GOTO 10930:REM no edits
10390 ON N0 GOSUB 10420,10470,10560
10400 IF ENTRY$="" GOTO 10930:REM ESC key pressed
10410 GOTO 10340
10420 REM-product name-
10430 GOSUB 10650:REM display prompt 1
10440 GOSUB 2000:REM call data input subroutine
10450 PRODNAME$=ENTRY$
```

Figure 6-22 Demonstration program that permits full-screen input as illustrated in Figures 6-14 through 6-21. (Requires subroutines shown in Figures 6-7 and 6-21.)

```
10460 RETURN
10470 REM-price-
10480 GOSUB 10750:REM display prompt 2
10490 GOSUB 2000
10500 PRICE=VAL(ENTRY$)
10510 IF PRICE)=1 AND PRICE<=999.99 GOTO 10550 ELSE 10520
10520 MESSAGE$="Range error. Value must be between 1 and 999.99. Reenter."
10530 GOSUB 4000
10540 GOTO 10480
10550 RETURN
10560 REM-no. units-
10570 GOSUB 10840:REM display prompt 3
10580 GOSUB 2000
10590 UNITS=VAL(ENTRY$)
10600 IF UNITS)=1 AND UNITS<=999 GOTO 10640 ELSE 10610
10610 MESSAGE$="Range error. Value must be between 1 and 999. Reenter."
10620 GOSUB 4000
10630 GOTO 10570
10640 RETURN
10650 REM--Prompt Definitions--
10660 REM Prompt 1
10670 ROW=5
10680 COL=5
10690 PROMPT$="1. Product name (2-12 char.):"
10700 SHORT=2
10710 LONG=12
10720 GOSUB 2350:REM display prompt
10730 GOSUB 2390:REM print length marker
10740 RETURN
10750 REM Prompt 2
10760 ROW=8
10770 COL=5
10780 PROMPT$="2. Price ($1-999.99):          $"
10790 SHORT=1
10800 LONG=6
10810 GOSUB 2350:REM display prompt
10820 GOSUB 2390:REM print length marker
10830 RETURN
10840 REM Prompt 3
10850 ROW=11
10860 COL=5
10870 PROMPT$="3. Number of units (1-999):   "
10880 SHORT=1
10890 LONG=3
10900 GOSUB 2350:REM display prompt
10910 GOSUB 2390:REM print length marker
10920 RETURN
10930 END:REM end of data input
```

Figure 6-22   (continued)

prompt and length marker without activating the cursor or otherwise initiating actual data input. This is exactly what will be done during step 1 when generating the screen—the prompts and length markers will be displayed by using these two subroutines, but data input will not be activated.

The second subroutine is the verification subroutine, which begins at line 4500, as shown in Figure 6-7. This subroutine must be modified for use in full-screen input to present not one but *two* prompts. The first and second prompts, respectively, are as follows:

```
Do you want to edit? (y/n)
Prompt number:
```

The second prompt is activated only if the operator responds y or Y to the first. Figure 6-21 is a modified version of the verification subroutine. Lines 4500 to 4600 of the subroutine are unchanged, but lines 4610 to 4710 are new. Line 4610 tests whether the operator has indicated that editing is desired. If an n or N has

TABLE 6-4   Line-by-Line Summary of the Listing in Figure 6-22

Lines	Function performed
10010	Turn off function key display.
10020 to 10220	Generate screen. Lines 10040 to 10180 generate title, horizontal lines, and MESSAGES: and VERIFICATION: indicators. Lines 10190 to 10220 call subroutines which assign arguments and display the prompts; these subroutines are also used during data input (see below).
10230 to 10260	Call first data-input subroutine at line 10420, and test whether the returned value is " ", indicating that the Escape key has been pressed; if so, line 10260 sends control to line 10930, terminating data input.
10270 to 10320	Call second and third data-input subroutines (see discussion of lines 10230 to 10260.)
10330 to 10410	Permit verification. Lines 10340 to 10360 define arguments for the verification subroutine, and line 10370 calls that subroutine. Line 10380 tests whether editing is required. If so, line 10390 calls the appropriate data-input subroutine: 10420 (entry 1), 10470 (entry 2), or 10560 (entry 3). Following entry, line 10400 tests whether the Escape key was pressed and terminates input if so. Otherwise, line 10410 sends control back to line 10340, which causes the initial verification prompt to be presented again.
10420 to 10460	First data-input subroutine. Line 10430 calls the subroutine at line 10650, which sets the arguments of the first prompt and also displays the prompt. Line 10440 then calls KEYS, which redisplays the prompt in highlighted video and collects the operator's input. Line 10450 assigns the program variable PRODNAME$, based on the entry.
10470 to 10640	Second and third data-input subroutines. See above discussion of lines 10420 to 10460.

been typed in, then no editing is required and control is sent to line 4710, which exits the subroutine with a RETURN statement. If editing is required, lines 4620 to 4700 will be executed. Lines 4620 to 4640 define the arguments for presenting the prompt "Prompt number:", and line 4650 calls KEYS. Line 4660 evaluates the number returned by KEYS and assigns it to the variable N0. Line 4670 then subjects N0 to a range test against the subroutine argument N (number of prompts). If the range test is passed, then control is sent to line 4710, terminating the subroutine. Otherwise, lines 4680 and 4690 generate an error message and control is sent back to line 4650, forcing the operator to enter a new prompt number.

Now let us consider the code required to permit full-screen input, as described, and with the prompts shown in Figures 6-14 through 6-19. Figure 6-22 is the listing of the program (excluding the subroutines in Figure 6-7 and 6-21). Table 6-4 is a line-by-line summary of the functions performed by the program.

Chapter

7

Error Management

Error management is a systematic approach to preventing errors and, failing that, minimizing their consequences. The starting point in error management is to understand the enemy—the error. Like most enemies, the error is not a single thing, but several. Three general classes of errors can occur within a program:

1. System—BASIC or DOS goes sour.
2. Programming—The programmer's code contains an error that produces an error condition. For example, a READ statement attempts to read more elements than are contained in the corresponding DATA statement.
3. Operator—The operator makes a data-input error or performs some other action that the system regards as illegal—such as attempting to print a report without an activated printer.

System errors are rare enough that they can be safely ignored, but programming and operator errors are quite common; this chapter focuses on them. The best approach to managing errors is to prevent them in the first place. Thus, the first two sections of this chapter discuss the prevention of programming and operator errors, respectively. The third section covers error handling. The final section offers advice on preventing disasters.

Preventing Programming Errors

Programming errors are common. Skilled programmers make many, unskilled ones even more. The only protection against such errors is adequate program quality control and testing. The ON ERROR GOTO statement can be used to build error-trapping routines that will minimize the consequences of many programming errors. However, while such a routine will prevent the program from crashing, the error's side effects—for example, a damaged file—will still be present, and so the routine does not actually solve the underlying problem. Consequently, ON ERROR GOTO routines should be one of the last things added to a program and should be built primarily to trap operator-caused errors, not programming errors.

Rigorous testing is necessary to detect programming errors during program development. Though there is more than one way to test a program, some testing principles are universal. The first of these is the familiar divide-and-conquer principle. In testing, you should always start with the smallest program module, test it, and then move upward in the scale of complexity to the level at which modules are combined.

The second principle is human myopia, which holds that every programmer has blind spots that make it impossible to discover certain types of errors. This is because each programmer develops habitual, stereotyped ways of doing things and will not explore every error path. Other people, with different biases, will use the program differently and explore different error paths. This is why it is so important for program testing to involve a team of individuals with different backgrounds and computer skills.

Some of the testing should be performed by "expert operators"—other programmers who act the role of operators in attempting to find the program's weak points. It is not enough to rely on the program's author, as the principle of human myopia tells us.

Each program should also be subjected to acceptance testing by typical operators to determine how well they can use the program. Such testing offers no guarantee that a program will be usable, but it will almost certainly highlight problems.

Preventing Operator Errors

How do you prevent operator errors? There are at least three ways. First, educate users about the program so that they are able to avoid errors; this is done mainly with documentation. Second, provide adequate prompting within the program to keep users on the right path. Third, write the program so that it minimizes exposure to potentially hazardous situations.

Educating Users

User documentation comes in two forms: internal and external. Internal documentation consists of help screens, directions, and other explanatory information within the program. To use this documentation, the program must be up and running. External documentation is, well, external, i.e., outside the program itself. Its most common form is the user's guide. The user documentation provided with most microcomputer programs has not been distinguished by its completeness, quality, or ease of use. In fact, much of it to date has been awful. Yet, good user documentation is extremely important to the success of a computer program. It is accurate to say that user documentation will govern whether a program can be used effectively.

All user documentation has the same purpose: to explain the features of a program and help the operator gain proficiency in using it. By imparting this information to the operator, the operator learns how to use the program correctly and thereby makes fewer errors. In other words, error reduction is the inevitable and very obvious side effect of using the program correctly.

While the purpose of internal and external documentation is the same, each has unique strengths and limitations and is more suited to certain things than the other. The two documentation approaches should be considered complementary rather than competing alternatives. Internal documentation is best used to aid the operator's memory concerning procedures (e.g., how to start a new file) and program vocabulary (e.g., the commands required for text formatting with a word processor). The small text window and memory overhead of internal documentation combine to make it a poor candidate for presenting a lot of detail. However, there is no question but that it is useful for the operator to be able to access detailed information concerning procedures and program vocabulary while using the program—without having to leaf through a user's guide. User documentation should be accessible within the program when and where needed. A written user's guide is an essential part of any software package. The guide must work at two levels:

1. As a step-by-step *tutorial* which guides new users until they gain the basic skills and confidence needed to operate the program effectively.

2. As a *reference* which provides experienced users with the information needed to use the program effectively and increase their proficiency.

The tutorial should contain hands-on exercises that require the operator to exercise every major facet of the program. The reference section of the guide should provide the operator with quick access to needed information in a form suitable for use while seated before the computer.

Providing Adequate Prompting

Prompting is any written (or coded) information within a program that tells the operator what to do. It includes data-input prompts, directions, help screens, and anything else explicitly intended to keep the operator on the right path. If prompting is adequate, then the operator will do what is required correctly and in the process avoid errors. If prompting is inadequate, then the operator will step off the path and into potentially hazardous territory.

Make sure that your program provides the necessary signposts and landmarks. For example, if a disk must be inserted or removed, the program should direct the operator to take the required action. If the action the operator is about to take may endanger an existing file, the operator should be warned. If a time delay is about to occur, the operator should be informed. The key word in these and innumerable other situations is *communication*. Let the operator know what must be done, what is happening, or what bad thing may happen. Tell the operator where your program's hazards lie and what must be done to avoid them.

Minimizing Exposure to Hazardous Situations

Design your program so that it is as simple as possible and requires the minimum of operator intervention to work properly. The simpler the program, the less the operator must learn and do, and the fewer opportunities there are to make an error. A short path through a crocodile-infested swamp is safer than a long, winding one—fewer places to take a misstep.

Minimize operator intervention within the program. The less the operator must do, the fewer things to do wrong. This principle can be applied in several different ways. Let us consider two concrete examples—one good, one bad. Let us start with the bad example. Many programs must be customized to suit a particular equipment configuration. For example, the number of disk drives, type of printer, communication interface, and so forth must be defined by the operator. Some programs require the operator to set these parameters by modifying BASIC code and then saving the program to disk. Since most operators are not skilled programmers, this requirement invites errors. Do not require operators to modify program code; leave programming to programmers. Instead of requiring the parameters to be set with code, write a utility program that permits the operator to enter the parameters through the keyboard, using a system setup screen. Have the program save the parameters to a disk file and recall them each time the program is initialized.

Now let us consider the good example—which is to build a "turnkey" system. A turnkey system is one that does the routine drudge work for the operator and minimizes the amount of operator intervention. The operator can get the program up and running simply by inserting a program disk and turning on the computer. Perhaps the most important feature of a turnkey system is that no DOS or BASIC commands have to be typed in by the operator. The operator simply interacts with an entity called "the program."

Automatic startup is quite easy to achieve simply by creating a BATCH file named AUTOEXEC.BAT. An AUTOEXEC.BAT file is an optional BATCH file that you may include on a diskette. When DOS is initialized, it searches for this file. If the file is present, then DOS goes ahead and executes the DOS commands contained in the file. Otherwise, it goes through the normal startup routine, requesting date and time, and then presenting the DOS prompt A>. You can write an AUTOEXEC.BAT file that will perform the DOS commands appropriate for your particular program. For example, here are the contents of one AUTOEXEC.BAT file.

```
CLS
DATE
TIME
BASICA MENU
```

When the commands in this file are executed, the following occurs: (1) the screen is cleared, (2) the date is requested, (3) the time is requested, (4) BASICA is activated, and (5) a BASIC program called MENU is run. Such a file can contain any DOS commands that make sense for the particular application. And, since a BASIC program can be executed from the BATCH file, BASIC statements can be executed as well.

You can create an AUTOEXEC.BAT file in a number of different ways. If it is a short file, the simplest approach is by using the COPY CON command. For example, to create the file described above, do the following:

1. Put the system in DOS.

2. Type in COPY CON: AUTOEXEC.BAT.

3. Press the Enter key.

4. Type in each DOS command, and then the Enter key, i.e.,
   CLS + Enter
   DATE + Enter
   TIME + Enter
   BASICA MENU + Enter

5. Press the Ctrl-Z combination (or function key 6) to terminate entry. Your batch file will be stored on disk.

If you make a mistake while typing in the file, type in the Ctrl-C combination to restart. (You cannot back up to change previous entries while using the COPY CON command.)

Once you have created a file named AUTOEXEC.BAT, that file will be executed each time DOS is initialized or restarted with the disk in drive A. The BATCH file will execute each command it contains in turn. It may contain as many commands as you want. It may be used to execute a series of BASIC programs, for each time a BASIC program ends and the PC returns to DOS, the next command in the BATCH file is executed. In addition, sequences of BASIC and DOS commands may be executed via BATCH files. In other words, a BATCH file permits you to combine various sequences of commands that may be necessary to perform the functions required by a particular program—a BATCH file is useful for a good deal more than automatic startup.

If you want to create a long BATCH file, it is best not to use the COPY CON approach, but rather to use a text file editor such as EDLIN. An editor makes it somewhat easier to create, edit, and modify the file than COPY CON. But for simple BATCH files, COPY CON works fine.

Error Handling

This section shows how to handle common system, programming, and operator errors. Errors vary in seriousness. Some—such as the printer being out of paper (error #27)—are not serious and can be fixed on the spot. Others—such as an internal error in BASIC (error #51)—are serious enough to require termination of the program. The consequence of a particular error depends upon the specific program. Running out of string space (error #14) may be no big deal in a game program but may spell disaster for your database program.

It is important to bear these two factors—varying seriousness of errors individually and within the specific program—in mind as you develop error-handling routines. The well-known ON ERROR GOTO statement enables you to trap errors and keep your program from crashing. However, sometimes a crash is exactly what is needed to deal with a problem. For example, you do not want the program to continue after BASIC has gone sour, if a directory or file may be blitzed, or in a host of other situations. In short, these routines must be designed with care and discretion.

This section is divided into two parts. The first part tells you how to "turn off" certain key combinations (such as Ctrl-Break) so that the operator cannot use them to interrupt a program. The second part tells you how to build error-handling routines based on the ON ERROR GOTO statement.

Turning Keys Off

Chapter 5 illustrated two simple techniques for averting data-input errors: (1) use of tests (e.g., range test) and (2) filtering (e.g., KEYS accepts only standard keyboard characters). These two approaches work fine for handling standard ASCII characters typed in during a data-input program. You can easily trap or filter the character "a" or # or any other character that can be typed in. However, the approach does not work for keys with nonstandard ASCII codes, such as the Ctrl key combinations, the Alt key combinations, or the function keys. These keys do not have standard ASCII codes, but instead use *Extended Codes* (see page G-7 of your IBM PC or PC*jr* BASIC manual*). Moreover, some of these key combinations generate an interrupt and can stop an ongoing program.

Fortunately, there is another method (i.e., beyond tests and filters) that can be used to deactivate any single key or key combination. The method requires DOS 2.1 and BASICA (or cartridge BASIC, if you have a PC*jr*), and uses the KEY, KEY ON, and ON KEY statements and key *scan* codes. In a nutshell, it amounts to defining the unwanted keys as function keys and having the PC call a subroutine when they are pressed instead of taking the action it normally would.

Scan codes are the codes the keyboard generates and sends to the System Unit. The unit then interprets the code and thereby reads the keys. Some of these codes are turned into standard ASCII codes and others into Extended codes. The scan codes of the IBM PC 83-key keyboard are shown in Figure 7-1.

Scan codes are shown to the left of the key legend. The scan code of the Ctrl key is 29, of the Alt key is 56, of the Del key is 83, and so on. The PC*jr* has a 62-key keyboard, but it is capable of producing all of the scan codes of the PC's standard 83-key keyboard. For example, the PC*jr* does not have separate function keys, but function keys can be activated by pressing the Fn key combined with number keys 1 through 0. The key-deactivation method that follows will work for either the IBM PC or PC*jr*.

Here is how you deactivate a key or key combination.

First, if you have an IBM PC, activate BASICA. If you have a PC*jr*, make sure that the BASIC cartridge is in place and active.

Select the key or key combination that you want to deactivate. Write down the scan code of each key. For example, suppose that you have an IBM PC and want to deactivate the key combinations Escape, @, Ctrl-Break, and Ctrl-Alt-k. The scan codes of these key combinations are as follows:

Escape—1

@   —3

Ctrl   —29   Break—70

Ctrl   —29   Alt   —56   k—37

Incidentally, if you have a PC*jr*, do *not* use the scan codes shown on the keys in your BASIC manual. Instead, use the scan codes of the standard PC keyboard (Figure 7-1).

---

* *BASIC by Microsoft Corporation,* IBM Corporation, 1982, and *BASIC (PC*jr*) by Microsoft Corporation,* IBM Corporation, 1984.

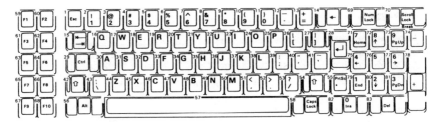

Figure 7-1 IBM PC keyboard. The number to the upper left of each key is the decimal scan code and is used in defining the key as a function key for key deactivation or other purposes. (*Courtesy of IBM Corporation.*)

Determine the appropriate *shift code.* The shift code of an unshifted key is 0, of a shifted key is 1, of a Ctrl key is 4, and of an Alt key is 8. For example, the shift codes of the individual keys used in our example are as follows:

Escape—0

@   —1

Ctrl   —4   Break—0

Ctrl   —4   Alt   —8   k—0

The shift code of a key combination is the sum of the individual shift codes. Thus, the shift code of the Escape key is 0, of the @ key is 1, of Ctrl-Break is 4, and of Ctrl-Alt-k is 12.

Now create a KEY trap using the KEY, KEY ON, and ON KEY statements and using key numbers 15 through 20. The first part of the trap is the KEY statement, which sets a soft key. The syntax of this statement, when used for key deactivation, is as follows:

```
KEY n, CHR$(shift code) + CHR$(scan code of final key)
```

To illustrate, these are the KEY statements for the four key combinations in our example, using key numbers 15 to 18:

KEY 15, CHR$(0) + CHR$(1)   Escape
KEY 16, CHR$(1) + CHR$(3)   @
KEY 17, CHR$(4) + CHR$(70)   Ctrl-Break
KEY 18, CHR$(12) + CHR$(37)   Ctrl-Alt-k

Next, add ON KEY and KEY ON statements to activate the newly defined function keys and to send control to a subroutine when they are pressed. To illustrate, let us do this for KEY 15.

```
10 KEY 15, CHR$(0) + CHR$(1):REM define Escape key as F15
20 ON KEY (15) GOSUB 1000:REM set up subroutine call
30 KEY (15) ON:REM activate F15
.
.
.
1000 REM—Key Response Subroutine—
1010 BEEP
1020 RETURN
```

In this code, lines 10 to 30 define the Escape key as function key 15, set up a subroutine call to line 1000 whenever F15 (the Escape key) is pressed, and activate F15. Once these lines have been executed, whenever the Escape key is pressed, the subroutine at line 1000—which simply beeps—will be called. In short, the Escape key will be deactivated.

Keys that have been deactivated using this method can be reactivated by having the program execute a KEY OFF statement. For example, to return the Escape key to normal operation, insert this statement in the program:

```
KEY (15) OFF
```

That is all there is to it. Although the emphasis of the above discussion was on deactivating keys, this method can be used to do other things as well. The undesirable key combinations are defined as function keys, and can be used like function keys. If you want to tell people not to press them when they are pressed, you can display an error message—do not feel limited to beeping. This method, in fact, gives you access to six additional, user-definable function keys, and you can use them anyway you like. It just happens that this method comes in handy for deactivating mischief-making key combinations.

Before leaving this subject, a general word of warning about troublesome key combinations. The ones to watch in most programs are these:

Ctrl-Break

Ctrl-C

Ctrl-Alt-Del

PrtSc

Ctrl-PrtSc

The first three of these can and usually do interrupt the program, and the Ctrl-Alt-Del combination restarts the system. The last two attempt to use the printer either to dump the screen or to echo the keyboard. You may want to give operators the freedom to interrupt the program or to use the printer. As a general rule, it is best not to allow interrupts, since they not only end the program but may also damage files or cause other problems. Thus, you should deactivate these key combinations while the program is running, and force the operator to exit the program via a standard route, such as a Quit or Sign Off option on a menu. Allowing the printer to be used is a different matter. Sometimes this is desirable, sometimes not. Code to trap these key combinations can readily be constructed by following the method described above. Figure 7-2 shows the required code.

A word of warning. Once you deactivate Ctrl-Break, Ctrl-C, and Ctrl-Alt-Del, you no longer have a way to interrupt a program. This may be fine for operators, but it makes the programmer's life difficult. If you install such code in your program, either keep it inactive during program development or provide another escape route. If you do not, you may find yourself pounding away helplessly at the keyboard, attempting to make the program stop, while nothing happens. At such moments, the only solution is to submit your PC to The Big Sleep.

```
10 REM--Ctrl-Break--
20 KEY 15,CHR$(4)+CHR$(70):REM key definition
30 ON KEY (15) GOSUB 1000
40 KEY (15) ON
50 REM--Ctrl-C--
60 KEY 16,CHR$(4)+CHR$(46):REM key definition
70 ON KEY (16) GOSUB 1000
80 KEY (16) ON
90 REM--Ctrl-Alt-Del--
100 KEY 17,CHR$(12)+CHR$(83):REM key definition
110 ON KEY(17) GOSUB 1000
120 KEY (17) ON
130 REM--PrtSc--
140 KEY 18,CHR$(1)+CHR$(55):REM key definition
150 ON KEY(18) GOSUB 1000
160 KEY (18) ON
170 REM--Ctrl-PrtSc--
180 KEY 19,CHR$(4)+CHR$(55):REM key definition
190 ON KEY(19) GOSUB 1000
200 KEY (19) ON
1000 REM--Key Response Subroutine--
1010 BEEP
1020 RETURN
```

Figure 7-2 Code that deactivates various key combinations by defining them as function keys. Key combinations deactivated and relevant line numbers are: Ctrl-Break (10), Ctrl-C (50), Ctrl-Alt-Del (90), PrtSc (130), and Ctrl-PrtSc (170).

ON ERROR GOTO Routines

Because there is no common solution to all errors, this section presents a general strategy for designing an error-handling routine. You must tailor this to meet the requirements of your specific program. This section contains separate subsections on error-handling mechanics, error codes, error-handling logic, local error-handling routines, and general-purpose error-handling routines. Specific examples of BASIC code are given, but you should use these as models, rather than adopt them directly for use in your programs.

Error-handling mechanics. The common element in all error-handling routines is the ON ERROR GOTO statement. This directs the program to send program control to a particular line number when an error condition is recognized by BASIC. The syntax of this statement is as follows:

```
ON ERROR GOTO line number
```

For example, to direct the program to send control to an error-handling routine starting at line 6000, a statement such as this would be used:

```
100 ON ERROR GOTO 6000:REM general-purpose error-handling routine
```

If the program employs a general-purpose error-handling routine, the initial ON ERROR GOTO statement is placed very early in the program so that it can direct error handling from that point on. The program can—and usually should—contain local error-handling routines as well to deal with certain specific, anticipated operator errors—such as not turning on the printer. Subsequent ON ERROR GOTO statements can be placed elsewhere in the program, as required, to activate these local routines. For example, to redefine the location of the error-handling routine within the program, a statement such as this would be used:

```
21500 ON ERROR GOTO 22470:REM local error-handling routine
```

(Chapter 5 presented date- and time-collecting data-input routines that employed local error-handling routines to handle anticipated input errors—see Figures 5-26 and 5-27.)

After the particular region of the program has been left, the general-purpose error-handling routine is reactivated.

The error-handling routine may be simple or complex. The only thing it *must* contain is a RESUME statement. RESUME enables the program to continue after the error. For example, this will work as a sort of minimal error-handling routine:

```
6000 REM—Error-Handling Routine—
6010 RESUME
```

This routine will simply send program control back to the line at which BASIC recognized the error. If the error recurs, then the program will be stuck in a loop and never get out. Moreover, this type of routine cannot solve a problem, since it does not even bring it to the operator's attention, let alone identify or locate the error. In other words, this type of error-handling routine is worse than worthless—it is bad.

In addition to using RESUME alone, it can be followed by the word NEXT or by a line number. If RESUME is followed by a line number, then program control will jump to that line and begin execution there following the error. If followed by the word NEXT, then control will jump to the line following the one at which the error was recognized.

Deciding whether to use RESUME alone or followed by a line number or NEXT is somewhat problematical and depends upon the particular situation. In general-purpose error-handling routines, it is probably best to use RESUME alone or followed by a line number. If RESUME is used alone, then a recurrence of the error will lock the program in a loop and force resolution before continuing. On the other hand, it might be desirable to have errors send control back to some central location, such as the program's main menu. One of the problems with using the line number and NEXT forms of RESUME is that pending loops (e.g., FOR-NEXT or WHILE-WEND) may be exited prematurely. A similar problem exists if the error occurs within a subroutine. When such premature exits occur, the program's pointers and counters can get very confused, and the end result may be disaster.

When an error occurs, BASIC assigns the error type and location data to the variables ERR (error code) and ERL (line number). For example, if error 25 (device fault) occurs in line 21000, the value of ERR is 25 and of ERL is 21000. Since BASIC makes this information available, it is easy to create code that identifies the error code and line number. To illustrate, let us modify the simplistic error-handling routine to provide the relevant information by adding lines 6005 and 6006, as shown below.

```
6000 REM—Error—Handling Routine—
6005 PRINT "Error code #: ";ERR
6006 PRINT "Line #: ";ERL
6010 RESUME
```

This is still a long distance from being a useful error-handling routine, but it will get the job done, i.e., keep the program from crashing and identify the type of error and its location. Later in this section we will see how to build more sophisticated error-handling routines.

But before doing this, it is necessary to explore error codes and error-handling logic. These topics are covered in the next two subsections.

BASIC Error Codes.   The error types and codes recognized by BASIC are given in Appendix A of the IBM PC and PC*jr* BASIC manuals.* The errors of these two computers are identical, except that PC*jr* cartridge BASIC recognizes three errors (74, 75, 76) that the IBM PC does not. With this exception, error-handling for the two computers is identical.

The error codes and messages for the two computers are shown in Table 7-1. This table also shows the probable source of the error—system, programming, or operator. There are fifty-one codes and messages in the list, of which the first forty-eight apply to both the PC and PC*jr*, and the last three only to the PC*jr*.

Of these codes and messages, the majority reflect programming errors. Roughly one-fifth represent operator errors. And a smaller number reflect system errors. Most of the assignments—system, programming, or operator—are straightforward, but some are either ambiguous or debatable. Let us consider each class of errors, in turn.

Errors 12 (illegal direct), 17 (can't continue), and 74 (rename across disks) do not count because they only occur in direct mode.

There are two system errors: 51 (internal error) and 57 (device I/O error). The first reflects a BASIC malfunction, the second an I/O error from which DOS cannot recover. The cause of the second *may* be the operator or a hardware malfunction, but the consequence—botched DOS—means that DOS is no longer operating properly.

Let us consider the operator errors. Two of these, 24 (device timeout) and 25 (device fault), are labeled "operator/hardware" errors. These may result either from malfunctioning hardware or from the hardware not being connected properly. In either case, if the device error is reported, the operator may be able to take corrective action. Error 61 (Disk full) could be either a programming or an operator error. It may be regarded as a programming error if the program permitted the disk to store too much data, or as an operator error if the operator is in charge of which disks files are being stored on. Once again, if the information is reported to the operator, corrective action may be possible. The remaining

---

BASIC by Microsoft Corporation, IBM Corporation, 1982, and *BASIC (PCjr) by Microsoft Corporation,* IBM Corporation, 1984.

TABLE 7-1 BASIC Error Codes, Messages, and Probable Sources

Code	Message	Source
1	NEXT without FOR	Programming
2	Syntax error	Programming
3	RETURN without GOSUB	Programming
4	Out of data	Programming
5	Illegal function call	Programming
6	Overflow	Programming
7	Out of memory	Programming
8	Undefined line number	Programming
9	Subscript out of range	Programming
10	Duplicate definition	Programming
11	Division by zero	Programming
12	Illegal direct	Not applicable
13	Type mismatch	Programming
14	Out of string space	Programming
15	String too long	Programming
16	String formula too complex	Programming
17	Can't continue	Not applicable
18	Undefined user function	Programming
19	No RESUME	Programming
20	RESUME without error	Programming
22	Missing operand	Programming
23	Line buffer overflow	Programming
24	Device timeout	Operator/hardware
25	Device fault	Operator/hardware
26	FOR without NEXT	Programming
27	Out of paper	Operator
29	WHILE without WEND	Programming
30	WEND without WHILE	Programming
50	FIELD overflow	Programming
51	Internal error	System
52	Bad file number	Programming
53	File not found	Operator
54	Bad file mode	Programming
55	File already open	Programming
57	Device I/O error	System
58	File already exists	Programming
61	Disk full	Programming/operator
62	Input past end	Programming
63	Bad record number	Programming
64	Bad file name	Programming
66	Direct statement in file	Programming
67	Too many files	Programming
68	Device unavailable	Operator
69	Communications buffer overflow	Programming
70	Disk write protect	Operator
71	Disk not ready	Operator
72	Disk media error	Operator
73	Advanced feature	Operator
74*	Rename across disks	Not applicable
75*	Path/file access error	Programming
76*	Path not found	Programming

*PC*jr* only.

operator errors are more clear-cut. For example, error 53 (File not found) means that the wrong disk is in the drive, error 68 (Device unavailable) means that a file or device is not accessible to the PC, and so on. In all, there are ten operator errors.

This leaves the programming errors. The list of these is long and most are fairly straightforward. For example, NEXT without FOR (error 1), Undefined line number (error 8), and the like all indicate careless programming.

This little analysis leads us to the following conclusions:

System errors: 51 and 57

Operator errors: 24, 25, 27, 53, 61, 68, 70, 71, 72, and 73.

Programming errors: everything else

Error-handling logic.   Since errors vary in seriousness both in their own right and in terms of the specific program, a decision must be made concerning how each error should be handled. The decision comes down to deciding whether a given error should (1) terminate the program or (2) let the program continue. In either case, the program must inform the operator of the error condition so that corrective action can eventually take place.

In general, it is advisable to terminate the program if a system error (51 or 57) occurs. When such errors occur, it is probable that it will be impossible to continue anyway.

Programming errors are more problematical. To begin with, such errors should *not* exist within a program, and their occurrence should be rare. On this basis, you can argue that it makes sense to terminate the program when they occur.

Operator errors are usually correctable. For this reason, they should be trapped, and the operator should be provided with enough information to take corrective action.

Let us examine the logic of three alternative general-purpose error-handling routines. A general-purpose routine is one designed to handle any error that may occur within a program. The program may also include local routines to handle certain specific, anticipated errors. The relationship between general-purpose and local routines is shown in Figure 7-3. The general-purpose routine is activated at the beginning of the program. It remains the active or default routine unless a local routine is activated. After the region of the program using the local routine is exited, the general-purpose routine is reactivated. Under certain conditions, the local routine may switch control to the general-purpose routine.

The logic of a conservative general-purpose routine is shown in Figure 7-4. Error handling begins when an error is recognized and the program sends control to the routine whose logic is shown in the figure. Step 1 is to test whether a system error has occurred. If so, a message identifying the error is presented and the program is terminated. Step 2 is to test whether an operator error has occurred. If so, a message is presented identifying the error and giving the recovery action, and the program then pauses until the operator is ready to continue. If the tests in both steps 1 and 2 are failed, then the error must be a programming error. In this case, a message is presented and the program is terminated.

The logic of a less conservative routine is shown in Figure 7-5. The difference

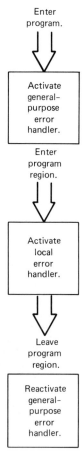

Figure 7-3 Relationship of general-purpose and local error-handling routines. The general-purpose routine is activated at the beginning of the program. Regions of the program may activate local error-handling routines of their own; upon exiting these regions, the general-purpose routine is reactivated.

between this and Figure 7-4 is that step 3 of Figure 7-5 tests whether the specific programming error is recoverable (step 3a). If recovery is possible, then an error message is presented and the program continues. If recovery is not possible, then the program is terminated. System and operator errors are handled as in Figure 7-4.

The logic of a liberal routine is shown in Figure 7-6. This routine will terminate the program only if a system error occurs. Otherwise, a message is presented and the program is continued.

The following subsection will show how to build a BASIC error-handling

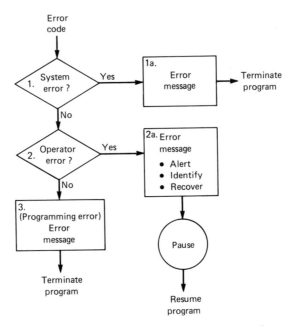

Figure 7-4 Logic of a conservative error-handling routine. Program will be terminated if a system or programming error occurs. Operator errors will cause an error message to be presented, and then the program will be resumed.

routine following the logic shown in Figure 7-4. This routine may be used as a model for building more conservative or liberal routines.

General-purpose error-handling routines. Let us create a general-purpose error-handling routine built on the error-handling logic in Figure 7-4. This routine will trap all errors but will terminate the program if a system or programming error is encountered. The routine will print an error message on row 21, opposite a "MESSAGES:" heading, as shown in Figure 7-7. If a nonrecoverable (i.e., system or programming) error occurs, then the error code and line number will be printed and the program will terminate, leaving the blinking message on the screen.

If a recoverable (i.e., operator) error occurs, then the message will remain on the screen and the program will pause until any key is pressed, at which time it will be erased and the program will continue (Figure 7-8).

The listing of the error-handling routine is shown in Figure 7-9. This routine consists of lines 6000 to 6310. The routine uses the temporary pause subroutine which starts at line 1000. In addition, the screen on which the message is printed requires the subroutines starting at lines 1300 and 1430.

Table 7-2 is a line-by-line summary of the functions performed by this routine.

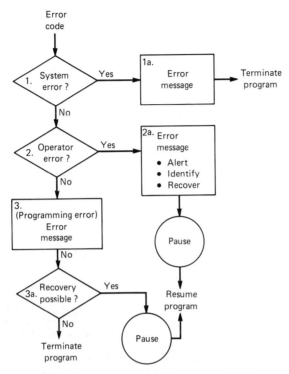

Figure 7-5 Logic of an error-handling routine which terminates the program if a system error or certain predefined programming errors occur. Operator errors and noncritical programming errors will cause an error message to be presented, and then the program will be resumed.

Incidentally, once you build an error-handling routine such as this one, you can test it by using BASIC's ERROR statement. The syntax of this statement is as follows:

```
ERROR code number
```

When BASIC encounters an ERROR statement, it acts as if the error condition indicated by *code number* exists in the line containing the statement. For example, if you include this line in your program,

```
50 ERROR 27
```

BASIC will act as if error 27 exists in line 50, and will assign 27 to ERR and 50 to ERL.

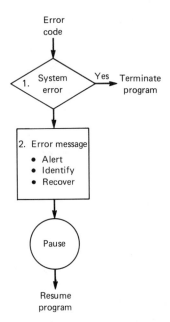

Figure 7-6 Logic of a very liberal error-handling routine. The program will be terminated only for system errors. Otherwise, an error message will be presented, and the program will be resumed.

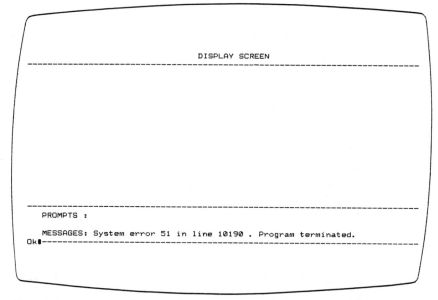

Figure 7-7 Appearance of screen after a system error has occurred. A blinking message identifying the error type and line number is displayed on the MESSAGES row, and the program has been terminated.

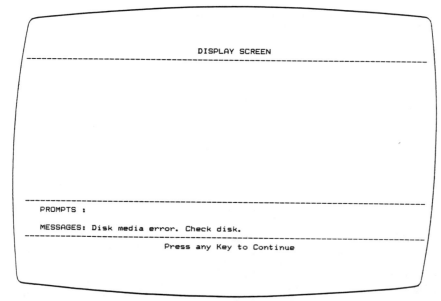

DISPLAY SCREEN

PROMPTS :

MESSAGES: Disk media error. Check disk.

Press any Key to Continue

Figure 7-8 Appearance of screen after an operator error has occurred. A blinking message identifying the error and giving the recovery action is displayed on the MESSAGES row, and the program has been paused temporarily.

```
6000 REM--General-Purpose Error-Handler--
6010 BEEP
6020 REM-Test for System Errors-
6030 IF ERR=51 OR ERR=57 THEN MSG$="System error": GOTO 6260 ELSE 6040
6040 REM-Test for Operator Errors-
6050 IF ERR=24 OR ERR=25 OR ERR=27 OR ERR=53 OR ERR=61 OR ERR=68 OR ERR=70 OR ER
R=71 OR ERR=72 OR ERR=73 GOTO 6060 ELSE 6240
6060 IF ERR=24 THEN MSG$="Device timeout. Retry operation."
6070 IF ERR=25 THEN MSG$="Device fault. Retry operation or check hardware."
6080 IF ERR=27 THEN MSG$="Printer error. Turn printer on and check paper."
6090 IF ERR=53 THEN MSG$="File not found. Check file name/insert correct disk."
6100 IF ERR=61 THEN MSG$="Disk full. Delete existing files or use new disk."
6110 IF ERR=68 THEN MSG$="Device unavailable. Check hardware and connections."
6120 IF ERR=70 THEN MSG$="Disk write protected. Remove protection or use a new d
isk."
6130 IF ERR=71 THEN MSG$="Disk drive not ready. Check drive door and disk insert
ion."
6140 IF ERR=72 THEN MSG$="Disk media error. Check disk."
6150 IF ERR=73 THEN MSG$="Advanced feature. Load advanced BASIC and restart prog
ram."
6160 COLOR 31,0:REM high-intensity blinking
6170 LOCATE 21,14
6180 PRINT MSG$
6190 COLOR 7,0:REM normal video
6200 GOSUB 1200
6210 LOCATE 21,14
6220 PRINT SPACE$(LEN(MSG$)):REM erase message
6230 RESUME
6240 REM-Programming Error-
6250 MSG$="Programming error"
6260 REM-Error Message for System & Program Errors-
6270 LOCATE 21,14
6280 COLOR 31,0:REM high-intensity blinking
6290 PRINT MSG$;ERR;"in line";ERL;". Program terminated."
6300 COLOR 7,0:REM normal
6310 END:REM terminate program
```

Figure 7-9 Code of a general purpose error-handling routine.

TABLE 7-2   Line-by-Line Summary of the Listing in Figure 7-9

Lines	Function performed
10	Activate error-handling routine at line 6000.
20	Send program control to line 10000. (Lines 10000 to 10180 create the screen.)
6020 to 6030	Test for system error. If the error code returned by BASIC (ERR) is 51 or 57 then a system error has occurred, and line 6030 assigns the message "System error" to MSG$, and then sends control to line 6260 so that the message can be printed. Otherwise, control flows to line 6040.
6050	Test for operator error. This line tests whether ERR corresponds to one of the operator errors. If so, control goes to line 6060. If not, control is sent to line 6240.
6060 to 6150	Test for specific operator errors and assign corresponding error messages. Each of these messages identifies the error and gives a recovery action. (The error code and line number are not included in the message.)
6160 to 6190	Print operator error message in high-intensity blinking.
6200	Call temporary pause subroutine. This holds the operator error message in place until the operator takes corrective action.
6210 to 6220	Erase operator error message.
6230	RESUME statement—this will resume the program at the line at which the error occurred.
6240 to 6250	Assign "Operator error" to MSG$. This line will only be executed if both system and programming errors have already been eliminated as causes of the error condition.
6260 to 6310	Print system or programming error message and terminate program. The message will identify the error code and line number and will remain on the screen after the program terminates.

Preventing Disasters

Certain keyboard entries can have far-reaching consequences. For example, the keystrokes that activate a file-purging program can, if made mistakenly, destroy part or all of an important database. If the file is not backed up, this may be a major disaster. In a menu-driven program, pressing the wrong key will select the wrong program. The consequence is not serious—only a delay.

These examples illustrate how important it is for you to be aware of such traps in your program and to take measures to protect the operator from them.

First, identify the points in your program where a wrong turn or data-input error may cause a problem. The following are examples of such points in a database management program:

- *Making menu selections.* Selecting the wrong option will cause a delay.

- *Loading files.* Loading a new file may destroy the file currently in memory and also cause a time delay.

- *Purging files.* Doing this by mistake will destroy the files.

- *Printing reports.* This will cause a delay and tie up the printer.

- *Creating a new file.* If done improperly, the new file may wipe out existing files.

```
                        *WARNING*
            You have selected the PURGE option.
            It will DESTROY your files.
            If you want to continue, type
            in the word "PURGE" and
            Press the Return key: _____
```

Figure 7-10   A screen designed to protect the operator from the serious error of purging files by mistake. Before purging actually occurs, the operator must verify the decision by typing in the word "purge" and then pressing the Enter key. Purging or other radical actions should never proceed on the basis of a single keystroke; these actions should require operator verification first. (*From Simpson:* Design of User-Friendly Programs for Small Computers, *copyright 1985, by permission of McGraw-Hill Book Company.*)

This list is not meant to be comprehensive but to illustrate the kinds of things to look out for in the average program. The list will vary with the type of program you are designing.

After you have identified the danger points, write software that will enable the operator to verify the action before the program proceeds. You must prevent the program from proceeding based on one or two keystrokes. Rather, the operator action must require *two* steps: (1) initial selection and (2) verification. This technique is not new. Verification is part of the data-input process described in Chapter 5 and was used in building the data-input screens shown in Chapter 6. However, those examples illustrated specific applications of the more general principle just described.

When error consequences are not severe, the initial selection may be one keystroke and the verification a press of the Enter key.

When error consequences are severe, display a warning screen to the operator after the initial selection is made. Require the operator to read the warning and to verify the choice before proceeding. For example, if the operator initially selects a purge files routine, display a message such as that shown in Figure 7-10. This tells the operator of the pending action and permits the operator to back out.

Chapter

8

Program Control
with Menus

This chapter is divided into four sections. The first gives an overview of program control. The remaining sections, respectively, tell how to design menus, create them using BASIC, and link them together into networks.

Overview of Program Control

Program control is the manner in which the operator interacts with the computer to get it to do something. To exercise control, the operator engages in a two-way conversation, or dialog, with the computer. The computer side of this dialog is carried on through its displays and through the prompts or questions that it asks. The human side is carried on through the keyboard or another input device.

Program control can be exercised in many different ways. One of the most popular ways with microcomputers is to use menus. In menu-driven programs, the computer displays a list of program options (Figure 8-1) and the operator selects one option. This is usually done by typing in the number or letter of the desired option, but it is also commonly done by pointing at the option with a light pen or finger (on a touch-sensitive screen), pressing a function key, or positioning the cursor over the option with a mouse.

Following operator selection, the program calls the subprogram or executes the function that the operator has selected. Menu-selection dialog is computer-initiated since the operator must respond to computer-presented options and cannot create them.

Most menu-driven programs have several menus organized into an overall control structure, or *network*. In this network, the menus may be thought of as nodes (or crossroads), with each menu option linking the menu to another menu or to a subprogram, as shown in Figure 8-2.

Menus can work well when the tasks operators perform are structured and predictable. The typical menu-driven program will have no more than a few dozen menu options, with each option corresponding to a separate subprogram. For example, menu control can be quite effective with database management

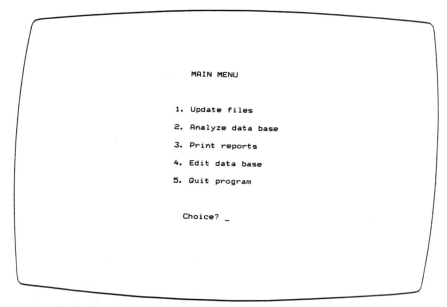

```
                    MAIN MENU


                    1. Update files

                    2. Analyze data base

                    3. Print reports

                    4. Edit data base

                    5. Quit program



                    Choice? _
```

Figure 8-1 Traditional menu, consisting of five numbered options. Menu is titled, and a prompt appears below it.

systems since the functions these programs perform are fairly predictable. That is, files must be planned, data entered, reports generated, and the database maintained. The task is structured enough that you can list the different things that must be done on a sheet of paper and group them by category.

The tasks performed with many programs cannot be structured so neatly. When the task is unpredictable, menu control is not very good because of its inflexibility. A command language permits the operator to exercise the computer's power more directly. However, it takes a sophisticated operator to use a command language effectively, and the operator must use the program regularly to maintain skill.

Researchers have pointed out that menu-driven programs make little demand on human recall memory, since the menu displays the acceptable commands at any given point in the program. However, such programs *do* make memory demands, and sometimes they are considerable. First, the operator must recognize and interpret the displayed menu options. Second, the operator must have some concept of the menu network itself—and be able to take acceptable paths around the network.

The menu-control method is often criticized by computer sophisticates for the limitations it puts on what the operator can do and for its lack of speed. These criticisms are valid but must be placed in perspective. First, as noted, menu selection requires tasks which are highly structured. With such tasks, the menu has advantages in terms of ease of learning and use. Second, the speed of one particular control method versus another (e.g., menus versus a command language) depends on several variables, the most important of which is operator

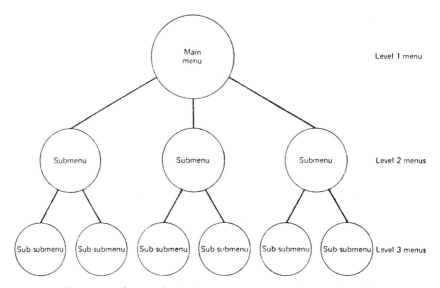

Figure 8-2   Menu-control network. Each menu is represented as a node, and the connections among menus are shown as links between nodes. (*From Simpson:* Design of User-Friendly Programs for Small Computers, *copyright 1985, by permission of McGraw-Hill Book Company.*)

experience. The advantages of command languages become evident only with highly experienced operators who use a program frequently enough to learn it inside out.

No single control method can be considered the best in every situation. Which one is best depends upon the application, the type of operator, how frequently the program is used, and a host of other factors.

Designing a Menu

Format

Menus come in many different forms. Perhaps the most common form is that shown earlier in Figure 8-1, which consists of a list of five numbered options. It is becoming increasingly common to create menus whose options are selectable with letters instead of numbers. A menu of this form is shown in Figure 8-3.

An improved version of the menu can be created by doing away with the prompt and using highlighting to identify the active prompt, as shown in Figure 8-4. When this menu is first displayed, its top option—which should be the one most frequently selected—is highlighted with reverse or high-intensity video. To change the option, the operator types in the letter of the desired option. That option is then activated by pressing the Enter key. This type of menu is better because the operator does not have to view the entry opposite the prompt in order to determine which option is currently active. In addition, having an automatic default option will save the operator keystrokes.

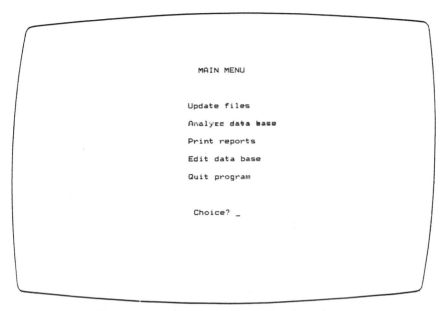

Figure 8-3 Traditional menu with options selectable with letters. Menu is titled, and a prompt appears below it.

Figure 8-4 Highlighted-option menu. The active option is highlighted. The menu is titled, but since the menu itself shows the active option, no prompt is required.

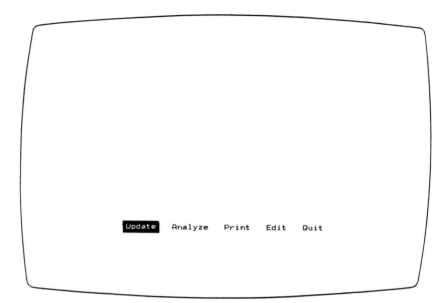

Update Analyze   Print   Edit   Quit

Figure 8-5 Highlighted-option menu which is compressed to fit onto a single row.

A menu does not have to consist of a series of options listed one below the other. It can also be squashed down to fit onto a few lines, as shown in Figure 8-5. This form of menu is required when there is insufficient room for a more traditional menu, or when the menu is used to control information appearing elsewhere on the screen.

Design Guidelines

Here are some general guidelines for designing menus.

Titling.   Each menu should be titled. This is especially important if a program uses several menus. The title should be descriptive and should have the word "menu" in it, e.g., "Main Menu" or "Edit Menu."

Number of options.   Limit the number of menu options. The ideal number is somewhere between four and six. In some programs, shorter or longer menus will be unavoidable. When a menu exceeds about ten options, it becomes, for all practical purposes, a directory. Rather than listing all programs on one long menu, organize your menus in levels or tiers. The only time it makes sense to have one long list of programs is if each one is totally unrelated to the others.

Order to list options.   On short menus, list the options according to their frequency of use—most frequent at top, least frequent at bottom. This reduces the operator's visual search time. On long menus (more than about ten options), list the options in an order that the operator will recognize, such as alphabetic, numeric, or chronologic order.

Option content.   There is no standard formula for writing menu options, although there are guidelines. First, the options should be consistent in the way they indicate the function they represent. Options commonly begin with a verb and end with the object to be acted upon. For example:

Save file

Set up plan

Define x-axis

In some cases, the object of action is left out. This is quite acceptable if the object is obvious. For example, in a word-processing program the menu option "Center" is acceptable because it is clear that text is being acted on. On the other hand, in most programs, the option "Set up" would not be acceptable without telling what was going to be set up.

It is also fairly common to frame options as concrete objects. For example:

File save

Plan setup

x-axis definition

This form is less desirable than the verb-object form since it is more difficult to interpret. The operator must mentally translate the noun forms of the verbs back to verbs to figure out what the options mean. This is extra work and can produce errors. Moreover, if the programmer mixes the verb-object and concrete object form of options, confusion can result. For example, consider these options:

File start

Set up plan

Program exit

The first and last options use the concrete object form and the second option uses the verb-object form. However, the first terms in all options can be interpreted either as nouns or verbs. If interpreted as verbs, then the first option means that something named "start" must be filed, the second option has the correct meaning, and the third option means that the exit is to be programmed. Similar confusions result if the first terms are interpreted as nouns. The lesson is to use a consistent form in writing the options—preferably the verb-object form.

Are long options desirable? For example, is it good to write options such as these?

Save your current file to disk

Set up your management plan

Define the x-axis of your plot

This may be good for naive or infrequent users of a program, but regular users will probably find such options unnecessarily descriptive. In general, frequent users will prefer the concise form of the prompt since it takes less time to read.

It is desirable to be able to select the menu option with the first letter of the option label, as illustrated in Figures 8-3 through 8-5. Designing a menu this way makes it easier to learn and use. If only a few menus are used and their options are semantically distinct, use alphabetic option selection throughout.

As the number of options on a menu increases, the availability of unique semantic labels decreases. When more than one option on a menu begins with the same letter, problems emerge. What do you do, for example, when your menu includes separate options for Save and Sort? One of the options must be re-named—perhaps by calling Sort something such as Reorder. To solve such problems, some programmers use their ingenuity to find synonyms for the duplicate options. Thus, you find commands such as Undo being called Oops, Save being called Transfer, and the like. This can and often does produce bizarre option labels that make learning the menu more difficult. Moreover, it can cause problems when the operator is used to using a particular letter to perform a function, and the program uses a different name for the function. For example, the operator who gets in the habit of using "S" to save a file may be quite distressed when the same command sorts all the rows in a spreadsheet. Technically, what is going on here is called "negative transfer"—the operator discovers that the rules learned in one place do not apply in another and can even be dangerous to follow.

In these cases, it is often better to number the options than to use letters. If you do use numbered options, then the lowest-numbered option should be number 1, not 0. Additional options should be separated by 1, i.e., numbers 1, 2, 3, etc., rather than 1, 3, 5, or some other series with missing numbers.

Note that if you use numbers for menu selection, then any list of numbered items appearing on one of your screens may be mistaken for a menu. Avoid numbered items on nonmenu displays, if possible. For example, in a list of instructions, precede each instruction by a bullet instead of a number.

Be consistent in how you design menus. If you design one full-screen menu with numbered options, then others should also be designed with numbered options. Do not design some with numbered options and others with options selected with letters. This does not mean that all menus in a program must be designed in the same way. For example, you may use full-screen menus such as Figure 8-4 for program selection, and also use one-line menus such as Figure 8-5 for screen control. As these two types of menus are used to perform different functions, one type may use numbered options and the others options which are selected with letters.

The prompt.   A prompt is required if the menu option is not highlighted to indicate the active choice. If you use a prompt, make it brief and explicit. For example, have it say something such as "Select option #: _."

Creating Menus with BASIC

There are two approaches to creating a menu. The first is to generate the menu directly, that is, to generate each of its options with separate PRINT statements. Additional code is required to print the menu's title, to generate its prompt, to collect the operator's keystrokes, and to perform error testing. The second approach is to use a subroutine to perform some or all of these functions. In general, the first approach is practical if the program contains a single menu, but the second approach is more efficient if the program contains two or more menus. This section will illustrate both approaches.

At first thought, it would seem a simple matter to create a menu. All it consists of, after all, is a list of options, a prompt, and perhaps a title. The problem is that the code must do more than merely print the menu on the display—it must do some combination of the following:

- Titling
    Print the menu title (if used)

- Displaying the options
    Position each option
    Print each option
    Highlight the active option (if highlighting is used)

- Collecting and testing operator entry
    Print the prompt (if a prompt is used)
    Generate the cursor (if a prompt is used)
    Collect the operator's entry
    Permit an Escape key exit
    Filter the entry to exclude unacceptable characters
    Perform character normalization (if letter entries are used)
    Test the entry for errors
    Permit operator verification of the entry via the Enter key

The major work appears to be to collect and test operator input. KEYS can do this job if a printed prompt is used. However, menu selections are normally made with a single character, and using KEYS is overkill. Moreover, if highlighted options are used, then KEYS is of no help. For these reasons, the code presented in this chapter does not use KEYS but shows how to handle data input with separate code.

This section shows three different ways to generate menus. The first is to generate the traditional type of menu directly in code. The second uses a subroutine to generate the same type of menu. The third shows how to use a subroutine to generate a menu with highlighted options.

Generating Menus Directly

Let us write the code to generate the menu shown in Figure 8-6. This is a traditional menu, consisting of a title, five numbered options, and a prompt. The title is printed at row 1 and the first option at row 4, with other options double-spaced below. The prompt is printed four rows below the last option. The options are double-spaced to make them easier to read but could be single-spaced if room were limited. The title and prompt must be set off from the options with extra space to assure that they are not confused with options. This is unlikely for the prompt, since it is printed in high-intensity video and has a blinking cursor to

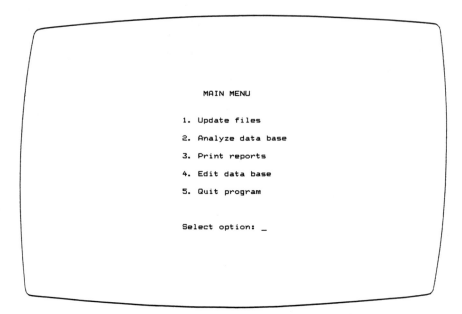

```
                    MAIN MENU

                1. Update files

                2. Analyze data base

                3. Print reports

                4. Edit data base

                5. Quit program


                Select option: _
```

Figure 8-6 Appearance of five-option traditional menu before a selection has been made.

make it stand out as a prompt, but possible for the title—especially if the options are not numbered. The title should be printed in capital letters.

This type of menu is usually centered on the display and used to select the next subprogram or to exit the program; options 1 to 4 select subprograms and option 5 exits the program. The menu selection is made by typing in a single number, 1 to 5, and then pressing the Enter key. This menu does not use highlighted options or have an Escape key exit. In short, it is about as simple a menu as can be designed.

To illustrate its use, suppose that the operator wants to select option 1. When the 1 is typed in from the keyboard, it appears opposite the prompt, as shown in Figure 8-7. The entry is verified by pressing the Enter key. If the operator presses any other key, then verification has not occurred, the prompt is reprinted, the entry is erased, and the menu returns to the state shown in Figure 8-6. The operator can then make a new entry.

The code required to generate the menu and perform the required input functions is shown in Figure 8-8. A line-by-line summary of this code is given in Table 8-1.

This code could be readily modified to accept character instead of numeric entries; to do this, changes would be required to the printed options and to the range test. The code is simple but also limited. If your program must use several menus of this type, then it is rather inefficient to duplicate such code in each menu. However, it is quite easy to devise a subroutine based on this model, as described below.

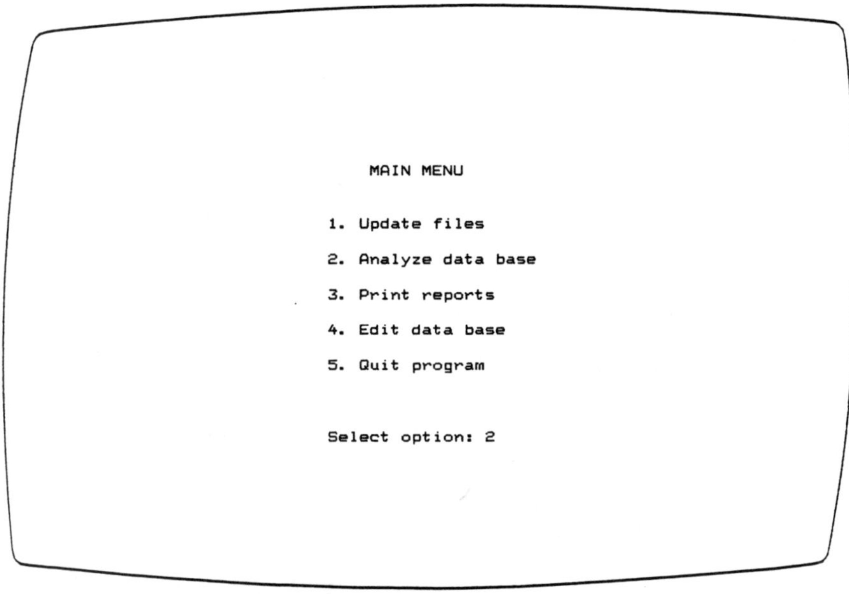

Figure 8-7 Appearance of five-option traditional menu after operator has selected option 2—the number of the selection is displayed opposite the prompt.

```
5 KEY OFF
10 CLS
20 LOCATE 1,34
30 PRINT"MAIN MENU"
40 REM-Generate Menu-
50 LOCATE 4,30
60 PRINT"1. Update files"
70 LOCATE 6,30
80 PRINT"2. Analyze data base"
90 LOCATE 8,30
100 PRINT"3. Print reports"
110 LOCATE 10,30
120 PRINT"4. Edit data base"
130 LOCATE 12,30
140 PRINT"5. Quit program"
150 REM-Collect Input-
160 LOCATE 16,30
170 COLOR 15,0:REM high intensity
180 PRINT"Select option: ";
190 COLOR 31,0:REM high-intensity blinking
200 PRINT CHR$(219);:REM print cursor
210 COLOR 7,0:REM normal
220 PICK$=INKEY$:IF PICK$="" GOTO 220
230 PICK=VAL(PICK$)
240 IF PICK)=1 AND PICK<=5 GOTO 250 ELSE BEEP:GOTO 220:REM range test
250 LOCATE ,POS(0)-1:REM position real cursor
260 PRINT PICK$
270 VER$=INKEY$:IF VER$="" GOTO 270
280 IF VER$=CHR$(13) GOTO 290 ELSE 160
290 END
```

Figure 8-8 Code required to generate menu shown in Figures 8-6 and 8-7 directly.

195

TABLE 8-1   Line-by-Line Summary of the Listing in Figure 8-8

Lines	Function performed
10 to 30	Clear display and print title.
40 to 140	Locate cursor, and print each menu option.
150 to 210	Print prompt and blinking cursor.
220 to 230	Collect single-key entry PICK$, and convert to numeric variable PICK.
240	Perform range test on entry. If the value of PICK is between 1 and 5, control flows to the next line. If not, the entry is rejected and control is sent back to line 220 to collect a new entry.
250 to 260	Reposition cursor, and print entry opposite prompt.
270	Collect verification keystroke.
280	Test verification keystroke. It must be the Enter key (CHR$(13)). If any other key is pressed, then the verification test is failed and control is sent back to line 160, where the prompt is reprinted and the old entry is erased; a new entry is then collected.

Generating Traditional Menus with Subroutines

Menus with numbered options.   Figure 8-9 is the listing of subroutine-based code for generating the menu shown in Figure 8-6. Lines 8 to 150 print the menu title, assign subroutine arguments, and perform a range test. The subroutine consists of lines 7000 to 7200. This subroutine displays the menu options and prompt, and collects the operator's entry. In other words, some of the menu functions listed in the introduction are performed directly and some by the subroutine. The title-printing and error-testing functions were left out of the subroutine purposely, for reasons described later.

A line-by-line summary of this code is given in Table 8-2.

This subroutine does not print the title or perform error-testing. It is not always desirable or necessary to print a title, and so it is best to print the title directly. Entry filtering is performed but not error testing. Testing is not performed because the subroutine must be capable of accepting any entry—numbers or letters—and setting up such tests with subroutine arguments is cumbersome. However, if the subroutine will be used only to generate standard menus—title at top and numbered options—then it would make good sense to perform these functions within the subroutine itself.

Providing an escape key exit.   In general, it is desirable to allow the operator to exit a menu via a standard, single-key procedure, such as pressing the Escape key. This provides a uniform escape route from all menus (except the main menu—see below). The menu shown in Figure 8-6 does not allow this: The operator must select option 5 to exit the menu. If a program uses several menus, with varying numbers of options, then the exit option will vary from menu to menu. Thus, it is a timesaver to be able to exit by simply pressing the Escape key; it is unnecessary to read the menu or press the Enter key.

Let us change the menu to allow an Escape key exit. The modified menu

```
5 KEY OFF
10 CLS
20 LOCATE 1,34
30 PRINT "MAIN MENU"
40 REM-Set Menu Arguments-
50 ROW=4:REM row of first option
60 COL=30:REM column
70 SPACES=2:REM double space between options
80 MENOPT$(1)="1. Update files"
90 MENOPT$(2)="2. Analyze data base"
100 MENOPT$(3)="3. Print reports"
110 MENOPT$(4)="4. Edit data base"
120 MENOPT$(5)="5. Quit program"
130 LAST=5:REM number of options
140 GOSUB 7000:REM call menu-generation subroutine
150 IF PICK$)="1" AND PICK$(="5" GOTO 160 ELSE BEEP: GOTO 140
160 END
7000 REM--Menu Generator--
7010 REM-Create Menu-
7020 FOR CHOICE=1 TO LAST
7030 LOCATE ROW+(CHOICE*SPACES),COL:REM position option
7040 PRINT MENOPT$(CHOICE)
7050 NEXT
7060 REM-Collect Input-
7070 LOCATE ROW+(LAST*SPACES)+4,COL
7080 COLOR 15,0:REM high intensity
7090 PRINT"Select option: ";
7100 COLOR 31,0:REM high-intensity blinking
7110 PRINT CHR$(219);:REM print cursor
7120 COLOR 7,0
7130 PICK$=INKEY$:IF PICK$="" GOTO 7130
7140 ASCII=ASC(PICK$)
7150 IF (ASCII)=48 AND ASCII(=57) OR (ASCII)=65 AND ASCII(=122) GOTO 7160 ELSE 7
130:REM letter & number filter
7160 LOCATE ,POS(0)-1:REM position real cursor
7170 PRINT PICK$
7180 VER$=INKEY$: IF VER$="" GOTO 7180
7190 IF VER$=CHR$(13) GOTO 7200 ELSE 7070
7200 RETURN
```

Figure 8-9 Code required to generate menu shown in Figures 8-6 and 8-7 with a menu-generation subroutine.

appears as shown in Figure 8-10. This menu is nearly identical to that shown in Figure 8-6. Differences are that the final option is now preceded by ESC instead of 5 and that the numbers of the first four options are followed by hyphens instead of periods so that the option labels are left-justified.

The code shown in Figure 8-9 can be easily modified to give this extra flexibility, as shown in Figure 8-11. Actually, this code contains only three changes; these changes are described in Table 8-3.

Note that both lines 141 and 7145 test for the Escape key before the entry is subjected to a range test that an Escape key entry would fail.

Using character options.   Now, to make things more interesting, let us suppose that we want to create a menu that uses letters instead of numbers for option selection. Selection with letters is preferable to selection with numbers; either type of menu may be used, depending upon a particular program's requirements. Thus, our menu-generation subroutine should be able to handle entries of both types. The modified menu is shown in Figure 8-12. This menu has the same five options as that in Figure 8-10, but the numbers preceding the options have been deleted. As before, the final option is selected with the Escape key.

What code is required to generate this menu? Actually, the subroutine shown in Figure 8-10 does not have any difficulty displaying such options or collecting

TABLE 8-2   Line-by-Line Summary of the Listing in Figure 8-9

Lines	Function performed
10 to 30	Clear display and print title.
40 to 130	Set subroutine arguments. ROW and COL are the row and column at which the top option should be printed. SPACES is the number of spaces between options. Options will be printed, one below the other, SPACES spaces apart, in column COL. MENOPT$(1) to MENOPT$(5) are the menu options. LAST is the number of menu options.
140	Call menu-generation subroutine. This subroutine will create the menu and return the operator's entry assigned to the variable PICK$.
150 to 160	Perform range test on PICK$. If PICK$ is between 1 and 5, then the entry is acceptable and control flows to line 160, which terminates input. If this test is failed, then control is sent back to line 140 to collect a new entry.
7000 to 7050	Display menu options.
7060 to 7120	Display prompt.
7130 to 7150	Collect and filter entry. Line 7130 collects the entry and assigns it to PICK$. Line 7140 computes the ASCII value and assigns it to the variable ASCII. Line 7150 then performs a range test on ASCII to assure that the entry is either a letter or number. If the test is passed, control flows to the next line; if not, the entry is rejected and control is sent back to line 7130 for a new entry.
7160 to 7200	Display entry, collect operator verification, and terminate the subroutine.

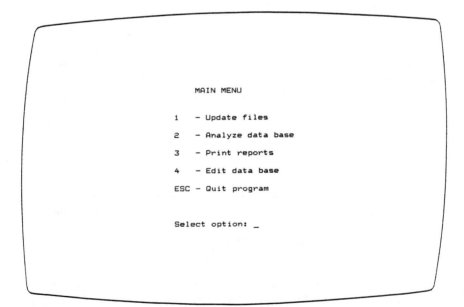

Figure 8-10   Appearance of five-option traditional menu with the final option modified to require single-keystroke (Escape key) selection.

```
5 KEY OFF
10 CLS
20 LOCATE 1,34
30 PRINT "MAIN MENU"
40 REM-Set Menu Arguments-
50 ROW=4:REM row of first option
60 COL=30:REM column
70 SPACES=2:REM double space between options
80 MENOPT$(1)="1   - Update files"
90 MENOPT$(2)="2   - Analyze data base"
100 MENOPT$(3)="3   - Print reports"
110 MENOPT$(4)="4   - Edit data base"
120 MENOPT$(5)="ESC - Quit program"
130 LAST=5:REM number of options
140 GOSUB 7000:REM call menu-generation subroutine
141 IF PICK$=CHR$(27) GOTO 160:REM ESC key pressed
150 IF PICK$)="1" AND PICK$(="4" GOTO 160 ELSE BEEP: GOTO 140
160 END
7000 REM--Menu Generator--
7010 REM-Create Menu-
7020 FOR CHOICE=1 TO LAST
7030 LOCATE ROW+(CHOICE*SPACES),COL:REM position option
7040 PRINT MENOPT$(CHOICE)
7050 NEXT
7060 REM-Collect Input-
7070 LOCATE ROW+(LAST*SPACES)+4,COL
7080 COLOR 15,0:REM high intensity
7090 PRINT"Select option: ";
7100 COLOR 31,0:REM high-intensity blinking
7110 PRINT CHR$(219);:REM print cursor
7120 COLOR 7,0
7130 PICK$=INKEY$:IF PICK$="" GOTO 7130
7140 ASCII=ASC(PICK$)
7145 IF ASCII=27 GOTO 7200:REM ESC key pressed
7150 IF (ASCII)=48 AND ASCII(=57) OR (ASCII)=65 AND ASCII(=122) GOTO 7160 ELSE 7
130:REM letter & number filter
7160 LOCATE ,POS(0)-1:REM position real cursor
7170 PRINT PICK$
7180 VER$=INKEY$: IF VER$="" GOTO 7180
7190 IF VER$=CHR$(13) GOTO 7200 ELSE 7070
7200 RETURN
```

Figure 8-11   Code required to generate menu shown in Figure 8-10.

them as entries. However, at present, it does not normalize capital and lowercase letters. Hence, the character returned by the subroutine will be whatever the operator types in, whether capital or lowercase. Since each entry must be error-tested, all characters should be normalized to either capital or lowercase to simplify testing. The code required to generate the modified menu and perform entry normalization and error-testing is shown in Figure 8-13. Again, only a few very simple changes are required, as described in Table 8-4.

The subroutine shown in Figure 8-13 is, at last, one with general utility. It is

TABLE 8-3   Line-by-Line Summary of the Listing in Figure 8-11

Lines	Function performed
80 to 120	Redefine menu option labels.
141	This line tests whether the entry returned by the subroutine is an Escape key press. If so, control is sent to line 160 to terminate entry. Otherwise, control flows to the range test in line 150.
7145	Test whether the Escape key has been pressed. If so, control is sent to line 7200 to terminate the subroutine. If not, control flows to line 7150, which conducts the usual range tests.

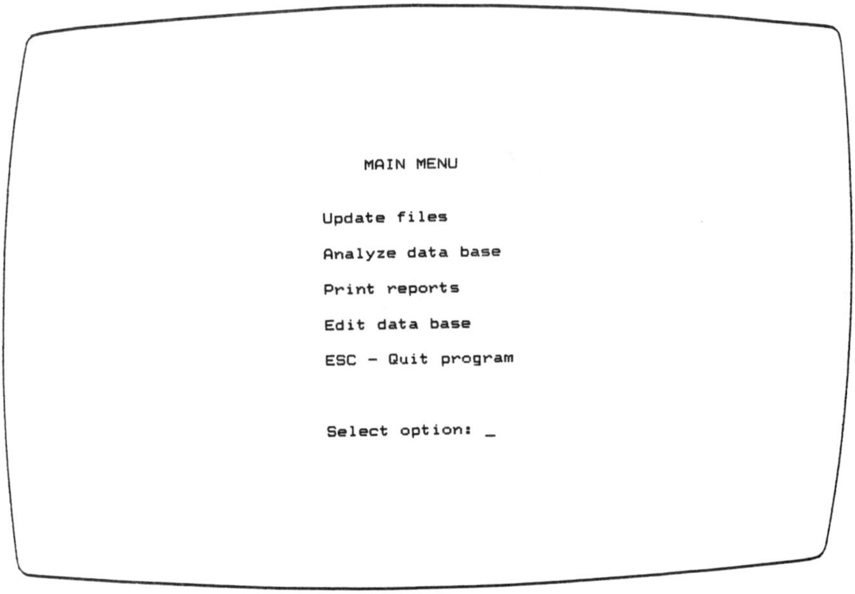

```
                        MAIN MENU

                   Update files

                   Analyze data base

                   Print reports

                   Edit data base

                   ESC - Quit program


                   Select option: _
```

Figure 8-12 Appearance of five-option traditional menu with character-selected options and an Escape key exit.

useful for generating a wide range of menus. Still, you might want to add some features and have it do such things as:

- Clear the display before printing the menu.
- Print the title.
- Compute ROW and COL to center the options or to print them in a standard location on the display.
- Perform error testing.

And so forth. Further changes are left to the reader.

The next subsection shows how to create a subroutine that does away with the prompt by highlighting the active option and using the menu itself to indicate which option is active. The subroutine is also more flexible in terms of menu formatting. Naturally, it is also more complex, but it also gives the programmer considerably more flexibility than the menu-generation methods shown so far.

Generating a Highlighted-Option Menu

Figure 8-4, presented earlier in this chapter, is a type of menu that uses highlighting to indicate the active option. The menu has no prompt; it does not need one because whatever option the user selects is highlighted to show that it is active. Figure 8-14a, b, c, d illustrate a dialog with this type of menu.

Figure 8-14a shows the appearance of the menu when first presented. The top

```
5 KEY OFF
10 CLS
20 LOCATE 1,34
30 PRINT "MAIN MENU"
40 REM-Set Menu Arguments-
50 ROW=4:REM row of first option
60 COL=30:REM column
70 SPACES=2:REM double space between options
80 MENOPT$(1)="Update files"
90 MENOPT$(2)="Analyze data base"
100 MENOPT$(3)="Print reports"
110 MENOPT$(4)="Edit data base"
120 MENOPT$(5)="ESC - QUIT PROGRAM"
130 LAST=5:REM number of options
140 GOSUB 7000:REM call menu-generation subroutine
141 IF PICK$=CHR$(27) GOTO 160:REM ESC key pressed
150 IF (PICK$="U" OR PICK$="A" OR PICK$="P" OR PICK$="E") GOTO 160 ELSE BEEP: GO
TO 140
160 END
7000 REM--Menu Generator--
7010 REM-Create Menu-
7020 FOR CHOICE=1 TO LAST
7030 LOCATE ROW+(CHOICE*SPACES),COL:REM position option
7040 PRINT MENOPT$(CHOICE)
7050 NEXT
7060 REM-Collect Input-
7070 LOCATE ROW+(LAST*SPACES)+4,COL
7080 COLOR 15,0:REM high intensity
7090 PRINT"Select option: ";
7100 COLOR 31,0:REM high-intensity blinking
7110 PRINT CHR$(219);:REM print cursor
7120 COLOR 7,0
7130 PICK$=INKEY$:IF PICK$="" GOTO 7130
7140 ASCII=ASC(PICK$)
7145 IF ASCII=27 GOTO 7200:REM ESC key pressed
7146 IF ASCII>=97 AND ASCII<=122 THEN PICK$=CHR$(ASC(PICK$)-32):REM convert
letters to uppercase
7150 IF (ASCII>=48 AND ASCII<=57) OR (ASCII>=65 AND ASCII<=122) GOTO 7160 ELSE 7
130:REM letter & number filter
7160 LOCATE ,POS(0)-1:REM position real cursor
7170 PRINT PICK$
7180 VER$=INKEY$: IF VER$="" GOTO 7180
7190 IF VER$=CHR$(13) GOTO 7200 ELSE 7070
7200 RETURN
```

Figure 8-13   Code required to generate menu shown in Figure 8-12.

option—which should be the one most frequently selected—is automatically highlighted. This option is the default; the operator can select it by simply pressing the Enter key.

To select a different option, the operator types in the first character of the option. For example, to select the Print option, the operator simply types in P. After doing this, the Print option is highlighted, as shown in Figure 8-14b. This option can then be verified by pressing the Enter key.

TABLE 8-4   Line-by-Line Summary of the Listing in Figure 8-13

Lines	Function performed
80 to 120	Redefine menu option labels.
150	Revised error test. This test determines whether the entry returned by the subroutine is a capital letter U, A, P, or E. These are the first letters of the first four menu options. (The Escape key option is handled separately, by line 141.) Tests for lowercase letters do not have to be conducted because the subroutine converts all letters to capital letters.
7146	Tests whether the ASCII value of the entry lies between 97 and 122. If so, a lowercase letter has been typed in, and it is converted to its capital letter equivalent.

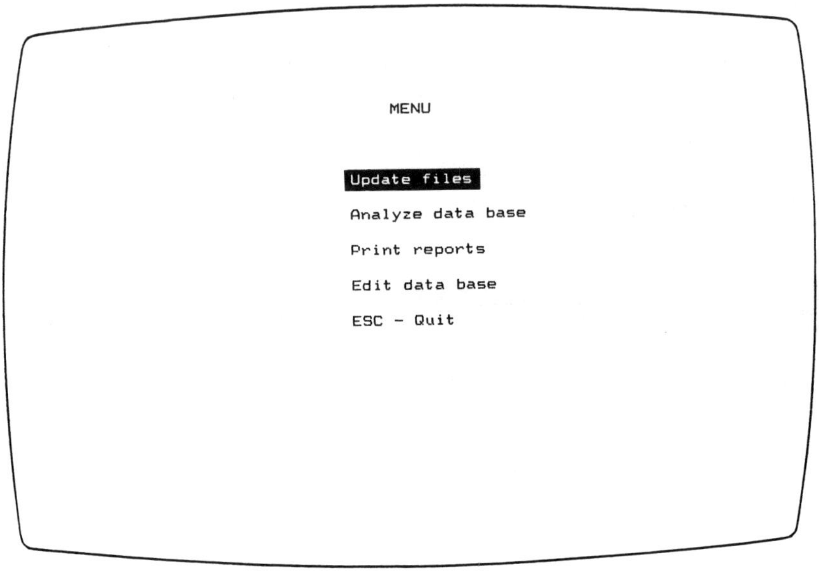

```
                    MENU

            ┌─────────────┐
            │Update files │
            └─────────────┘
            Analyze data base

            Print reports

            Edit data base

            ESC - Quit
```

(a)

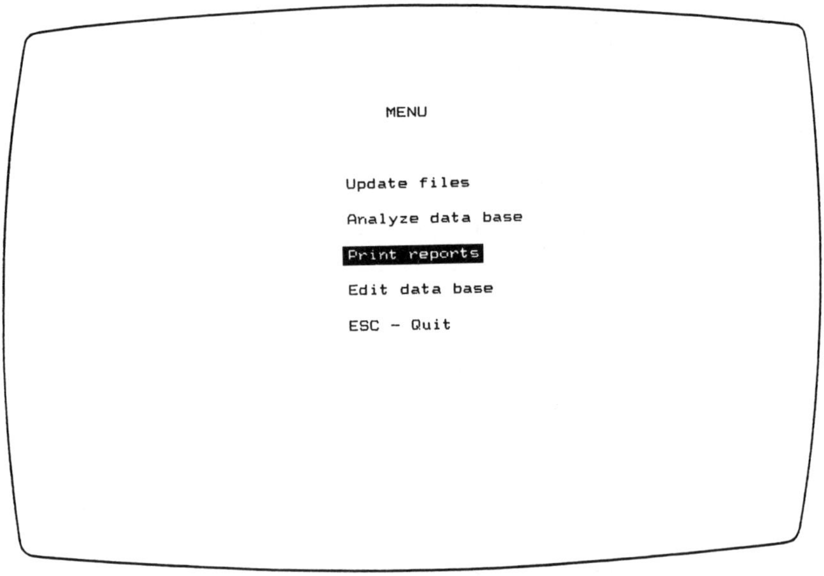

```
                    MENU

            Update files

            Analyze data base

            ┌─────────────┐
            │Print reports│
            └─────────────┘
            Edit data base

            ESC - Quit
```

(b)

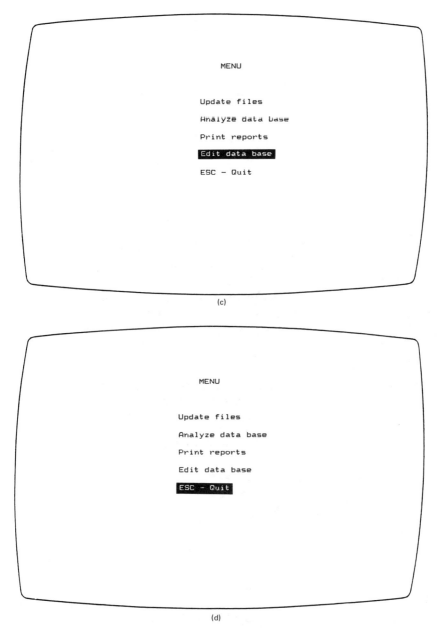

(c)

(d)

Figure 8-14 Appearance of highlighted option menu (*a*) when first presented, (*b*) after typing P key, (*c*) after typing E key, and (*d*) after typing Escape key.

But if the operator decides to make another change, to, say, edit the database, then typing in E will cause that option to be highlighted, as shown in Figure 8-14c.

And if the operator gets tired of all of this, pressing the Escape key will cause the ESC option to become highlighted and the menu will be exited—it is unnecessary to press the Enter key this time. This final action is shown in Figure 8-14d.

When menus of this type are used, it is fairly common to permit the operator to select an option not only with letter or number keys but also by using the space bar or cursor keys. For example, the space bar is used to step through the menu options, one by one. When the desired option is highlighted, the operator presses the Enter key to activate it. For example, when the menu is first presented, the top option is highlighted; each time the space bar is pressed, highlighting moves down one option (Figure 8-15a). When the bottom option is reached, an additional space bar press causes the highlight to cycle back to the top option (Figure 8-15b). Incidentally, when the ESC option is highlighted, it does not become active until the Enter key is pressed—in this sense, the final option works differently when selected with the space bar than when the Escape key itself is pressed.

Cursor keys are also commonly used to move the highlight. One advantage they have over the space bar is that they have two directions. For example, the Cursor Down key is used to move the highlight down the menu and the Cursor Up key to move it up. Cursor Left and Cursor Right keys can be used analogously, if the menu is presented on one or two lines, as in Figure 8-5.

The highlight can also be moved in other ways—for example, by using the + and − keys to increment or decrement the active option or by using the function keys. While various techniques are possible, we will focus in this chapter on the first three mentioned: using (1) the first character of the desired option, (2) the space bar, and (3) the cursor keys. And to save a digression later, let us spend a little time here showing how to read the cursor keys with BASIC.

Reading the cursor keys with BASIC.   As you may be aware, the cursor keys—as well as several other keys—do not generate standard ASCII characters. You can prove this to yourself by typing in and running this little program:

```
10 CHAR$=INKEY$:IF CHAR$="" GOTO 10
20 PRINT ASC(CHAR$)
30 GOTO 10
```

Run the program and type in some letter and number keys. These will return standard ASCII values. For example, the program will return ASCII values 48 to 57 for number keys 0 to 9, ASCII values 65 to 90 for the capital letters, and ASCII values 97 to 122 for lowercase letters.

But now try the cursor keys. What you get is 0. The same thing happens with the Insert or Delete keys, alternate key combinations, and certain Control key combinations. The 0's are not the true ASCII values of these keys and key combinations because they have *Extended Codes*. (The extended codes are given

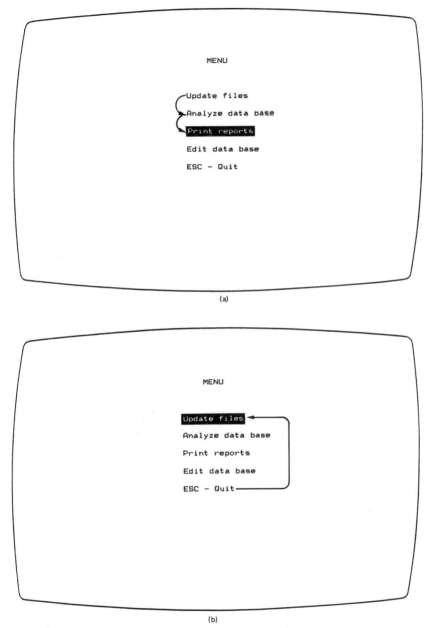

Figure 8-15 Effect on highlighted option menu of pressing the space bar: (*a*) Repeated pressing moves the highlight down the list of options, and (*b*) after the last option is reached, the highlight moves back up to the top option.

TABLE 8-5 Character and ASCII Values for Certain Keys

Key	Number of characters	ASCII value
Cursor Up	2	72
Cursor Down	2	80
Cursor Left	2	75
Cursor Right	2	77
Insert	2	82
Delete	2	83

at the end of Appendix G of the IBM PC and PCjr BASIC manuals.*) You must read these keys differently than, say, the letter or number keys.

The difference is that the INKEY$ variable returns two characters instead of one. The first character is a null character with ASCII value 0; the relevant ASCII value is contained in the second character. Thus, to read a key with an extended code, you must extract the second character returned by INKEY$. By adding lines 11 and 12, as shown below, the technique can be illustrated.

```
10 CHAR$=INKEY$:IF CHAR$="" GOTO 10
11 PRINT LEN(CHAR$);
12 IF LEN(CHAR$)>1 THEN CHAR$=RIGHT$(CHAR$,1)
20 PRINT ASC(CHAR$)
30 GOTO 10
```

Line 11 simply prints the length of CHAR$. Line 12 tests whether CHAR$ is more than one character long; if so, it redefines CHAR$ as its rightmost character.

Type in and run this program, and you will gain some perspective on the problem. The number and letter keys produce the same results, but the cursor keys and the other keys that previously produced ASCII values of 0 now have more substantial values. For example, Table 8-5 gives the result you should get when typing the indicated key.

This is the technique that must be used to read the cursor keys—as well as the other keys and key combinations that return nonstandard ASCII values. Now that this has been gotten out of the way, we can move on with our discussion of menus.

Creating and reading a highlighted menu. Let us create the code necessary to generate the highlighted menu shown in Figure 8-14a, b, c, d such that the menu option can be selected by typing the first character of the option or using the space bar or cursor keys. As before, the menu will be titled, and the title will be generated in separate code, rather than in the subroutine itself. However, this time error-testing will be built into the subroutine so that external error-testing will not be required.

---

*BASIC by Microsoft Corporation, IBM Corporation, 1982, and BASIC (PCjr) by Microsoft Corporation, IBM Corporation, 1984.

```
5 KEY OFF
10 CLS
20 LOCATE 1,32
30 PRINT "MAIN MENU"
40 REM—Set Menu Arguments—
50 MENOPT$(1)="Update files"
60 MENOPT$(2)="Analyze data base"
70 MENOPT$(3)="Print reports"
80 MENOPT$(4)="Edit data base"
90 MENOPT$(5)=CHR$(27)+"ESC - Exit program"
100 LAST=5:REM number of options
110 FOR CHOICE=1 TO LAST
120 ROW%(CHOICE)=2*CHOICE+4:REM set rows
130 COL%(CHOICE)=30:REM set cols
140 NEXT
150 GOSUB 7500:REM call menu-generation subroutine
160 END
7500 REM—Menu Generator—
7510 PICK=1:PICK$="":REM initialize & set default option
7520 REM—Create Menu—
7530 FOR CHOICE=1 TO LAST
7540 LOCATE ROW%(CHOICE),COL%(CHOICE)
7550 IF PICK=CHOICE THEN COLOR 0,7:REM set highlighting
7560 PRINT MENOPT$(CHOICE):REM print option
7570 COLOR 7,0:REM normal
7580 NEXT
7590 IF PICK$=CHR$(27) GOTO 7760:REM ESC key exit
7600 REM—Collect Input—
7610 PICK$=INKEY$:IF PICK$="" GOTO 7610
7620 ASCII=ASC(PICK$)
7630 IF ASCII=13 GOTO 7760:REM Enter key pressed
7640 IF PICK$ =" " THEN PICK=PICK+1: IF PICK>LAST THEN PICK=1:GOTO 7520:REM
Space Bar
7650 IF ASCII>=97 AND ASCII<=122 THEN PICK$=CHR$(ASC(PICK$)-32):REM convert
letters to uppercase
7660 IF LEN(PICK$)=1 THEN 7720 ELSE 7670:REM test for cursor keys
7670 PICK$=RIGHT$(PICK$,1):REM extract cursor character
7680 ASCII=ASC(PICK$):REM Extended ASCII code
7690 IF ASCII=72 THEN PICK=PICK-1: IF PICK=0 THEN PICK=LAST:REM Curs Up
7700 IF ASCII=80 THEN PICK=PICK+1: IF PICK>LAST THEN PICK=1:REM Curs Down
7710 GOTO 7520
7720 FOR CHOICE=1 TO LAST
7730 IF PICK$=LEFT$(MENOPT$(CHOICE),1) THEN PICK=CHOICE:REM compare entry with
first character of option
7740 NEXT
7750 GOTO 7520
7760 RETURN
```

Figure 8-16 Code required to generate menu shown in Figures 8-14*a, b, c,* and *d.*

Figure 8-16 is the listing of the code required to generate the menu shown in Figure 8-14*a, b, c, d.* Lines 10 to 150 print the menu title, assign subroutine arguments, and call the menu-generation subroutine. The subroutine consists of lines 7500 to 7760. This subroutine displays the menu options, highlighting the currently active one. It initially sets the first option as the default but permits the operator to reset the active option by typing in the first character of an option label or by pressing the space bar or Cursor Up or Cursor Down keys. The active option can be changed only by making a valid entry; hence, the subroutine performs an automatic validity test on the entry. The manner in which options are selected requires that no two options on the menu begin with the same character. After the operator has made a selection and pressed the Enter key (or simply pressed the Escape key), the subroutine returns the first character of the option label in the variable PICK$ and the option number in the variable PICK.

A line-by-line summary of this code is given in Table 8-6.

Varying the menu format. This subroutine is able to generate a menu with any appearance you like. If you want, you can display one menu option in each corner

TABLE 8-6   Line-by-Line Summary of the Listing in Figure 8-16

Lines	Function performed
10 to 30	Clear screen and print title.
40 to 140	Set subroutine arguments. MENOPT$(1) to MENOPT$(5) are the menu options. The first character of each option must be identical to the key that is to be pressed to select that option. Any number or letter can be used. Note that the Escape option (line 90) begins with CHR$(27), which is the Escape character. LAST is the number of menu options. CHOICE is a local counting variable. ROW%(CHOICE) and COL%(CHOICE) are the row and column at which menu option CHOICE is to be printed. By defining the location of each menu option separately, it is possible to create a menu whose individual options are positioned however desired. Line 120 sets ROW%(1) to 4, ROW%(2) to 6, ROW%(3) to 8, and so on. Line 130 sets all column arguments to 30. And line 150 calls the menu-generation subroutine. Note that no error-testing occurs within this code, since the subroutine will only return a valid menu option.
7510	Set default menu option (PICK) to 1. This will cause the top option to be highlighted when the menu is first displayed.
7520 to 7580	Display menu options. Lines 7530 and 7580 start a counting loop that counts from 1 to the number of options (LAST), using the counting variable CHOICE. Line 7540 positions the menu option. Line 7550 tests whether the option being displayed is the active option by comparing PICK (the default or operator-selected option) with the counting variable CHOICE. If this test is passed, then reverse video is set to highlight the option. Line 7560 then prints the option, and line 7570 resets normal video.
7590	Test whether the Escape key has been pressed and, if so, send control to the exit line from the subroutine.
7610	Collect operator entry and assign to variable PICK$.
7620	Calculate ASCII value of PICK$.
7630	Test for verification of the active option with the Enter key. If this key has been pressed, control is sent to the exit line from the subroutine.
7640	Test whether the space bar has been pressed. If so, then the active option (PICK) is incremented by 1. PICK is then tested to see if it exceeds the number of options (LAST) and, if so, PICK is reset to 1. Control is then sent back to line 7520 to redisplay the menu.
7650	Test whether ASCII is between 97 and 122. If so, a lowercase letter has been typed in, and it is converted to its capital letter equivalent.
7660	Test whether length of PICK$ is 1. If so, then a key with a standard ASCII code has been pressed and control is sent to line 7720. If the test is failed, then the pressed key has an Extended ASCII code and may be one of the cursor keys. In this case, control is sent to line 7670.
7670 to 7710	Extract rightmost character from PICK$, compute ASCII value, test for Cursor Up key (ASCII = 72) or Cursor Down key (ASCII = 80), and increment or decrement PICK accordingly. Control is then sent back to line 7520 to redisplay the menu.
7720 to 7750	These lines will be executed only if a letter or number key has been pressed. They compare the letter or number typed in with the first character of the menu. If a match is found, then PICK is set to CHOICE. If no match is found, then PICK is not changed. This code therefore filters out invalid entries and eliminates the need for further error testing. Line 7750 sends control back to line 7520 to redisplay the menu.
7760	Exit from subroutine. Note that this is the only way out of the subroutine and that it can only be jumped to from line 7590 (Escape key pressed) or 7630 (Enter key pressed).

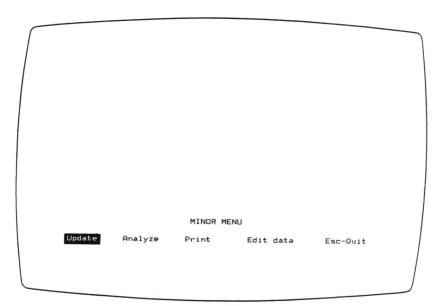

Figure 8-17 Appearance of a highlighted-option menu with menu compressed to a single line.

of your display (not recommended), in a geometric shape (also not recommended), or according to any other whim. To illustrate, let us use it to create the one-row menu shown in Figure 8-17. Since all options are presented on a single row, the option labels must be shortened as shown.

Figure 8-18 is the listing of the code required to generate the menu shown in Figure 8-17. This listing is very similar to that shown in Figure 8-16. Lines 10 to 150 print the menu title, assign subroutine arguments, and call the menu-generation subroutine. These lines set the subroutine arguments differently than the corresponding lines in Figure 8-16 but are otherwise very similar. The subroutine consists of lines 7500 to 7760 and is identical to that in Figure 8-16 except

```
5 KEY OFF
10 CLS
20 LOCATE 20,32
30 PRINT "MINOR MENU"
40 REM-Set Menu Arguments-
50 MENOPT$(1)="Update"
60 MENOPT$(2)="Analyze"
70 MENOPT$(3)="Print"
80 MENOPT$(4)="Edit data"
90 MENOPT$(5)=CHR$(27)+"ESC - Exit"
100 LAST=5:REM number of options
110 FOR CHOICE=1 TO LAST
120 ROW%(CHOICE)=22:REM set rows
130 COL%(CHOICE)=(CHOICE-1)*15+1:REM set cols
140 NEXT
150 GOSUB 7500:REM call menu-generation subroutine
160 END
```

Figure 8-18 Code required to generate menu shown in Figure 8-17. (Requires menu-generator subroutine starting on line 7500.)

that lines 7690 and 7700 must be changed to act on Cursor Left and Cursor Right keys instead of Cursor Up and Cursor Down keys. Naturally, with a single-row menu such as this, Cursor Up and Cursor Down do not have much meaning.

Menu-Control Networks

So far, this chapter has told how to design and generate menus. While this may be a useful exercise in character graphics, it says nothing about how these menus should be used to control a program. The code presented had a convenient END statement where the next step, program control, would ordinarily be located. This section takes up where that END statement left off. It addresses menu-control networks—the networks used to link individual menus together into the network used to control the program. The section begins with an overview of such networks and offers guidelines for design. Code is then presented showing how to link menus together into networks.

Design of Menu Networks

Most menu-driven programs have several menus that are organized into an overall control structure, or *network*. In this network, the menus may be thought of as nodes (or crossroads), with each menu option linking the menu either to another menu or to a subprogram (Figure 8-2). Such networks can be designed in many different ways. The simplest possible network consists of a single menu node (Figure 8-19). This is the form of the network if the program uses only one menu.

Design criteria.   Most programs with menus use more than one menu, however, and so the simple form shown in Figure 8-19 is seldom applicable. A program may, for example, use two, three, a dozen, or several dozen different menus throughout its structure. Since these menus can be linked together in many different ways, it is not immediately obvious which is best or, for that matter, if there is a single "best" way.

In fact, though there are guidelines for designing such networks, there is no simple formula that can be followed in every instance. To a large degree, the organization of these menus should mirror the organizational structure of the program itself. If this structure is logical, then a menu network modeled on it will also be logical. If the program's structure is not logical, then organizing the menus in a particular way cannot correct the underlying defect in the program. But assuming that the program's basic structure is sound, what is the best way to organize the menus? To answer this question, we must define the criteria by

Figure 8-19   The simplest possible menu network consists of a single menu node.

which to evaluate different control networks. When the primary goal is to make the program user-friendly, two such criteria are obvious:

1. *Speed.* How quickly does the network permit movement within the program?
2. *Ease of learning and use.*

A simple way to assess speed is to count the number of keystrokes to get from any given menu to any other. The fewer the keystrokes, the easier transportation is and the more efficient the program.

Ease of learning and use will be influenced by how logically the menus are organized. A key factor here is whether the menus are organized in a hierarchical fashion. This network is usually both easy to learn and easy to use.

The tree.   Perhaps the most common control network in menu-driven programs is the familiar tree (Figure 8-20). This is a multilevel, hierarchical network. The main menu is the highest node. Selecting a program from it leads to a level 2 node or menu, selecting an option from a level 2 menu leads to a level 3 menu, and so on. There are no links or crossovers between different menus at the same level. In order to move from one level 3 menu to another, the operator must first return to the previous level 2 menu and then the main menu, and then work back down through another level 2 menu to the desired level 3 menu. If the final option on the menu is an Escape key exit, as illustrated in the previous section, then the main menu may be reached very quickly simply by pressing the Escape key until the main menu appears. If the exit option is numbered and varies from menu to menu, then it is, of course, more time-consuming to reach the main menu.

This network has the advantage that it is symmetrical and therefore easy to learn. However, if it is several levels deep, moving between branches is very time-consuming. The obvious solution to this problem is to provide some shortcuts or

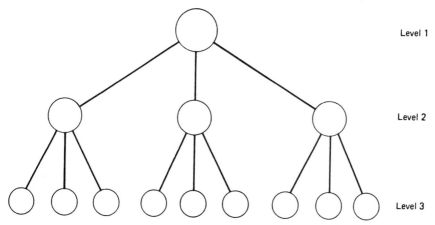

Figure 8-20   A hierarchical menu network. Each node is linked only to the node above it. Moving from one branch to another requires a return to the highest node, or main menu. (*From Simpson:* Design of User-Friendly Programs for Small Computers, *copyright 1985, by permission of McGraw-Hill Book Company.*)

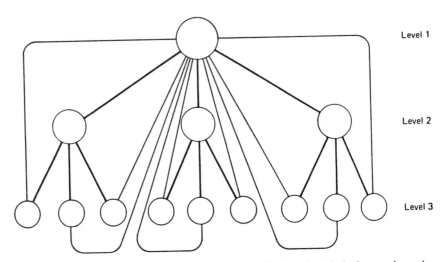

Figure 8-21 A modified hierarchical menu network. Each node is linked not only to the node above but also to the highest node. This permits faster movement around the program. (*From Simpson:* Design of User-Friendly Programs for Small Computers, *copyright 1985, by permission of McGraw-Hill Book Company.*)

links between different parts of the network. One way of simplifying things is to provide an option on every menu that links it directly back to the main menu (Figure 8-21). This provides a shortcut that does not disrupt the functional integrity of the different branches of the network. If the Escape key exit technique is used (see above), then there is really no need for a separate option on each menu that goes to the main menu, since the operator may press the Escape key repeatedly (or simply hold it down and let it repeat) until the main menu is reached.

Shortcuts.   While the Escape key exiting technique provides fast movement home to the main menu, working back down through the network can still take considerable time. If the network is several levels deep, and movement between branches must occur frequently, the only solution is to provide some additional links between branches (Figure 8-22). However, this must be done with care or the network will begin to lose its symmetry. The more crossovers that are permitted, the less predictable the network and the more difficult it is for the operator to model it mentally and learn it. Moreover, as you start to multiply the options on your program's menus, the menus get longer and more difficult to work with. What should be avoided at all costs is a network with crossovers between branches that follow no particular pattern or rule (Figure 8-23). This is like having a road system in which some streets come to dead ends and others have cross streets. The more symmetric you make your network, the easier it will be for the operator to learn it. If your control network is complex, the operator will need a road map to find the way around it.

Probably the best solution to the speed problem when fast movement around the network is required is to include "invisible" options on the menus, that is, options that are active but not listed. This is a bit devious, but the options are not

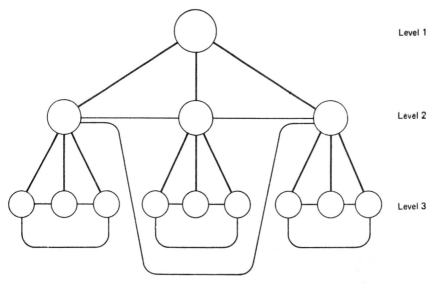

Figure 8-22 Another alternative menu network. In this one, each node is linked not only to the node above but also to the node at the same level in other branches. (*From Simpson:* Design of User-Friendly Programs for Small Computers, *copyright 1985, by permission of McGraw-Hill Book Company.*)

designed for everybody to use. These options are activated by pressing Function keys or Alternate or Control key combinations, and permit a jump from any menu to any other menu in the program (Figure 8-24). These hidden options are provided mainly for the expert user who memorizes the codes required to activate them. The program can be used quite effectively without them but is faster with them. The use of invisible options is illustrated later in this section.

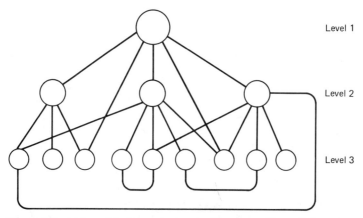

Figure 8-23 A hierarchical menu network with many arbitrary links among menus that follow no pattern or rule.

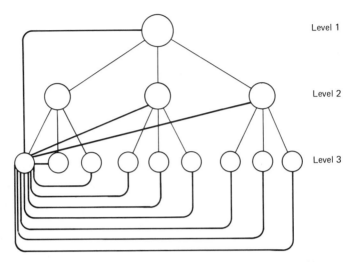

Level 1

Level 2

Level 3

Figure 8-24 A hierarchical menu network showing the "invisible" options available from a single node (lower left). The invisible options are not displayed on the menu but can be activated with commands that the operator has memorized.

Depth-breadth tradeoff.   In designing a menu-control network, sometimes you must make a depth-breadth tradeoff. That is, you must decide whether to use more menus with fewer options or fewer menus with more options. Make the trade-off in favor of longer menus. For example, if your program has a total of sixty-four different functions, it is better to use two levels of menus with eight options each than three levels with four options each or six levels with two options each. No single menu should contain more than ten options, however.

Linking Menus into Networks with BASIC

Menus may be thought of as multiple-choice switches. The menu presents the choices to the operator, and the operator types in the choice. The menu-generation code also collects the operator's choice in the form of a variable. The variable returned by the menu code is then used to decide what line in the program to send control to.

The variables returned by the menu-generation code are either string variables, real (or integer) variables, or a combination of both. The previous section of this chapter showed how to generate menus directly in code and with two different types of subroutines. Before we show how to use these returned variables to switch control, let us take a little inventory of what variables the menu-generation code presented earlier will return to us.

Figure 8-8 showed the code for generating a traditional menu. This code returns the operator's choice in the form of the string variable PICK$. For example, if option 1 on a menu is selected, PICK$ = "1". Figure 8-9 showed a subroutine form of this code that returns the operator's choice with the same variable. Both types of code could be used to generate menus with nonnumbered items. If this is done, then PICK$ will take on letter values, such as A, B, and so on.

Figure 8-11 showed how to modify the subroutine to permit an Escape key exit. When the operator presses the Escape key, PICK$ is set to CHR$(27).

Figures 8-16 and 8-18 both used a new subroutine that generates menus with highlighted options. This subroutine returns the operator's choice in the form of both the real variable PICK and the string variable PICK$. The options do not have to be numbered to return a valid value of PICK; PICK is simply the ordinal position of the selected option. For example, if the fifth option is the Escape key exit and that option is selected, then PICK will be 5 and PICK$ will be CHR$(27).

This may seem rather tedious, but it has the point that some of the code demonstrated earlier returns character strings and some both character strings and numbers. We must take this into account in writing control code. To illustrate, let us consider first the case of string variables and then that of numbers.

Control with string variables.   When the selection variable is a string, IF-GOTO logic must be used to do the control switching. For example, code such as this would be used following the menu subroutine call:

```
160 IF PICK$="1" GOTO 12000:REM option 1 selected
170 IF PICK$="2" GOTO 14000:REM option 2 selected
180 IF PICK$="3" GOTO 16000:REM option 3 selected
190 IF PICK$="4" GOTO 20000:REM option 4 selected
200 IF PICK$=CHR$(27) GOTO 210:REM ESC key pressed
```

This type of code is not compact; as many IF GOTO statements are required as there are menu options.

To illustrate this control technique a little more tangibly, let us build the simple menu-control network shown in Figure 8-25. This network has three menus: a main menu (titled "Main Menu") and two branch menus (titled "Branch 1 Menu" and "Branch 2 Menu"). Each menu has three options. The first and second option on the Main Menu lead, respectively, to the Branch 1 Menu and Branch 2 Menu. The final option on the Main Menu terminates the program. Each branch menu also has three options. The first two lead to dummy displays, and the third leads back to the Main Menu.

The code required to generate this network is shown in Figure 8-26. This may look bewildering at first, but it is actually quite simple. To begin with, the overall organization of the program is given in Table 8-7.

Let us start with the Main Menu. Lines 5 to 170 set subroutine arguments and call the menu-generation subroutine. The lines of interest here are 130 to 170, which perform a range test and control switching. Line 130 tests for the Q key. If it has been pressed, the screen is cleared, an "End of program" message is printed, and the program is terminated. Incidentally, do not design a menu that lets the operator exit the program by pressing a single key, such as Escape—this makes it much too easy to terminate the program accidentally. Instead, require the operator to type in something (such as Q for Quit) and verify the choice with the Enter key, as is done here.

Line 140 performs a range test on PICK$. If PICK$ is valid, then control is sent

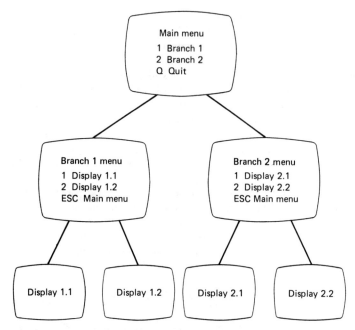

Figure 8-25 A two-level menu network consisting of three menus and four displays. Each branch menu provides access to two displays.

```
14 KEY OFF
5 REM--Main Menu--
10 CLS
20 LOCATE 1,34
30 PRINT "MAIN MENU"
40 REM-Set Menu Arguments-
50 ROW=4:REM row of first option
60 COL=30:REM column
70 SPACES=2:REM double space between options
80 MENOPT$(1)="1 - Branch 1"
90 MENOPT$(2)="2 - Branch 2"
100 MENOPT$(3)="Q - Quit program"
110 LAST=3:REM number of options
120 GOSUB 7000:REM call menu-generation subroutine
130 IF PICK$="Q" OR PICK$= "q" THEN CLS:PRINT"End of program":END
140 IF PICK$)="1" AND PICK$(="2" GOTO 150 ELSE BEEP: GOTO 120
150 REM--Switch Control--
160 IF PICK$="1" GOTO 180
170 IF PICK$="2" GOTO 460
180 REM--Branch 1 Menu--
190 CLS
200 LOCATE 1,32
210 PRINT "BRANCH 1 MENU"
220 REM-Set Menu Arguments-
230 ROW=4:REM row of first option
240 COL=30:REM column
250 SPACES=2:REM double space between options
260 MENOPT$(1)="1   - Display 1.1"
270 MENOPT$(2)="2   - Display 1.2"
280 MENOPT$(3)="ESC - Main Menu"
290 LAST=3:REM number of options
300 GOSUB 7000:REM call menu-generation subroutine
310 IF PICK$=CHR$(27) GOTO 5:REM ESC key pressed
320 IF PICK$)="1" AND PICK$(="2" GOTO 330 ELSE BEEP: GOTO 300
330 REM--Switch Control--
340 IF PICK$="1" GOTO 360
350 IF PICK$="2" GOTO 410
```

```
360 REM--Display 1.1--
370 CLS
380 PRINT"DISPLAY 1.1"
390 GOSUB 1200
400 GOTO 180
410 REM--Display 1.2--
420 CLS
430 PRINT"DISPLAY 1.2"
440 GOSUB 1200
450 GOTO 180
460 REM--Branch 2 Menu--
470 CLS
480 LOCATE 1,32
490 PRINT "BRANCH 2 MENU"
500 REM-Set Menu Arguments-
510 ROW=4:REM row of first option
520 COL=30:REM column
530 SPACES=2:REM double space between options
540 MENOPT$(1)="1    - Display 2.1"
550 MENOPT$(2)="2    - Display 2.2"
560 MENOPT$(3)="ESC - Main Menu"
570 LAST=3:REM number of options
580 GOSUB 7000:REM call menu-generation subroutine
590 IF PICK$=CHR$(27) GOTO 5:REM ESC key pressed
600 IF PICK$)="1" AND PICK$(="2" GOTO 610 ELSE BEEP: GOTO 580
610 REM--Switch Control--
620 IF PICK$="1" GOTO 640
630 IF PICK$="2" GOTO 690
640 REM--Display 2.1--
650 CLS
660 PRINT"DISPLAY 2.1"
670 GOSUB 1200
680 GOTO 460
690 REM--Display 2.2--
700 CLS
710 PRINT"DISPLAY 2.2"
720 GOSUB 1200
730 GOTO 460
1200 REM--Temporary Pause--
1210 LOCATE 23,28:REM (use LOCATE 23,8 for 40-column display)
1220 COLOR 30,0:REM high intensity blinking
1230 PRINT"Press any Key to Continue"
1240 A$=INKEY$:IF A$="" GOTO 1240
1250 LOCATE 23,28
1260 PRINT SPACE$(25)
1270 COLOR 7,0:REM normal video
1280 RETURN
7000 REM--Menu Generator--
7010 REM-Create Menu-
7020 FOR CHOICE=1 TO LAST
7030 LOCATE ROW+(CHOICE*SPACES),COL:REM position option
7040 PRINT MENOPT$(CHOICE)
7050 NEXT
7060 REM-Collect Input-
7070 LOCATE ROW+(LAST*SPACES)+4,COL
7080 COLOR 15,0:REM high intensity
7090 PRINT"Select option: ";
7100 COLOR 31,0:REM high-intensity blinking
7110 PRINT CHR$(219);:REM print cursor
7120 COLOR 7,0
7130 PICK$=INKEY$:IF PICK$="" GOTO 7130
7140 ASCII=ASC(PICK$)
7145 IF ASCII=27 GOTO 7200:REM ESC key pressed
7150 IF (ASCII)=48 AND ASCII(=57) OR (ASCII)=65 AND ASCII(=122) GOTO 7160 ELSE 7
130:REM letter & number filter
7160 LOCATE ,POS(0)-1:REM position real cursor
7170 PRINT PICK$
7180 VER$=INKEY$: IF VER$="" GOTO 7180
7190 IF VER$=CHR$(13) GOTO 7200 ELSE 7070
7200 RETURN
```

Figure 8-26 Code required to create menu network shown in Figure 8-25. Control switching is done with IF-GOTO clauses.

TABLE 8-7 Program Organization, Figure 8-26

Line block	Function
5 to 170	Main Menu
180 to 350	Branch 1 Menu
360 to 450	Dummy displays for Branch 1 Menu
460 to 630	Branch 2 Menu
640 to 730	Dummy displays for Branch 2 Menu
1200 to 1280	Temporary pause subroutine
7000 to 7200	Menu generator subroutine

to line 150; otherwise, control is sent back to line 120 to collect another entry. Lines 160 and 170 perform control switching, using IF GOTO logic of the type illustrated above. If the first option on the menu has been selected, control is sent to line 180, the Branch 1 Menu. If the second option has been selected, control is sent to line 460, the Branch 2 Menu. Now let us consider the Branch 1 Menu. This is very similar to the Main Menu: arguments are set, the menu-generation subroutine is called, entries are error-tested, and control is switched with IF-GOTO logic. Here an Escape key exit, to the Main Menu, is permitted, however. Lines 360 to 400 contain one of the dummy displays. This could just as well be another menu, a program, or any other function that might be called within the program. In this case, the code clears the screen, prints a title, calls the temporary pause subroutine, and then sends control back to line 180—the starting line of the Branch 1 Menu. The code for the Branch 2 Menu and its dummy displays is essentially the same. Just for the record, the lines in this code which perform control switching are 130, 160, 170 (Main Menu); 310, 340, 350 (Branch 1 Menu); and 590, 620, 630 (Branch 2 Menu).

As indicated earlier, this code is actually quite simple. And it illustrates the use of IF-GOTO logic to switch control to different parts of the program.

Control with numeric variables.   When the selection variable is a number, control switching can be done with IF-GOTO logic, as shown above. However, it is more efficient to use the ON-GOTO or ON-GOSUB statements. The syntax of the ON-GOTO statement is as follows:

```
ON n GOTO line x, line y, . . . .
```

When this statement is executed, BASIC will send program control to the nth line in the list following the GOTO statement. For example, if $N = 3$ and this statement is executed,

```
ON N GOTO 300,400,500,600,1000
```

control will be sent to line 500.

The GOSUB form of this statement works identically, except that it treats the jumped-to code as a subroutine. After the RETURN is encountered, control is sent back to the line following the ON-GOSUB statement.

Clearly, ON-GOTO or ON-GOSUB are more efficient than IF-GOTO logic since one statement handles all switching; a separate statement for each menu option is not required.

To illustrate this control technique, let us build a program that uses it to generate the menu network shown in the previous example. Since control switching requires a numeric variable, this code must use the highlighted-menu subroutine, and the lines handling the actual switching must be changed. However, the new program can be built on the same model as the previous one. The required code is shown in Figure 8-27.

```
4 KEY OFF
5 REM--Main Menu--
10 CLS
20 LOCATE 1,34
30 PRINT "MAIN MENU"
40 REM-Set Menu Arguments-
80 MENOPT$(1)="1 - Branch 1"
90 MENOPT$(2)="2 - Branch 2"
100 MENOPT$(3)="Q - Quit program"
110 LAST=3:REM number of options
114 REM-set row & column arguments-
115 FOR CHOICE=1 TO LAST
116 ROW%(CHOICE)=CHOICE*2+4
117 COL%(CHOICE)=30
118 NEXT
120 GOSUB 7500:REM call menu-generation subroutine
130 IF ASCII=27 GOTO 120:REM trap ESC key
150 REM--Switch Control--
160 ON PICK GOTO 180,460,170
170 CLS:PRINT"End of program":END
180 REM--Branch 1 Menu--
190 CLS
200 LOCATE 1,32
210 PRINT "BRANCH 1 MENU"
220 REM-Set Menu Arguments-
260 MENOPT$(1)="1    - Display 1.1"
270 MENOPT$(2)="2    - Display 1.2"
280 MENOPT$(3)=CHR$(27)+"ESC - Main Menu"
290 LAST=3:REM number of options
300 GOSUB 7500:REM call menu-generation subroutine
330 REM--Switch Control--
340 ON PICK GOTO 360,410,5
360 REM--Display 1.1--
370 CLS
380 PRINT"DISPLAY 1.1"
390 GOSUB 1200
400 GOTO 180
410 REM--Display 1.2--
420 CLS
430 PRINT"DISPLAY 1.2"
440 GOSUB 1200
450 GOTO 180
460 REM--Branch 2 Menu--
470 CLS
480 LOCATE 1,32
490 PRINT "BRANCH 2 MENU"
500 REM-Set Menu Arguments-
540 MENOPT$(1)="1    - Display 2.1"
550 MENOPT$(2)="2    - Display 2.2"
560 MENOPT$(3)=CHR$(27)+"ESC - Main Menu"
570 LAST=3:REM number of options
580 GOSUB 7500:REM call menu-generation subroutine
610 REM--Switch Control--
620 ON PICK GOTO 640,690,5
640 REM--Display 2.1--
650 CLS
```

Figure 8-27 Code required to create menu network shown in Figure 8-25. Control switching is done with ON *n* GOTO clauses.

```
660 PRINT"DISPLAY 2.1"
670 GOSUB 1200
680 GOTO 460
690 REM--Display 2.2--
700 CLS
710 PRINT"DISPLAY 2.2"
720 GOSUB 1200
730 GOTO 460
1200 REM--Temporary Pause--
1210 LOCATE 23,28:REM (use LOCATE 23,8 for 40-column display)
1220 COLOR 30,0:REM high intensity blinking
1230 PRINT"Press any Key to Continue"
1240 A$=INKEY$:IF A$="" GOTO 1240
1250 LOCATE 23,28
1260 PRINT SPACE$(25)
1270 COLOR 7,0:REM normal video
1280 RETURN
7500 REM--Menu Generator--
7510 PICK=1:PICK$="":REM initialize & set default option
7520 REM-Create Menu-
7530 FOR CHOICE=1 TO LAST
7540 LOCATE ROW%(CHOICE),COL%(CHOICE)
7550 IF PICK=CHOICE THEN COLOR 0,7:REM set highlighting
7560 PRINT MENOPT$(CHOICE):REM print option
7570 COLOR 7,0:REM normal
7580 NEXT
7590 IF PICK$=CHR$(27) GOTO 7760:REM ESC key exit
7600 REM-Collect Input-
7610 PICK$=INKEY$:IF PICK$="" GOTO 7610
7620 ASCII=ASC(PICK$)
7630 IF ASCII=13 GOTO 7760:REM Enter key pressed
7640 IF PICK$ =" " THEN PICK=PICK+1: IF PICK)LAST THEN PICK=1:GOTO 7520:REM
Space Bar
7650 IF ASCII)=97 AND ASCII(=122 THEN PICK$=CHR$(ASC(PICK$)-32):REM convert
letters to uppercase
7660 IF LEN(PICK$)=1 THEN 7720 ELSE 7670:REM test for cursor keys
7670 PICK$=RIGHT$(PICK$,1):REM extract cursor character
7680 ASCII=ASC(PICK$):REM Extended ASCII code
7690 IF ASCII=72 THEN PICK=PICK-1: IF PICK=0 THEN PICK=LAST:REM Curs Up
7700 IF ASCII=80 THEN PICK=PICK+1: IF PICK)LAST THEN PICK=1:REM Curs Down
7710 GOTO 7520
7720 FOR CHOICE=1 TO LAST
7730 IF PICK$=LEFT$(MENOPT$(CHOICE),1) THEN PICK=CHOICE:REM compare entry with
first character of option
7740 NEXT
7750 GOTO 7520
7760 RETURN
```

Figure 8-27 (continued)

Control switching in this program is handled by just three lines—160, 340, 620—a considerable saving over using IF-GOTO logic. And, of course, the saving is compounded as the number of options per menu increases.

The rest of the program is essentially unchanged.

Shortcutting Techniques—Using "Invisible" Options on a Menu

As noted above, probably the best solution to the speed problem when fast movement around a menu network is required is to include "invisible" options on the menus. These are unlisted options that permit the operator to move anywhere in the program by typing in control codes.

These options are activated by using predefined Alternate key combinations, function keys, or Control key combinations. Of these three choices, the Alternate key combinations are the best. All Alternate key combinations produce extended codes that can be read by extracting the second character from the INKEY$ variable, as described earlier in this chapter (refer to the discussion of the cursor keys). The Alternate keys are also fairly available to the programmer since they do not have standardized uses. The programmer can use a wide range of Alternate key combinations—Alternate plus all of the number and letter keys. Menus can be coded by number or letter to make it easier to relate a particular code to a particular menu. For example, you might permit the operator to return to a program's main menu with Alt-1 or with Alt-H (H for "home") or Alt-M (M for "main"), to access an analysis menu with Alt-A, and so forth.

The function keys can be used but have two drawbacks. First, there are only 10 of them. Additional meanings can be assigned to combinations of the function keys and the shift, Control, or Alternate keys, but this makes the coding system more complicated and difficult to remember. Second, if they are used for selecting hidden options, they cannot be defined as soft switches with the KEY statement. When left undefined, they produce extended codes, but if defined with a KEY statement, their definition string will be returned instead of their ASCII code.

The Control key combinations also have several drawbacks. First, most do not produce extended codes. Second, those that do, e.g., Ctrl-End, Ctrl-Home, have other meanings already. Hence, it is best to leave them alone.

To illustrate "invisible options," let us assume that the Alternate key combinations will be used and that we want to modify the network shown in Figure 8-27 so that the operator can use a hidden option to access any other menu from any given menu. The menus will be labeled 1, 2, and 3, as shown in Figure 8-28.

To go to another menu, the operator will type the combination of the Alternate key and the number of the menu. For example, if the Branch 1 menu is being displayed, the operator can access the Main Menu with Alt-1 or the Branch 2 Menu with Alt-3. Obviously, there is not much point in having this ability in such a simple network, but it will serve the purposes of our illustration. The same technique can be extended to networks containing up to ten menus (using Alter-

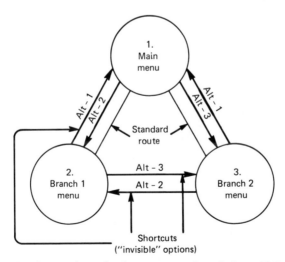

Figure 8-28 A two-level menu network with "invisible" options. Each menu is assigned a number code, and any menu can be reached from any other by typing in an Alternate key–menu number combination.

```
4 KEY OFF
5 REM--Main Menu--
10 CLS
20 LOCATE 1,34
30 PRINT "MAIN MENU"
40 REM-Set Menu Arguments-
80 MENOPT$(1)="1 - Branch 1"
90 MENOPT$(2)="2 - Branch 2"
100 MENOPT$(3)="Q - Exit program"
110 LAST=3:REM number of options
114 REM-set row & column arguments-
115 FOR CHOICE=1 TO LAST
116 ROW%(CHOICE)=CHOICE*2+4
117 COL%(CHOICE)=30
118 NEXT
120 GOSUB 7500:REM call menu-generation subroutine
125 IF JUMP$="up" GOTO 7800
130 IF ASCII=27 GOTO 120:REM trap ESC key
150 REM--Switch Control--
160 ON PICK GOTO 180,460,170
170 CLS:PRINT"End of program":END
180 REM--Branch 1 Menu--
190 CLS
200 LOCATE 1,32
210 PRINT "BRANCH 1 MENU"
220 REM-Set Menu Arguments-
260 MENOPT$(1)="1   - Display 1.1"
270 MENOPT$(2)="2   - Display 1.2"
280 MENOPT$(3)=CHR$(27)+"ESC - Main Menu"
290 LAST=3:REM number of options
300 GOSUB 7500:REM call menu-generation subroutine
305 IF JUMP$="up" GOTO 7800
330 REM--Switch Control--
340 ON PICK GOTO 360,410,5
360 REM--Display 1.1--
370 CLS
380 PRINT"DISPLAY 1.1"
390 GOSUB 1200
400 GOTO 180
410 REM--Display 1.2--
420 CLS
430 PRINT"DISPLAY 1.2"
440 GOSUB 1200
450 GOTO 180
460 REM--Branch 2 Menu--
470 CLS
480 LOCATE 1,32
490 PRINT "BRANCH 2 MENU"
500 REM-Set Menu Arguments-
540 MENOPT$(1)="1   - Display 2.1"
550 MENOPT$(2)="2   - Display 2.2"
560 MENOPT$(3)=CHR$(27)+"ESC - Main Menu"
570 LAST=3:REM number of options
580 GOSUB 7500:REM call menu-generation subroutine
585 IF JUMP$="up" GOTO 7800
610 REM--Switch Control--
620 ON PICK GOTO 640,690,5
640 REM--Display 2.1--
650 CLS
660 PRINT"DISPLAY 2.1"
670 GOSUB 1200
680 GOTO 460
690 REM--Display 2.2--
700 CLS
710 PRINT"DISPLAY 2.2"
720 GOSUB 1200
730 GOTO 460
1200 REM--Temporary Pause--
1210 LOCATE 23,28:REM (use LOCATE 23,8 for 40-column display)
1220 COLOR 30,0:REM high intensity blinking
1230 PRINT"Press any Key to Continue"
1240 A$=INKEY$:IF A$="" GOTO 1240
1250 LOCATE 23,28
1260 PRINT SPACE$(25)
1270 COLOR 7,0:REM normal video
1280 RETURN
7500 REM--Menu Generator--
7510 PICK=1:PICK$="":REM initialize & set default option
7520 REM-Create Menu-
7530 FOR CHOICE=1 TO LAST
```

```
7540 LOCATE ROW%(CHOICE),COL%(CHOICE)
7550 IF PICK=CHOICE THEN COLOR 0,7:REM set highlighting
7560 PRINT MENOPT$(CHOICE):REM print option
7570 COLOR 7,0:REM normal
7580 NEXT
7590 IF PICK$=CHR$(27) GOTO 7760:REM ESC key exit
7600 REM-Collect Input-
7610 PICK$=INKEY$:IF PICK$="" GOTO 7610
7620 ASCII=ASC(PICK$)
7630 IF ASCII=13 GOTO 7760:REM Enter key pressed
7640 IF PICK$ =" " THEN PICK=PICK+1: IF PICK>LAST THEN PICK=1:GOTO 7520:REM
Space Bar
7650 IF ASCII>=97 AND ASCII<=122 THEN PICK$=CHR$(ASC(PICK$)-32):REM convert
letters to uppercase
7660 IF LEN(PICK$)=1 THEN 7720 ELSE 7670:REM test for cursor keys
7670 PICK$=RIGHT$(PICK$,1):REM extract cursor character
7680 ASCII=ASC(PICK$):REM Extended ASCII code
7685 IF ASCII>=120 AND ASCII<=122 THEN JUMP$="up":GOTO 7760:REM jump code entry
7690 IF ASCII=72 THEN PICK=PICK-1: IF PICK=0 THEN PICK=LAST:REM Curs Up
7700 IF ASCII=80 THEN PICK=PICK+1: IF PICK>LAST THEN PICK=1:REM Curs Down
7710 GOTO 7520
7720 FOR CHOICE=1 TO LAST
7730 IF PICK$=LEFT$(MENOPT$(CHOICE),1) THEN PICK=CHOICE:REM compare entry with
first character of option
7740 NEXT
7750 GOTO 7520
7760 RETURN
7800 REM--Jump Control Center--
7810 JUMP$="":REM reset jump flag
7820 IF ASCII=120 GOTO 5:REM Alt-1 Main Menu jump
7830 IF ASCII=121 GOTO 180:REM Alt-2 Branch 1 Menu jump
7840 IF ASCII=122 GOTO 460:REM Alt-3 Branch 2 Menu jump
7850 REM etcetera
```

Figure 8-29 Code required to create the menu network shown in Figure 8-28 containing "invisible" options.

nate-number key combinations) or twenty-six (with Alternate-letter combinations).

What code is required to do this? Actually, this can be done in several different ways, but here is a simple one that works. It requires three modifications to the program shown in Figure 8-27. These modifications consist of the following three elements:

1. Add an Alternate key combination filter to the highlighted-menu subroutine that sets a "jump" flag and exits the subroutine if an acceptable Alternate key combination is made. Line 7685 does this. It is included after the extended ASCII code has been extracted by line 7680 but before the cursor keys are read. The extended ASCII values of Alt-1, Alt-2, and Alt-3, respectively, are 120, 121, and 122, and so the filter tests for these values. If one is found, then the jump flag JUMP$ is set to "up" and control is sent to the exit point from the subroutine.

2. Add jump flag detection code in the main part of the program immediately following each call to the menu-generation subroutine. The added lines in Figure 8-29 are 125, 305, and 585. Each of these lines routes control to centralized switching code.

3. Add centralized switching code to route program control to the appropriate part of the program. In Figure 8-29, this code consists of lines 7800 to 7850. Note that the first thing this code does is to reset the jump flag to the null string.

And that, as they say, is all there is to it.

BOB KIRCHGESNER

INDEX

Active error tests, 121
Alternate key combinations and menu
   control switching, 220–221, 223
ASCII values:
   of important input characters, 111–112
   use of, in range tests, 124–125
AUTOEXEC.BAT files, 169–170

BATCH files (*see* AUTOEXEC.BAT files)
Blinking, 92–97
Blinking cursor, 102–104
Boxing for display separation, 65, 66

Centering:
   of information on screen, 53–55
   of title, 49–51
Clearing of screen, 40–45
Codes, keyboard, 171–174
Color:
   conventions for use of, 91
   mechanics of setting, 66–69
   selection of, 69–73
   undesirable combinations of, 72
   use of, to separate parts of display
     screen, 59–60, 64
COLOR statement, 92–93
Compound entries, parsing and analyzing,
   141–143
Consistency in design:
   importance of, in designing data-input
     screens, data-input forms, and
     database-review screens, 144–145
   principle of, 4, 55–57
Contrast, image, 70–71
Control of program:
   design of, 17–18

Control of program (*Cont.*):
   with menus, 188–223
     (*See also* Menus)
   methods of, 186
   by operator, 4–5, 119
Conventions, design, 8, 88–92
COPY CON command, 169–170
Cursor:
   blinking, 102–104
   positioning of, 31–37
   size, control of, 38–40
Cursor keys, reading of, 204, 206

Data input (*see* Input, program)
Data-input forms, 144–145
Data-input screens, 144–165
Database-review screens, 144–145
DATE$:
   statement, 89
   use of, in BASIC programs, 137–141
Dates, presentation of, 88–91
Default values during user input, 117–
   118
Delays, keeping operator posted on, 119–
   120
Depth-breadth tradeoff in menu networks,
   214
Design:
   consistency in, 4, 55–57, 144–145
   conventions of, 8, 88–92
   evaluation of, 18
   inside-out, method of, 10–11
   outside-in, method of, 10–20
   principles of, 1–9
   testing of, 20
Directories, presentation of, 77–78
Disasters, prevention of, 184–185

Display screens (*see* Screens, computer display)
Documentation, program:
  role of, in reducing operator errors, 167–168
  types of, 19–20

Echoing user inputs on the screen, 104–105
Editing during user input, 136–137
ERL (line number) variable, 175, 181, 183
ERR (error code) variable, 175, 181, 183, 184
Error-testing philosophy, 120–121
Errors:
  BASIC codes for, 176–178
  correction of, during user input, 118–119, 128
  due to hazardous situations, 168–170
  logic for handling, 178–182
  management of, 8–9, 166–185
  messages in response to, 128–136
  operator, prevention of, 167–170
  programming, prevention of, 166–167
  routines for handling, 170–184
  tests for, 121–128

Feedback, operator, 4
Filtering of keystrokes, 111–112, 121
Full-screen input, 153–165
Function keys, defining, 171–174

Hazardous situations and operator errors, 168–170
High-intensity video (*see* Special video modes)
Highlighting, use of, to aid visual search, 87
  (*See also* Special video modes)

Identity test, 126
IF-GOTO logic for menu control switching, 215, 218–220
INKEY$ statement:
  blinking cursor for, 102–104
  data-input routine based on, 108–112
  displaying entry of, 104–105
  Enter key verification with, 105–106
  multiple-keystroke entries with, 106–112

INKEY$ statement (*Cont.*):
  properties of, 101–102
Input, program:
  with INKEY$ statement, 101–112
  with INPUT statement, 98–100
  with LINE INPUT statement, 100–101, 112–114
  screens, design of, 16–17, 144–165
  (*See also* Screens, computer display)
INPUT statement, 98–100
Input-validation sequence, 114–137
"Invisible" options on menus, 220–223

Justification of text, recommendations for, 75–76

KEY and KEY ON statements, 171–174
Keyboard codes, 171–174
Keys:
  cursor, reading of, 204–206
  deactivation of, 171–174
Keystrokes, filtering of, 111–112, 121

Labeling of display screens, 49–55
Language, use of, recommendations for, 74–75
Layout of display screen, 22–24, 48–73
LINE INPUT statement, properties and use of, 100–101, 112–114
Lists and directories, presentation of, 77–78
LOCATE statement, use of:
  for controlling cursor size, 38–40
  during screen generation, 36–37
Logical expressions, use of, in error-testing, 125
  (*See also* Errors)
LPRINT USING statement, 84

Memory, human:
  and menu-driven programs, 187
  recall, 6
  recognition, 6
  short-term, 5–6
Menus:
  depth-breadth tradeoff, 214
  design guidelines for, 190–192
  formats of, 188–190
  generation of, 192–210

Menus (*Cont.*):
  limitations of, 187–188
  networks of, 186, 210–223
  overview of, 186–188
Miller's magic number 7, 5

Negative images, 69–70
Networks, menu, 186, 210–223
Numeric information, presentation of, 78–88

ON ERROR GOTO statement:
  description of, 138–141
  use of, in error-handling routines, 174–184
ON-GOSUB statement, 218
ON-GOTO statement, 218
ON KEY statement, 171–174
Operators, human:
  control of program by, 4–5, 119
  definition of, 13
  errors, prevention of, 167–170
  feedback to, 4
  memory of, 5–6
  orientation of, 6, 8
  types of, 1–2
  work for, minimizing, 2–3
Output, program (*see* Screens, computer display)
Outside-in method of design, 10–20

Paging:
  among display screens, 26–28
  partial, 47, 48
Parsing compound entries, 141–143
Pauses in program, 45–47
Positive images, 69–70
PRINT USING statement, 79–84
Priority information, presentation of, 94–95
Program:
  control of (*see* Control of program)
  design approach for, 10–20
  documentation of, 19–20, 167–168
  functions, definition of, 13–14
  objectives, definition of, 13
  pauses in, 45–47
  testing of, 20
  users, definition of, 13
Program input (*see* Input, program)

Prompting:
  role of, in reducing operator errors, 168
  rules for, 114–118
  (*See also* Input, program)

Range testing, 122–125
Readability of text, 75–76
Recall memory, 6
Recognition memory, 6
Relational operators, use of, in error-testing, 125
  (*See also* Errors)
RESUME and RESUME NEXT statements, 175, 184
Reverse video (*see* Special video modes)

Screens, computer display:
  clearing of, 40–45
  design of, 14–17, 144–165
    with full-screen input, 153–165
  generation of, 21–22, 31–37
  layout of, 22–24, 48–73
  movement among, 24–31
  with scrolling prompts, 145–146
  separating information on, 59–66
  with single-row input, 146–153
  titling and labeling of, 49–55
Scrolling:
  among display screens, 24–25
  of prompts on screen, 145–146
Search, visual, aiding with graphic techniques, 85–88
Separating information on display screens:
  with color, 64
  with lines and bars, 60–66
  methods of, 59–60
Simplicity in design, principle of, 3–4
Single-row input, 146–153
Sorting information to display, 77–78
Special video modes:
  guidelines for use of, 94–97
  mechanics of use of, 92–94
Strings, presentation of, 91–92
Subroutines:
  center and print title, 49–51
  clear to end of row, 44
  clear part of one row, 41–44
  clear range of rows, 44–45
  date formatters, 90
  DATE$-based date collector, 139
  draw box, 65

Subroutines (*Cont.*):
draw vertical bar, 62, 63
editing query, 163
error handler, 183
error-message generator, 133–136
INKEY$–based data-input routine, 108–111
interrupt key deactivator, 174
LINE INPUT–based data-input routine, 112–114
menu generator, highlighted options, 206–207
menu generator, traditional, 201
pause, 45–47
print horizontal line, 62
right-justify title, 52–53
TIME$-based time collector, 139
verification prompt, 150
Syntax-dependent entries, handling of, 137–143

TAB statement, 33–36
Telephone numbers, presentation of, 91

TIME$, use of, in BASIC programs, 138–141
TIME$ statement, 91
Title page, 51–54
Titling of display screens, 49–55
Turnkey systems, 9, 168–170

Underlining (*see* Special video modes)
Users, program (*see* Operators, human)

Verification:
to prevent disasters, 184–185
during user input, 103–106, 136–137, 146–165
Video modes (*see* Special video modes)

Windowing among display screens, 28–31
Work of operator, minimizing, 2–3

ABOUT THE AUTHOR

Henry Simpson is an independent consultant and software developer. Most recently, he was senior scientist at Anacapa Sciences, Inc., a human factors research firm in Santa Barbara, California. Previously, he was west coast editor of *Digital Design* magazine. For several years before that, he was research engineer and project director at Human Factors Research, Inc. He has conducted research, served as consultant to industry, and developed management information systems and other programs for microcomputers. He is the author of *Design of User-Friendly Programs for Small Computers* (McGraw-Hill), and his articles have appeared in such magazines as *BYTE, Microcomputing,* and *Digital Design.*